EGYPT ———

Hot Spots in Global Politics Series

EGYPT ————————————

Robert Springborg

polity

First published in 2018 by Polity Press

Polity Press
65 Bridge Street
Cambridge CB2 1UR, UK

Polity Press
101 Station Landing
Suite 300
Medford, MA 02155, USA

ISBN-13: 978-1-5095-2048-0
ISBN-13: 978-1-5095-2049-7(pb)

A catalogue record for this book is available from the British Library.

Library of Congress Cataloging-in-Publication Data

Names: Springborg, Robert, author.
Title: Egypt / Robert Springborg.
Other titles: Hot spots in global politics.
Description: Malden, MA : Polity Press, 2017. | Series: Hot spots series | Includes bibliographical references and index.
Identifiers: LCCN 2017007693 (print) | LCCN 2017010789 (ebook) | ISBN 9781509520480 (hardback) | ISBN 9781509520497 (pbk.) | ISBN 9781509520510 (Mobi) | ISBN 9781509520527 (Epub)
Subjects: LCSH: Egypt–Politics and government–1981- | Political culture–Egypt.
Classification: LCC DT107.88 .S67 2017 (print) | LCC DT107.88 (ebook) | DDC 962.056–dc23
LC record available at https://lccn.loc.gov/2017007693

Typeset in 10.5 on 12 pt Sabon by Toppan Best-set Premedia Limited
Printed and bound in Great Britain by Clays Ltd, St Ives PLC

For further information on Polity, visit our website: politybooks.com

FOR ZIYAD AND GEORGE, LEYLA AND LUKE

Contents

Preface

Egypt, China, and Iran are the three great empires of antiquity that exist today as nation states, the sovereignty of which extends over much the same territory ruled by those ancient empires. This remarkable durability attests to the special if not unique natures of both rulers and ruled in these countries. Those ruling have been able to assert their authority and claim on loyalties for millennia, while the ruled have shared sufficient in common to remain united as political communities over this longue durée.

Egypt is especially remarkable in these regards, reflecting the unique unifying force of the Nile River. Relative ease of communication and transportation, combined with remarkably fertile arable land, enabled successive governments to organize and control populations and to extract the resources necessary to sustain centralized government. Further benefits to the state and its peoples derived from Egypt's strategic location at the junction of two continents and the gateway to a third. Since Roman times trade between Asia and Europe has passed through Egypt. The most important legacies of Egyptians having been governed as a united people over millennia have been a sense of common national identity combined with loyalty to political community and the institutions governing it.

Given this extraordinary record of national endurance and unity it would seem rash to even speculate that Egypt's contemporary nation state is at risk of fracturing. Yet, the pressures to which it is currently subjected and which are bound to intensify are already straining the ties that hold the political community together, while rendering ever more difficult the task of governing it. As Egyptians become steadily more divided by class, religion, region, ethnicity, gender, and contrasting views of how, by whom, and for what purposes they should be governed, so do their rulers become ever more fearful, repressive, and unrepresentative. Caught in a downward spiral in which poor governance is both cause and consequence of mounting political, economic, environmental, regional, and other pressures, Egypt is facing a future so uncertain that it could come to resemble neighboring countries that have essentially collapsed under similar loads, albeit having had weaker states to bear them.

Egypt, in sum, is not just a temporary hotspot, it is an exemplar of a broader trend in the Middle East and North Africa (hereafter, MENA) of the collapse of political orders and of the economies, environmental resources, and societies upon which those orders have been based. No small political changes, such as replacement of Egypt's President Abd al Fattah al Sisi by another general, or even by a civilian so long as he remains subordinate to the existing power structures, will arrest the decline. So Egypt exemplifies a broader problem and in that sense is a hotspot, but not one that is going to cool any time soon.

This book will seek to explain how a country with such a long and impressive history—successfully transitioning from empire to a modern state that came to dominate its region and become a leader of the then Third World—has arrived at this parlous condition. The structure of the argument and the book is that the key explanatory variable is the manner in which state power has been acquired and exercised, while the dependent variables are measures of the country's performance, whether economic, societal, environmental, demographic, infrastructural, or its role in the region and the world. As the economy and society weaken, the environment and infrastructure deteriorate, population growth accelerates, and Egypt's roles in the region and the world become more marginal, the task of governing becomes ever more challenging.

The performance decline also indicates that the country faces not just a temporary political crisis, but an existential one, aggravated yet more by the forces of economic globalization to which the country is ill-prepared to adjust.

Egypt is thus caught up in a vicious circle. Its unaccountable, unrepresentative, authoritarian government undermines the structural and resource foundations upon which a more accountable, representative, and capable government could be built. Such a government is essential if Egypt is to confront the rising tide of domestic threats and take advantage of the opportunities provided by the forces of economic globalization, rather than just be buffeted by them. Reversing this downward spiral is an ever more difficult challenge, not only because of continued erosion of the structural and resource foundations upon which government rests, but because alternatives to the political status quo become steadily fewer, less appealing and less likely to have the competence and support to reverse the downward spiral. The Egyptian "hot spot" thus seems destined to become steadily hotter, with ominous implications for its peoples, its neighbors in the MENA, and for Europe and beyond.

The book's chapters can be thought of as composing four steps. The first, comprised of Chapter 1, will provide an historical account of the rise and decline of the capacities of state and nation, thereby setting the stage for the investigation of the causes and consequences of that decline. The second step in the following three chapters will be to investigate the nature of the military government in order to explain why it has failed to adequately develop the polity and economy and the human and physical contexts in which they operate. Chapter 2 focuses on the "deep state" itself. Chapter 3 then investigates how it controls the state "superstructure," while Chapter 4 focuses on its manipulation of political and civil societies. The third step will be to review in Chapter 5 the intensifying crises of the economy, of human and physical resources, and of foreign relations. The conclusion in Chapter 6 will present and assess three scenarios for the country's future as its rulers and people grapple with the challenges outlined in the preceding chapters.

Acknowledgments

Having lived and worked in and studied Egypt intermittently for more than half a century, my debts of gratitude to scores of friends, colleagues, and fellow students of the country are huge. Regrettably many of them cannot be acknowledged here without fear of retribution as they continue to live or visit there. I would like to single out those who read and commented on the manuscript or who indirectly contributed to it through discussing with me either theoretical or empirical material contained in it. In alphabetical order they are Zeinab Abul-Magd, Amr Adly, Soha Bayoumi, Gerhard Behrens, Kirk Beattie, Guilain Denoeux, Philippe Droz-Vincent, Khaled Fahmy, Anthony Gorman, Hazem Kandil, Giacomo Luciani, Tamir Moustafa, Roger Owen, Donald Reid, Glenn Robinson, Ron Wolfe, and Polity's anonymous reviewers.

Most of the book was written while I was the Kuwait Foundation Visiting Scholar at the Middle East Initiative of the Belfer Center at the Kennedy School of Harvard University. Harvard faculty Middle East specialists Nicholas Burns, Melani Cammett, Ishac Diwan, Tarek Masoud, and Gary Samore went out of their way to welcome me into their ranks and share their information and thoughts about contemporary Egypt, as did Bill Granara, Director of Harvard's Center for Middle Eastern Studies. The staff of the Middle East Initiative, led by Director Hilary Rantisi and including Chris Mawhorter and Julia Martin, spoiled me far beyond the call of duty.

Nathalie Tocci, Deputy Director of the Istituto Affari Internazionale in Rome, allowed me the opportunity on several occasions to present at the Istituto thoughts about Egypt and benefit from the feedback she and her colleagues provided.

The idea for the book was that of Louise Knight, my editor at Polity Press. She and her assistant, Nekane Tanaka Galdos, encouraged and guided me expertly through the writing and production processes. Tim Clark's editing greatly improved my frequently awkward prose.

I appreciate permission being granted by the editor of *The International Spectator*, Gabriele Tonne, to reproduce herein some of the material that first appeared in my article "Caudillismo along the Nile," Vol. 51, Issue 1 (2016).

Finally, I have benefitted from the friendship, advice, and assistance of scores of Egyptians who over the years have welcomed me into their lives and country while candidly providing me with their thoughts and views on many of the subjects taken up in this book. It is to them and their fellow Egyptians that this book is primarily addressed, in the hope that it may be of some use to them in their struggle to overcome the baleful legacy of authoritarian government from which they have suffered most, if not all of their lives.

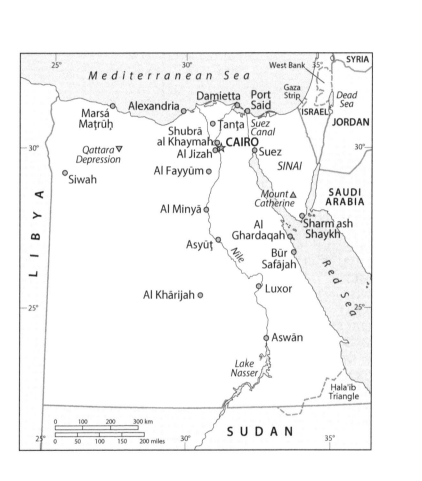

Abbreviations

EFITU	Egyptian Federation of Independent Trade Unions
ETUF	Egyptian Trade Union Federation
FDI	Foreign Direct Investment
GCC	Gulf Cooperation Council
GDP	Gross Domestic Product
IMF	International Monetary Fund
LAO	Limited Access Order
MENA	Middle East and North Africa
NDP	National Democratic Party
NGO	Non-governmental Organization
OAO	Open Access Order
ODA	Overseas Development Assistance
POMED	Project on Middle East Democracy
PRM	Popular Resistance Movement
R&D	Research and Development
SCAF	Supreme Council of the Armed Forces
SCC	Supreme Constitutional Court
SJC	Supreme Judicial Council
SSI	State Security Investigations
UNICEF	United Nations Children's Fund
USAID	United States Agency for International Development

1 | Eroding Historical Legacies _____

By late 2010 former Air Force General Husni Mubarak had been ruling Egypt for almost thirty years. His primary preoccupation had become securing his younger son Gamal's succession as president. Otherwise there were relatively few clouds on his political horizon. The military, a perennial if intermittent challenger to presidential rule, he had successfully defanged in 1989 by discrediting and purging the charismatic minister of defense, Field Marshal Abd al Halim Abu Ghazala. Security and intelligence forces, which he had beefed up as counterbalances to the military and to repress autonomous political expression, were held securely in check by his key aide, General Umar Suliman, head of General Intelligence. He had already handed the ruling National Democratic Party (NDP) over to son Gamal, who was busy extending its reach into the organs of the state and the patronage networks through which organized political life had long been controlled. Parliamentary elections held earlier in the year had, through a record amount of fraud and intimidation, produced a supermajority for the NDP, upping its seat total to 420 of the 444 possible from the 330 it had won in the more free and fair 2005 election. Conversely, the Muslim Brotherhood, the only effective organized opposition force, saw its record eighty-eight seats won in the 2005 elections reduced to one. So the newly elected parliament in 2010 promised to be docile, posing no threat to the father-son presidential succession.

As for the third branch of government, the judicial system, it was no longer the thorn in President Mubarak's side it had once been. He turned his attention to it in the wake of the 2005 elections, combining constitutional changes, intimidation of the small cadre of independent-minded judges entrenched in the Judges' Club, and direct interventions into court management to effectively subordinate this third branch to the all-powerful executive by 2010. Civil society organizations were being choked by a yet more restrictive legal framework and interdiction by the Egyptian government of their sources of funding, primarily foreign. Newly emerged, privately owned media outlets had come grudgingly to accept the regime's more tightly drawn "red lines." Mubarak, in sum, appeared on the 2010–11 New Year to be sitting astride an increasingly repressive but nevertheless stable authoritarian system that he could reasonably hope to bequeath to his son, albeit with some pushback from the military and ineffective grumbling from opposition elements and civil society activists.

As it transpired, this was a myopic view. On January 25, 2011, a veritable political explosion occurred as thousands of demonstrators, encouraged by civil society activists networked through social media—the *Facebookiyyin* as they were dubbed in Arabic—poured into the streets to voice their discontent with Mubarak, shouting for the fall of his regime. Within days the largest demonstrations since the funeral of President Nasser in 1970 were rocking Cairo, Alexandria, Port Said, Ismailiya, and various urban centers in the Delta. As the crowds continued to swell in the face of remarkably poorly prepared security forces and with the tacit approval of the military, the Mubarak regime that had been in place for just shy of three decades collapsed in a remarkably brief eighteen days, with comparatively little bloodshed. The president fled to his villa at Sharm al Shaikh on the southern tip of the Sinai Peninsula to await his fate.

At first blush these dramatic events appeared to be a classic example of a "color revolution," akin to those that had swept through the former Soviet Union and the Balkans. Essentially non-violent and led by non-governmental organizations, they relied on sheer "people power" to overthrow authoritarian regimes and begin transitions to democracy. The hundreds of thousands of demonstrators in Cairo's Midan al Tahrir (Liberation Square) appeared to embody this inclusive people power, including as they did Muslims and Coptic Christians, middle-class professionals and workers, youths and retirees, women and men. But virtually from the moment of its success this broad-based if loose coalition began to fracture and be overwhelmed by two other, competitive forces. One was the military, which had deceptively claimed to be "of one hand" with the demonstrators, but which under Mubarak's long-serving minister of defense, Muhammad Husayn Tantawi, immediately began to assert its authority and reel in what it viewed as the excessive exuberance and inappropriate clamoring for democracy of the "mob." The other was the Muslim Brotherhood, which had provided the most dedicated shock troops in dramatic battles with security forces in and around Midan al Tahrir and whose leaders and members believed that it was they, not the more secular *Facebookiyyin* demonstrators, who had engineered Mubarak's downfall. They thus felt entitled to exercise power in the new order they, in collaboration with the military, would establish.

Over the next two years the military played the mongoose against the Brotherhood cobra, first handing civilian power to it as a check on the more radical, democratic secular forces, then skillfully undermining it before dramatically overthrowing it by coup d'état in July 2013. In the interim the officers and Brothers collaborated to rehabilitate the much discredited security services, as both sought to use them against the other and against their common enemy, the civil society activists who had initially triggered the uprising. They also cooperated in drafting a new constitution that awarded the military powers it had never previously exercised, the tradeoff being an electoral law that virtually guaranteed the Brothers victory, hence control over parliament. State institutions, including the judiciary, parliament, and virtually the entirety of the public administration, suffered extensive collateral damage from this struggle for power that was frequently played out within and between those institutions, destroying any pretense to their impartiality and professionalism. As for civil society, it was marginalized through the application of brute force by the reconstituted security services, now backed by the military, and by its own internal fragmentation and weakness. Nobel Prize winner Muhammad al Baradei, a prominent international symbol of the uprising and the sole elder statesman with the potential to unify its forces, resigned his post as vice-president in protest against the killings by military and security forces of more than 800 Brotherhood supporters in Rabaa al Adawiyya and al Nahda Squares in Cairo in August 2013. He went into self-declared exile and has yet to return, his absence symbolizing that of civil society more generally.

The uprising thus turned out to be not a color revolution, but a "coup-volution," aptly named such by an analyst of the country's armed forces.[1] The military had "sucker punched" both civil society activists and the Muslim Brothers, leading the former to believe that officers would midwife fundamental political reforms, and the latter to surmise that those officers would depend upon the Brotherhood as its chief instrument of civilian rule. In reality the high command, constituted as the Supreme Council of the Armed Forces (SCAF), had from the outset intended to jettison Mubarak, but then protect him, in order to preserve, even expand the military's political role and their command of it. Although it took considerable maneuvering for the SCAF to accomplish this—including a change of its leadership, with Field Marshal Tantawi being replaced by the politically more adroit General Abd al Fattah al Sisi in September 2012—the outcome was never much in doubt. The SCAF first used the Brothers to crush the enthusiastic but weak and disorganized secular "revolutionaries," then rehabilitated some of those very same marginalized, youthful elements to advocate and justify the coup they were planning against the Brothers' president, Muhammad al Mursi.

If this was a color revolution, its color was black. Its net result was to strip away the civilian accretions on top of the military regime that had originally been established with Gamal Abdel Nasser's July 1952 coup d'état that overthrew King Faruq and ended the monarchy. Those accretions in the form of state institutions and processes, such as a formally civilian presidency, parliament, and elections, organizations of political society such as political parties, and a range of civil society actors, had over the years diluted military rule, hiding its residue from view. But the 2013 coup-volution restored direct military rule, paving the way for the officers to undermine virtually all manifestations of civilian rule, whether administrative, political, or even economic. The repression required to erode these civilian institutions, organizations, and actors exceeded that which Nasser and his Free Officer colleagues had employed when they destroyed the remnants of monarchial and constitutional government and politics back in the 1950s. In both cases the Brotherhood was a primary target of the crackdown, with General Sisi employing more draconian means than Nasser had, including cold-blooded killings of hundreds of its members in Cairo's Rabaa al Adawiyya and al Nahda squares, inglorious firsts in the history of Republican Egypt.[2] Once Sisi was sworn in as president in June 2014, discredited Mubarak-era officials were gradually rehabilitated, albeit more with the style than the substance of their former powers. The coup-volution, in sum, inverted the power relationship between Mubarak and his immediate entourage, on the one hand, and the military on the other, leaving in place an officer republic more brutal than any since the darkest days of the Nasser era, causing many "revolutionaries" and Brothers to long for the "good old days" of Mubarak, indeed, even for the monarchy.

The dramatic events since January 2011 raise four interrelated questions. First, what caused the 2011 uprising? Second, why did so few, including those who participated in it, not anticipate it? Third, why did it fail? And finally, what consequences have these tumultuous few years had for the political foundations of the country?

Causes of the Uprising

Of these queries, that of the uprising's causes is the easiest to answer, both because they are the most apparent and because they have been extensively analyzed, due primarily to the fact that the Egyptian uprising was but one case of the wider "Arab

Spring" of 2011, exploding first in Tunisia in the last month of 2010. Indeed, cross-border learning was a primary cause of Egypt's and then other countries' uprisings. The dramatic events on the streets of Tunis were graphically depicted in the pan-Arab media. Egyptians could see and easily identify with Tunisian protesters. It did not take a great stretch of their imagination to transpose the hated Ben Ali regime there to the unpopular Mubarak regime at home. Once the uprising had occurred in Egypt, others erupted in Libya, Yemen, Syria and elsewhere in the Arab world, adding further regional pressure to the gathering momentum for change along the Nile.

The causes of the Arab Spring were both economic and political. The global economic downturn that commenced in 2008 had placed additional pressure on economies that were already underperforming. In Egypt's case, GDP per capita growth had been stagnating at a paltry 1 percent or so for years, the rapidly growing population eating up much of the economic growth that did occur. Unemployment hovered around 10 percent even during the boom period of 2003–7 that was fired by an export surge of natural gas. Youth unemployment was double, then growing to triple the overall proportion. Almost three quarters of new jobs were in the informal sector, meaning without contracts, social or medical insurance, serious prospects for advancement, or adequate remuneration. The absolute and proportionate growth of the middle class, one of the achievements of the Nasser era and still occurring under Sadat, had ground to a halt by the mid-1980s, then gone into reverse. The "desertion of the middle class," a warning and cause of revolutions, was more pronounced in Egypt than other Arab countries.[3] As middle-class prosperity became an ever more distant dream and unemployment and poverty spread, so did inequality grow. By the time of the uprising four of the ten richest Africans were Egyptians, but one quarter of the entire population and more than half the population in Upper Egypt lived in dire poverty. According to Facundo Alvaredo and Thomas Piketty, a careful analysis of available data reveals Egypt as having one of the highest degrees of income and asset inequality among lower middle income countries.[4] Not surprisingly, most Egyptians suffered from relative deprivation, profoundly resenting the wealthy and the corruption commonly believed to have made them rich.

As the Mubarak regime ground on, it provided ever fewer vents for the political steam generated by the malfunctioning economy. Never an adroit politician and having a bland public persona, Mubarak seemed to lose interest in playing the public political game, spending longer periods in his villas on the Mediterranean Coast and in Sinai, and relying on his security and intelligence services to intimidate other active and potential players. Under pressure from the Bush administration after 9/11 to liberalize and even democratize, Mubarak grudgingly conceded relatively free and fair elections in 2005. The outcome frightened him and his security specialists, threatening as it did to derail plans for Gamal Mubarak's succession.

So despite lingering, albeit declining, pressure from President Bush and Secretary of State Condoleezza Rice, then virtually none from President Obama, Mubarak ordered a political U-turn. His security and intelligence forces commenced a crackdown in 2006 that continued virtually until the day of his removal five years later. Hopes for democratic reforms were dashed, so those associated with them, essentially the leaders of the long-tamed political parties, lost what little credibility and influence they still had. Moving into the breach were increasingly active and radical civil society activists. The Brotherhood bided its time, assuming that at some stage the regime would again have need of it, as it had at various times in the past dating back to the monarchy. Its leadership continued to express support for democratic change, especially to western audiences, but as subsequent events were to amply demonstrate, those words did not reflect the Brothers' true belief or calculation—namely, that the primary and probably only pathway to power was through a combination of democratic and undemocratic means of gaining control over state institutions. So by the end of 2010 the political game, tame as it had long been, had come to a virtual standstill, opening the door to those who argued that taking to the streets was the only way to secure change, even if they did not really believe it would have much effect.

The political psychology of uprisings reflects relative deprivation and political repression. One key element of it is the desire for human dignity. Egyptians, like Tunisians, believed that the regime simply did not care whether they lived or died, or how they lived. They felt denied of human dignity, so desperately wanted to assert it. The second vital element is fear. Repression works so long as it instills fear. If coercive forces are challenged and found to be ineffective, fear morphs into confidence and a willingness to take risks, including physical ones. That is what happened in the streets of Cairo, Alexandria, and the Canal Zone cities. The chief riot-control forces, Central Security and State Security, had over the years grown soft from meeting few challenges from crowds that were typically small and easily dispersed. When on January 25 they confronted thousands and then tens of thousands of demonstrators, they did not know how to respond. As other Egyptians, in person, on TV or on social media, watched the demonstrations grow and then overwhelm security forces, their innate fear gave way to a desire for justice, revenge and assertion of dignity. When the security forces belatedly toughened up and began brutalizing, even killing demonstrators, it was in vain. The crowds were by then of overwhelming size and commitment. Most importantly, the military chose to abandon the hapless riot-control troops to their fate. The SCAF had other plans.

Why the Uprising Was Not Anticipated

Roger Owen aptly described the Arab republics prior to the 2011 uprisings as ruled by "presidents for life."[5] These rulers, including Mubarak, were among the longest serving in the world, many actively seeking to hand power to a son. Given the presidents' longevity, participants and analysts alike believed their "hybrid" authoritarian regimes, which alternated political liberalizations with crackdowns of varying intensities, would indeed survive father-son successions. None did. Of them, only Tunisia and Egypt now have states that govern more or less all of their sovereign territory and political communities which, if more divided than before the uprisings and generally less loyal to their governments, are at least not embroiled in civil wars.

The comparative durability of state and nation in Tunisia and Egypt has not occurred by chance. These two Arab republics have the longest traditions of coherent and effective statehood and unified national identities. Of the two, Egypt's traditions are longer and stronger. Egypt's was the first modern state to emerge in the Arab world, resting on already firmly established foundations of centralized, legitimate authority. Egyptian identity was also the earliest to form and the most uniform Arab national consciousness.

Almost uniquely in the Arab world, and central to its persistence in the face of centrifugal forces currently assailing virtually every country in the Middle East and North Africa (MENA), Egypt's beneficial legacies of state and nation are the product of their interaction. The state forged the nation, the coherence of which in turn reinforced the state and its administrative powers. At the heart of that reciprocal relationship was the ability of the state to enforce its writ throughout the land. The comparative dearth of rugged, remote territory to host insurrections rendered that task easier. Relative ease of transport and communications along the Nile, readily controlled from Cairo, the point at which the River fans out to form the Delta, combined with ample material surplus produced by agriculture and trade, were also key factors making possible successive, powerful Egyptian states dating back to 4000 BCE. The Romans, for example, marveled at Ptolemaic Egypt's extensive governance, including its capacity to oversee the harvest and distribution of grain throughout the land, to say nothing of its support for institutions of learning and research that were the envy of the Mediterranean and indeed, the entire world. In the fourteenth century, Egypt under its Mamluk rulers dominated the Far Eastern spice trade, the Eastern Mediterranean coast up to what is now Turkey, and the Nile Valley into Sudan. When the famous Moroccan traveler, Ibn Battuta, arrived in Cairo, its population of 600,000 made it the largest city west of China, fifteen times the size of London. Alexandria was the biggest port on the Mediterranean. Mamluk architecture was structurally and artistically the most sophisticated then known.

Since most Egyptians reside along the Nile, they have for millennia had little chance of successfully resisting central government, so have accommodated to it. For their part, governments have facilitated that acceptance by propagating legitimating ideologies, the earliest of which were religious. Kingship has its origins in pharaonic Egypt. The pharaoh-king was a god on earth whose legitimacy was an integral, indeed essential feature of the Egyptian religion. The Greeks and then the Romans did not supplant the Egyptian religion when they conquered the country. Instead they wisely adopted it themselves to gain popular acceptance. Christianity subsequently legitimated Byzantine rule. Islam, brought to Egypt from the Arabian Peninsula by the Arab conquest of 642, did not deify rulers but instructed people to submit to them so long as they obeyed the tenets of the faith. Since Islam was the belief system that legitimated the government, its rulers, whether Mamluks, sultans, khedives, or kings, had only to be of that religion. They did not have to be native Egyptians, none of whom strictly speaking were, from the defeat of the Pharaohs by the Greeks, to the rise of Gamal Abdel Nasser in 1952. Egyptians are in fact of diverse origins. The Nilotic majority are descended from the original population along the Nile, while minorities include those originally from elsewhere on the African continent; Semites from the Arabian Peninsula; "Turks," referring to Muslims whose family origins were in lands controlled by the Ottoman Empire in what is now Turkey or the Transcaucasian region; and Syro-Lebanese, meaning Christians who typically migrated from the Levant to Egypt from the late eighteenth century to the mid twentieth. None of these ethno-religious subgroups is considered more essentially Egyptian than another, or characterized by a distinctive accent. All have been Egyptianized in a society penetrated and homogenized by centralized rule. By contrast, the populations of many other MENA countries, much less subject to continuous, effective central governance, are cleaved by ethnic divisions far deeper and more recalcitrant to being "melted down" by governmental action.

The one distinction that does assume major sociopolitical importance is that between Muslims and Christians. This is the only subcultural divide in which some believers on one side seek to excommunicate those on the other from the national political community, to say nothing of disputing estimates of proportions of the respective populations. Christian–Muslim antagonisms are, however, muted by the fact that they are not reinforced by other deep, overlapping cleavages, whether linguistic, regional, class or otherwise. Although historically Christians were wealthier than Muslims and began entering middle-class professions earlier and in greater numbers, differences in wealth, education, and professional attainment steadily declined in Republican Egypt. Egypt has not experienced a war of religion in the more than 1,300 years since Islam was established as the faith of the state and majority of its citizens. Intermittent hostilities, however, have occurred, such as those that broke out in Alexandria at the time of the British invasion in 1882. Members of both faiths were active in the nationalist movement against the British.

The religious tension that has been growing since the late Sadat era results not from age-old antagonisms, but from the contemporary politicization of religion, in both Egypt and the surrounding Arab world. As Islamists, especially the Muslim Brothers, gained influence under Presidents Sadat and Mubarak, Christians, suffering from discrimination of various sorts and increasingly marginalized in public life, reinforced their own intra-communal organizational solidarities, including those based in monasteries on the periphery of the Nile Valley, and in overseas Coptic communities.[6] In the wake of Mubarak's removal, to which Copts contributed by joining rallies in Cairo's Tahrir Square and elsewhere, tensions between the two communities resumed when the Muslim Brotherhood won control of parliament and the presidency in 2012 and, from the Coptic perspective, began to try to Islamize the country. Most Christians welcomed the coup that removed President Mursi. Many of his Brotherhood supporters believed the coup to be the manifestation of a Christian plot against them and Islam more generally. Muslim–Christian tensions thus now threaten the nation's sense of political community, although

Egypt's comparatively benign history of Muslim–Christian relations and the lack of overlapping cleavages render that threat less profound than are religious or ethnic cleavages in Lebanon, Syria, Iraq, or within or between the two Sudans.

In sum, there are two answers as to why the 2011 uprising was not anticipated. The simple, immediate one is that the authoritarian status quo was so long established, so complete, and so lacking visible, potent challengers, whether domestic or foreign, that it seemed inevitable it would continue into the indefinite future. The second answer, which occasioned this digression into Egypt's distinctive record as an effective, centralized state sitting astride a unified political community sharing a common national consciousness, is that by regional standards Egypt has enjoyed remarkably stable politics for centuries, precisely because historically it has been the region's most impressive nation state. The Mamluks and the Ottomans ruled separately and in cooperation for half a millennium before Napoleon's invasion in 1798. The regime of Muhammad Ali that emerged from the several years of tumult following that invasion ruled alone or under British tutelage until 1952. The coup that overthrew that dynasty was bloodless. The successor republican regime survived catastrophic defeat in the 1967 war against Israel, the assassination of President Sadat in 1981, and some thirty years of uninspiring leadership under President Mubarak. After a partial, one-year interlude under the Muslim Brotherhood, the military-dominated republican government has been restored. Given this record of the longevity and durability of regimes, owing to the sturdy underpinnings of state and nation, it is hardly surprising that the default assumption has been one of continuity and persistence, not change and disruption. That this key assumption may no longer be correct is suggestive of the magnitude of change the country is presently undergoing.

Why the Uprising Failed

The uprising did not develop into a color revolution because it did not produce a transition to anything resembling democracy. While not all of those who joined or just passively supported the demonstrators were ardent democrats, and indeed economic motivations were probably just as determinative as political ones for their behavior, most were searching for something other than the military-backed authoritarian order under which they had lived for so long. So most were disappointed with the outcome of the coup-volution. So, too, were reformers regionally and globally disappointed that a potential democratic transition aborted in Egypt. Had it succeeded there it might have reverberated in other Arab countries, as a group the world's least democratic. In the event, the restoration of draconian military rule along the Nile, coupled with the return to power of much of the Mubarak *ancien regime*, dashed the reform hopes of Egyptians and Arabs more generally.

The failure of the eighteen-day, sadly misnamed Tahrir, or January 25, Revolution, to produce a more liberal political order can be explained on two levels. On the surface it was a political cacophony, with a hopelessly diverse cast of individual and institutional players vying for center stage, such as the *Facebookiyyin*, the Muslim Brothers, yet more fundamentalist Islamists known as Salafis, the military high command, Mubarak loyalists, and so on. This type of explanation centers on the political dramatis personae, their relative powers, strategies and tactics. An attempt will be made in the following chapter to sketch out this drama in order to illustrate the workings of the country's political system at the time and more generally. A second level of analysis focuses on the substructural conditions of the political economy that facilitate or impede a democratic transition. It is that level to which we shall now turn as those conditions constitute the political and economic legacies bequeathed to Egypt's rulers and peoples as they commenced their intense political struggle in early 2011.

A country's political legacy is reflected in its human resources, the endowment of which is of vital political importance. Recent empirical research on preconditions for democratization has identified seven dimensions of a population that render it more or less supportive of a democratic transition.[7] On none of those dimensions does Egypt score highly. First, its population is too young. The probability of a democratic transition increases as the median age of the population rises. Thirty years of age appears to be the threshold above which such transitions have a far higher chance of success. Egypt's median age is twenty-four, about average for the Arab world, in which only Tunisia's median age almost reaches the thirty-year threshold.

Second, Egypt's population is too rural. Democratization is facilitated by urbanization, presumably because moving to cities not only broadens political horizons and opens new avenues for political participation, but also reflects economic conditions. In East Asia, for example, urbanization has been driven by economic growth in general and industrialization in particular. In Egypt, by contrast, the stagnating industrial sector has been economically too inconsequential to act as a strong magnet attracting dwellers in the countryside into cities. Egypt was more urban in the period between 1975 and 1991, when 44 percent of Egyptians were urban residents, than it has been since. To express the ratio differently, Egypt has the world's twenty-third largest urban population, but its eleventh largest rural one.[8] With flagging industrialization young Egyptians have chosen to stay at home in rural and semi-urban areas, where living expenses are lower and where their chances of eking out a living in the informal sector are about the same as they are elsewhere in the country. Only external migration offers real hope of a dramatic change in income and lifestyle, but such migration undermines pressure for democratic reforms rather than intensifying it.

A third demographic deficiency in Egypt is that its people are too poor. Cross-national comparative research has established that the GDP per capita threshold above which regressions to authoritarianism are unlikely following the establishment of at least a partial democracy is about $11,000. In 2016 Egypt's GDP per capita was some $2,700. Even if measured according to purchasing power parity, with Egypt's being 58 percent of the world's average, per capita GDP in the country still only reaches about 60 percent of the threshold figure.[9] Averages aside, Egypt's high and growing incidence of poverty must surely add an additional obstacle to democratic transition. Between 2000 and 2010, the proportion of Egyptians living on the equivalent of less than $2 per day rose from 20.2 percent to 29.2 percent and by 2017 may have reached as much as 40 percent in the wake of the halving of the pound's value in December 2016.[10] As many as 18 million Egyptians were living on less than $1 per day in 2016. So poverty, reinforced by profound inequality, militates against democracy in Egypt.

A fourth drag effect on Egypt's potential democratization results from the shrinking of its middle class. One of the most secure empirical findings on the correlates of democratization is that which links it to the growth of the middle class. Among other reasons for this correlation is that the security provided by middle-class status is essential for thought and action by citizens on policy matters, for otherwise they are consumed with the struggle for material existence. Having been built primarily on the steady expansion of public employment from the Nasser era until recently, the Egyptian middle class has suffered disproportionately from the slowing of recruitment into the civil service and the relative deterioration of wages and conditions within it. At its high point, public employment accounted for at least one third of the non-agricultural labor force, a proportion that by 2016 had dropped to around one quarter, albeit with 7 million of the country's total labor force of around 28 million still employed in it. The vast majority of them, however, are finding it ever more difficult to make ends meet, so do not have the security provided by true middle-class status. Private sector employment has not picked up the slack. A recent study of middle-level employment in the private sector revealed it as having declined by 5 percent in numbers and its total share of wages/salaries by more than 9 percent between 2000 and 2009, years that incorporated the gas-fired boom.[11] Within the Middle East, according to the World Bank, only in Egypt and Yemen did the middle class contract in the first decade of the twenty-first century, falling in the former from 14.3 to 9.8 percent of the population.[12] The Egyptian middle class is, in short, a shrinking demographic enclave, neither large nor robust enough to provide a solid foundation upon which democratic institutions and practices could readily be built.

A fifth correlate of democratization, and one related to but more encompassing than an expanding middle class, is that of the material security of the entire population. Insecurity is the enemy of democracy and Egyptians suffer greatly from it. Unpaid family work and own-account workers are, according to the World Bank, in "vulnerable employment." Twenty-one percent of all male and 44 percent of all female members of Egypt's labor force are so classified. The rate for both is increasing. In 1998, 12 percent of the employed were irregular wage workers, meaning intermittent or seasonal. As the economy grew in the early 2000s that proportion dropped, by 2006 to 8 percent. But over the next six years as the economy slowed, the rate more than doubled to 17 percent. Almost three quarters of new entrants to the labor market are now absorbed into the informal sector. About one third of all workers in 2012 were either irregular or informal workers, more than three times the proportion of those employed on contracts in the private sector.[13] In 1988 firms employing fewer than five workers accounted for 54 percent of all employment, a ratio that grew to two thirds by 2008. Similarly, the average size of micro firms in Cairo fell from 3.6 to 2.5 employees in the dozen years from 1986. So the decline of the public sector, paralleled by the downward slide in formal employment and the proliferation of micro businesses and own-account workers, all point to an ever tighter labor market, one increasingly unable to provide security for even a constant proportion of the population, much less an expanding one.

A sixth obstacle to democratization also involves material security, but turns on the question of who provides it. If it is primarily the government, the inevitable consequence will be its use of resource allocations to foster vertical, patron-client relations of dependency. They in turn militate against the strengthening of horizontal ties necessary for vibrant civil and political societies.[14] The Arab population as a whole is more dependent upon government than the peoples of any other region, that dependence determined by the world-leading proportion of public employees in the workforce, combined with the highest level globally of consumer subsidies. Dependence is further augmented by selective allocation of financial credit on grounds other than sheer creditworthiness. By these three measures, Egyptians are extraordinarily dependent upon their government for their material welfare.

As just noted, of the country's labor force of 28 million, fully 7 million, or one quarter, are employed in the civil service. Another half a million serve in the armed forces. Assuming an average family size of just over four, this suggests that as many as 33 million people, more than a third of the total population, depend for their income primarily on government. It is all the more remarkable that profound dependence on government employment also characterizes even farming communities in rural Egypt. A 2005 survey revealed that 40 percent of such households relied on at least one government salary as their largest income source, compared to 37 percent who derived the bulk of their income from agriculture.[15]

In addition to dependence on government for employment, Egyptians also rely on it to subsidize their food and energy consumption. Those subsidies have for many years consumed between 25 and 30 per cent of the government's budget, with other shares of that magnitude allocated to civil servant salaries and, since 2013, to debt repayment, leaving only about 10 percent of the budget for all other expenditures. The budget, in sum, is eaten up mainly by annual transfers and repayments for previous ones. Ninety percent of the population is entitled to at least some subsidized foodstuffs. Egyptians are the world's largest per capita consumers of bread, primarily as a consequence of its very low price due to heavy subsidization. Egypt is the world's biggest importer of wheat. As for energy subsidies, all consumers benefit from both fuel and electricity subsidies, but the wealthy benefit disproportionately. As much as three quarters of those subsidies have been consumed by processing industries, such as steel, fertilizer, cement, and ceramics, owned principally by regime cronies and increasingly by the military or its retired officers. A final "subsidy" takes the dubious form of extending bank credit to political favorites. Almost one quarter of all loans held by the country's banks were declared non-performing at the time of the coup-volution, a rate that has diminished since then largely because most new bank credit has been absorbed by the cash-strapped government.

Egyptians, in short, depend to an extraordinary degree on their government to provide them with jobs; to subsidize their consumption of food, fuel and electricity; and in the case of the rich, to furnish their factories with cheap energy or simply to loan them money without necessarily expecting it to be repaid. This in turn provides the government with extensive leverage over the population, choosing as it can who obtains a job, a subsidy, or a bank loan. Democracy is unlikely to take root and flourish when those who might challenge the authoritarian order must first calculate the potential personal material cost of governmental retribution.

Finally, democratization is positively if weakly correlated with education and training.[16] In neither does Egypt perform well. Its illiteracy rate, which has been hovering around 25 percent for several years, is well above that of most lower middle income countries. Moreover, instead of declining, it has been creeping up slowly since the coup-volution, rising from 24.9 percent in 2012 to 25.9 percent a year later. Even more disturbing is that among those aged fifteen to twenty-four the illiteracy rate is almost 30 percent, higher than in the ascending age decile of the population.[17] Egypt's primary and secondary educational systems, as reflected by the high and accelerating rate of illiteracy, are underperforming, to say the least. President Sisi himself has declared the country needs 30,000 new school teachers, but cannot afford to hire them. As for the universities, they are performing rather better, although only one has in recent years ranked in the top 500 in the world as listed by any of the relevant ratings agencies. That was the American University of Cairo, which in 2012 jumped more than 100 places to 398th on QS World University Rankings, rising further to 345th in 2016.[18] Other measures of educational achievement, such as citations of faculty publications, registration of patents, and expenditure on research and development, all place Egypt more or less in the middle of Arab countries, which produce 5.9 percent of the world's GDP, but account for less than 1 percent of total global R&D expenditure. Egypt spends 0.7 percent, a bit less than either

Tunisia or Morocco.[19] The investment in tertiary education is not matched by payoffs for those with university degrees, as they are substantially more likely to be unemployed than those with fewer educational attainments. The calculated national return to investment in university education is extremely low. Even the personal return from a university education, which is an annual increment of only 9 percent over those without, compares unfavorably to every other MENA country except Yemen and to all other comparator lower middle income countries assessed on this measure by the World Bank.[20] Another World Bank survey found that only the private sector companies in Guinea-Bissau commit fewer resources to training than do those in Egypt.[21] So, to the extent that democratization is propelled by education and training, those drivers appear too weak in Egypt to provide momentum.

The demographic cards were thus stacked against the "Tahrir Revolution" producing a transition to democracy. Comparative experience indicates that the Egyptian population was just too young, too rural, too poor, too lacking a middle class, too materially insecure, too dependent upon government and too poorly educated and trained to perform the political organizational tasks required to construct a democracy out of the ashes of a collapsed authoritarian order. That the *Facebook-iyyin* utterly failed to translate popular momentum into coherent political organizations that could confront other challengers—whether at the ballot box, in civil society organizations such as professional syndicates, or in the streets—was due not just to their youth and political inexperience. It was due also to the huge magnitude of the task of trying to organize and lead a population that in the aggregate has few if any of the characteristics of a people apt to democratize.

Consequences for State and Nation of the Coup-Volution

The legacies of a comparatively strong state and coherent political community that were inherited by those who seized power in 1952 had by 2011 already been much squandered, as reflected in the deterioration of the country's human resources and its ill-preparedness for a democratic transition. The dramatic events of that and subsequent years have further debased these vital legacies, while also undermining yet further the endowment of human resources, thereby raising the question of whether these now much eroded legacies and resources will be sufficient to sustain a viable nation state as it faces ever more pressing challenges.

Weakening of state institutions

Since 1996 and the launch by the World Bank of its six Worldwide Governance Indicators, those measures have become the standard means by which state capacities are evaluated and compared.[22] Three of the indicators (government effectiveness, regulatory quality, rule of law) measure the state's core administrative abilities, while the other three (voice and accountability, political stability and absence of violence/terrorism, control of corruption) focus more on the context in which the state operates, although of course its actions do have an impact, hence feed back into that context.

The dramatic impact of the coup-volution on the Egyptian state's capacity for administration is reflected in the precipitate decline on the three most relevant indicators since 2010. In that year the relative effectiveness of the Egyptian government placed it in the 43rd percentile of countries, from which it commenced a steady decline, taking it to the bottom 20th percentile by 2014. This downward trajectory similarly characterizes regulatory quality, which dropped from the 47th to the 25th percentile, and the rule of law, which fell from the 51st to the 31st percentile during those five years. In sum, according to these rankings, the Egyptian state's core capacities have declined by almost half since the coup-volution and are at their lowest point since measurement commenced in 1996. Indeed, on all three of these indicators the highest scores were obtained in that initial year—48th, 53rd, and 54th, respectively, making the aggregate decline of core governance since that time in excess of 50 percent, one of the most precipitate declines in the world. Put simply, by 2014 things were not working even half as well in Egypt as they had been back in 1996.

Deterioration of the environment within which the government administers is both cause and consequence of this governance decline. Voice and accountability, an indicator of the degree of freedom and democracy in the system, was by 2014 at about the same level it had been during the most repressive years of the Mubarak era, at the 15th percentile, indicating that 85 percent of the world's countries were more democratic than Egypt. Its comparative score on political stability and absence of violence/terrorism was even worse, having by 2014 fallen to just below the 8th percentile from a high point in 2000 of almost the 45th. At least as concerning is the fact that there has been little change in Egypt's ranking on this indicator since the tumultuous period of 2011–13, during which time the country experienced the coup-volution and then an actual coup, both of which were associated with political instability and violence. Finally, the government's control of corruption in 2014, at the 32nd percentile, is just slightly less than its ranking back in 2010, the final year of the Mubarak era, which came to an end in significant measure because of perceived widespread corruption.

Egypt's rankings on these direct and indirect measures of state institutional capacities reflect the decline that set in during the Mubarak era and which has subsequently accelerated. It is interesting to speculate on what Egypt's rankings on the World Bank's Governance Indicators would have been from, say, 1952, had they been available. Although they would have fluctuated over that period, in general they would likely have traced a secular downward trajectory from the time at which the military took control and brushed aside established institutional capacities for administration, regulation, and provision of rule of law. All that is really new since 2010 is that this rate of decline accelerated, taking Egypt's state down to the bottom fifth of those in the world in the overall quality of the governance it provides. In 1952 Egypt was one of the better administered states in the then Third World, suggesting how truly mediocre its performance has been over the past some six decades, recently becoming even worse.

The impact of the coup-volution on two state institutions, the legal-judicial system and local administration, can serve to illustrate why and how governance is poor and declining. The former has primary responsibility for providing rule of law. There are four levels of courts, the highest being the Supreme Constitutional Court (SCC), charged with judicial review of legislation to ensure its constitutionality. When the newly established Mubarak regime liberalized in the wake of Sadat's assassination in 1981 it led to almost two decades of judicial activism by the SCC that expanded political and civil rights. In 2000 it finally overstepped the limits of court autonomy the executive was willing to grant when it ruled that, to be free and fair, elections had to be supervised by judges present in every polling station. This challenge to executive supremacy was met by the appointment of a new head of the SCC, Fathi Naguib, pulled from the Ministry of Justice, which is of course in the executive branch. He packed the Court with Mubarak loyalists. Executive interference cascaded down the court system, with a variety of interventions intended to encourage judicial self-restraint and discourage judicial activism. Authority over the Supreme Judicial Council (SJC), which administers the judiciary, was in effect transferred from judges to the executive. The minister of justice was awarded the power to choose the heads of lower courts, while the judicial inspection department, which falls under the Ministry of Justice, hence under the executive, began to interfere more in judicial administration, including court assignments and promotions.

So by 2011 executive interference had served to politicize the judiciary and erode its professionalism. Worse was soon to come. This politicized judiciary mostly sided with the military, with one of its key members, Tahani al Gabali, the first woman to serve on the SCC and its vice-president, becoming an advisor to the SCAF. She assisted its efforts to draft a constitution that would weaken the *Facebookiyyin*, and then advised on ways and means to undermine the Muslim Brotherhood. Scores if not hundreds of judges who objected to the suborning of their profession and the courts by either the SCAF or the Muslim Brotherhood were sidelined in various ways. Following the coup that overthrew the Brotherhood, a purge of judges commenced that carried on intermittently through 2015, in March of which forty-one more high-ranking judges, alleged Brotherhood sympathizers, were sacked. Three months later the Prosecutor General, the state's principal defender in the legal-judicial system, was assassinated, the first time in the country's republican history that such a high-ranking official associated with the administration of justice had been murdered. Such politicization and erosion of professionalism in the legal-judicial system also aggravated the systemic corruption of the court system, including rampant bribery of court officials, that had already spread from the time of Mubarak, if not before.[23] Coupled with the steady decline in the quality of legal education in the universities as the number of law students exploded from a few hundred to tens of thousands, and of judicial training, which has fallen from a year to a week for new judges, this helps explain the dramatic decline in the World Bank's indicator of rule of law, which fell by twenty percentile points between 2010 and 2014.

The World Bank's indicator of government effectiveness depends significantly on how well local government performs, for it is the level at which most citizens conduct day to day business with the authorities, whether in the fields of education, transport, communication, agriculture, or other. In Egypt, as in most of the Arab world, local *government* is really local *administration*, meaning that it reports not to local citizens, but to central executive authorities. Governorates, districts, and cities, towns or villages comprise in Egypt the three levels of local government, each of which collects into its own central administration employees of ministries, all headed by an executive appointed by the Ministry of Interior. The most powerful such executive is the governor, who heads the governorate. Since the Sadat era there have existed appointed executive councils, comprised of administrators who report to the chief executive, and elected popular councils, theoretically intended to represent citizens and oversee local executive authorities. The popular councils under Mubarak lost whatever dynamism they may have once had under Sadat for several reasons, key of which were that local civil servants report to national, not local level authorities, and that the overwhelming majority of members of popular councils were civil servants and members of the ruling National Democratic Party as well, with most elections not even contested.

Folk wisdom in Egypt is that local government is both profoundly corrupt and inefficient. It is accurate on both counts. A recent study found that two-thirds of governmental corruption in Egypt took place in the governorate, district or local level units.[24] Successive governments since the Sadat era have pledged to decentralize it as the chief means to combat corruption and improve performance. Indeed, demands for such were an important component of reforms advocated by participants in the uprising in 2011. A watered-down version of those demands was then embodied in article 180 in the 2014 constitution, which mandated decentralization within five years. Implementing legislation has yet to be enacted. Local government has essentially atrophied since the coup-volution. The last election to popular councils was a political non-event held in 2008. Councils elected at that time were disbanded in the wake of the coup-volution. They have yet to be reconstituted by election or appointment. As for the most powerful actors on the local government scene, governors, they are appointed by the president and report directly to him. The majority in Republican Egypt have been former military or police officers, their proportion increasing significantly once the military gained control of government in July 2013. By 2015, seventeen of the twenty-seven governors were retired generals, while another two were former police generals. Serving under governors are other retired military officers, typically colonels or generals, acting as deputy governors, secretaries-general, and/or assistant secretaries-general. In sum, after the coup-volution local government became less responsive to local citizens and more directly dominated by the armed forces than at any previous time in Egypt's modern history. Its profound shortcomings contribute in no small way to Egypt's ranking in the bottom one fifth of countries on the World Bank's government effectiveness indicator, that abysmal performance reflecting both the absolute degree and accelerating pace with which the legacy of competent central government is eroding.

Weakening of political community

Paralleling the decline of the state has been a weakening of the ties that bind Egyptians together in their shared sense of nationhood—the belief that they all are members of a common political community. As those ties erode, increased inter-communal tensions ultimately give way to violence, so its relative degree and pervasiveness provide ready indicators of the coherence, or lack thereof, of the overall political community.

Violence between Muslims and Christians has sharply escalated since the coup-volution, reflecting the growing sense of separateness within both religious communities. The governorate with the highest proportion of Coptic Christian inhabitants, Minya in Upper Egypt, is wracked by inter-communal violence that has taken the lives of many members of both religions, but predominantly of Copts, since the coup-volution. Intermittent Muslim–Christian violence has also flared up elsewhere in Upper Egypt, in the western Delta close to the important monasteries in Wadi Natrun, and in Cairo and Alexandria. But this violence, intense and expanding as it is, tends to be sporadic, incident driven, and not a manifestation of an insurrection or systematic campaign to destroy the other. Tanks, aircraft, and armored regiments are not engaged in this violence.

In the northern Sinai Peninsula, by contrast, attacks on government installations that commenced with the coup-volution, most notably on the critical gas pipeline to Israel, subsequently blossomed into a full-blown insurrection in reaction to the July 2013 overthrow of the Muslim Brotherhood government. It is still being fought out with heavy armor, helicopter gunships, F-16s, artillery, improvised explosive devices and other accoutrements of asymmetric warfare. This violence reflects the absolute breakdown of relations between local citizens and the central government and the contempt each side has for the other. The native population of the Sinai has a strong sense of its own, tribally based, sub-national identity and deeply resents the discriminatory treatment to which it has long been subjected by the Cairo-based government. Indeed, Sinai natives refer to their countrymen who are not from the Sinai as "Egyptians," suggesting that they do not consider themselves such. Egyptians from the Nile Valley tend to look down on the tribalized population of Sinai as primitive, lawless, and violent, to say nothing of their being compromised by their various relations with Palestinians in the bordering Gaza Strip, ranging from smuggling to shared kinship ties. Initially adopting the name Ansar Bait al Maqdis (Partisans of Jerusalem), these Bedouin-based insurrectionists pledged their allegiance in 2014 to the then powerful Islamic State (IS) based in Syria and Iraq, changing their organization's name to the "Sinai Province" of that claimed caliphate. This symbolized the first major, violent penetration by an external force into Egyptian domestic political strife in centuries. Weaker, less cohesive Arab states, such as Lebanon, Iraq, Syria, Libya, and Yemen, have long wrestled with problems of irredentism, secessionism, and external meddling. But for Egypt this is a novel challenge, suggestive of the degrees to which state capacity and national solidarity have eroded.

Moreover, the Sinai is not the only location in Egypt that manifests violent disaffection with the government, even with the nation itself. There are troubling parallels between the psychological exit from Egypt of residents of the northern Sinai and those in Upper Egypt, known as *saidis*. They, too, feel with good reason they have been short-changed by Cairo. Like residents in the Sinai, *saidis* are united not only by shared grievances against a government which discriminates against them, but by a dense network of tribal, kinship, and regionally based ties, which are overlaid with a shared identity as Upper Egyptians, akin to that of Sinai residents. They share a common Arabic accent, which along with other distinctive features serves as a butt for jokes at their expense among Cairenes and other Egyptians who perceive themselves as more sophisticated, superior to *saidi* "country bumpkins."

Jihadi Islamists have since the assassination of Sadat considered the *said* a fertile breeding ground for their message and actions. Islamic Jihad, the organization that assassinated Sadat in 1981, took a page out of Fidel Castro and Che

Guevara's revolutionary playbook by seeking to stimulate a rural uprising simultaneously with the October 6 presidential assassination. They seized control of Asyut, the capital of the governorate of that name, which they managed to hold for several days before being routed by paratroopers, who incurred some seventy casualties, but did stop the insurrection from spreading. About a decade later another jihadi organization, al Gama'a al Islamiyya (the Islamic Group), with its origins in student organizations principally in Cairo's universities, also based their nascent uprising in the *said*. Its sugar-cane fields and escarpments along the Nile River Valley provided refuge, but even more importantly, the rebels calculated that their message would have greatest appeal to *saidis*, disenchanted as they were even then with the central government. The insurrection sputtered off and on, with extensive loss of life and damage to property, until finally collapsing in the wake of the killing of almost sixty foreign tourists at Queen Hatshepsut's Temple on the West Bank of Luxor in November 1997.

Upper Egypt is afflicted with violence from other sources as well. As mentioned above, Asyut is the epicenter of the country's Muslim–Christian violence. In addition, the long-simmering disaffection of another section of the *saidi* population, the Nubians, whose main center is Aswan, the southernmost city in Egypt, finally boiled over into violence in April 2014. The al Dabudiyya Nubian clan, acting on long-harbored grudges against the Bani Hilal Arab tribe and non-Nubians in general, battled the Bani Hilal in the streets and alleyways of Aswan. Like other *saidis*, Nubians harbor profound resentments against some of their fellow countrymen and, most of all, against the central government. In the case of Nubians their sense of being wronged is based primarily on having been forcibly displaced from their ancestral homeland along the Nile River when that land was flooded by Lake Nasser, formed behind the High Dam, construction of which was completed in 1964.[25]

Saidi identity as separate from that of the rest of Egypt also rests on historical foundations. Qina Province, which is the key land bridge between the Red Sea and the Nile, has, as Zeinab Abul-Magd observes, "a long tradition of expressing discontent and rebelling. For many centuries, Qina Province was the vibrant capital of an autonomous state in Upper Egypt."[26] The fact that Qina is the poorest governorate in Upper Egypt, a region which as a whole suffers from profound neglect by the central government, is suggestive of the multiple causes and justifications presently driving intensification of anti-national sentiments and outbreaks of violence throughout the *said*.

Yet another widening fault line in the national political community with which at least some violence is associated is that based on gender. The coup-volution seemed to lift constraints on harassment and worse of Egyptian women by their male compatriots, including those in uniform. General Sisi himself was involved with so-called "virginity tests" of female demonstrators apprehended by the military in the spring of 2011, paradoxically justifying these egregious violations of women's rights on the grounds that the military did not want to be accused of sexual mistreatment of detainees. In the final years of the Mubarak era, national holidays had become occasions on which scores of women were physically assaulted on the streets of downtown Cairo and Alexandria. Such assaults increased dramatically in number and severity almost from the moment of the "Tahrir Revolution." The causes of this "gender war" are multiple, including increased societal tension overall; greater sexual frustration as a result of postponed marriage due to lack of economic wherewithal; the breakdown of authority during and after the revolution; the rise of Islamism and the gender-related values it propagates; and the growing political assertiveness of women which challenged both institutional authority, especially that of the military and security services, as well as men in general. Driving that assertiveness is the widespread societal discrimination and limited access to decision-making positions for women in both the polity and the workplace. The parliament elected from November 2011 to January 2012, for example, included only eleven women, about 1 percent of total membership, a profound insult to the country's women in the wake of the "revolution" to which they had contributed so much. The first woman to serve as governor was appointed in 2017 and only one, as mentioned above, has served on the Supreme Constitutional Court. Because they do not serve in the military other than in the medical corps, its dominant role in the country's political, governmental, and economic systems inevitably compounds their marginalization and exclusion from decision-making roles, including those in the economy. The Sisi government formed in July 2014 took some symbolic steps to increase female participation. It appointed, for example, twenty-six new female judges in June 2015, taking the total number to around eighty, or about 2 percent overall. The 2014 electoral law stipulated that parliament include at least fifty-six elected women. The limits of these initiatives, however, coupled with continuing violence directed against women by men in general and the security forces in particular, suggests that the new president was seeking less to bolster the status of women and protect them against violence than he was to cultivate their support against the Muslim Brotherhood, widely perceived as an enemy of women's rights. In the cabinet formed under Sisi's tutelage in September, 2015, only 3 of 33 ministers were women, none of whom was assigned a significant portfolio.

Violent street crime, including muggings, kidnappings and murder, has also dramatically increased since the fall of Mubarak. Some of this increase is due to a rise of organized crime, made possible by a general deterioration of policing as it has been focused increasingly on political rather than criminal activities. Other causes of criminal violence are increasing financial desperation, the spread of more politically motivated violence, and, what is most relevant to our concerns here, the general decay of community. It is not just that Muslims and Christians, Sinai and Upper Egyptian residents on the one hand and those from elsewhere in Egypt on the other, or Nubians as opposed to Arab Egyptians, or women as opposed to men, are intensifying sub-national identities that attenuate the sense of broader community. It is that individual Egyptians are increasingly alienated from one another and willing to perpetrate violent acts on others. Maybe most central to this broader breakdown of community is the profound and growing inequality, the impacts of which are accentuated by spreading poverty. Gated communities, private security guards, armored vehicles, personal weapons, and other indicators of the fear of violence have all dramatically increased since the coup-volution. Egypt is a country on edge, one in which the legacy of a shared national identity that the overwhelming majority of citizens once professed and in which they took pride has dramatically eroded, albeit after that legacy was much abused over the preceding years, largely as a result of the government's acts of omission and commission.

Conclusion

Egypt, in sum, has failed to capitalize on its almost unique legacies of state and nation, as the general deterioration of its comparative performance suggests. Charles Issawi, for example, noted that Egypt in the nineteenth century was generally more developed than Japan.[27] By the 1830s the Egyptian government was more aware of European science and technology than was its Japanese equivalent. At the turn of the century, Egypt's railway system was more extensive than Japan's. Just before the outbreak of World War I, Egypt's GDP per capita was higher than Japan's and its per capita imports and exports were double. Today, Japan's GDP per capita of some $40,000 is at least twelve times greater than Egypt's. Issawi pointed to several factors that account for Japan rapidly overtaking Egypt in the twentieth century, key of which was the high quality of the educational system and widespread literacy.

Similar if more recent comparisons can be made with other countries. South Korea's GDP per capita in 1965 was $105, $60 less than Egypt's. Twenty years later South Korea's had risen by more than twenty times to over $2,500, whereas Egypt's had risen only by some four and a half times to $690. In that year, 1985, Thailand's GDP per capita was about $50 greater than Egypt's. Today it is at least $2,500 more. Even in the MENA, where growth rates have been lower than those in East Asia, Egypt has been outperformed by comparator countries. Morocco's GDP per capita in purchasing power parity, for example, was $5,700 in 2006, more than double

Egypt's of $2,270. Ten years later Morocco's had risen to $7,300 while Egypt's only to $2,700, so in that decade Morocco's GDP per capita went from being double to more than triple Egypt's.

By failing to capitalize on its favorable, millennia-old endowments of centralized governance coupled with cohesive national consciousness, Egypt has not only underperformed economically, it has undermined those very endowments, as reflected in the increasingly dysfunctional government and a disunited, worryingly violent national political community. Economic performance is both a measure of the combined capacities of state and nation and a determinant of those capacities. If that performance sags over time, it places increased pressure on the ability of government to administer, adjudicate, and legislate, as well as on citizens to work together cooperatively. At the end of the period of colonial rule, which in Egypt was the mid-1950s, the country was undisputedly still the leading Arab nation state, but about to begin a steep comparative economic descent which has yet to be arrested. The causes of the decline of state capacities, of national cohesiveness, and hence of economic performance, are to be found primarily in the political system, which is the subject of Chapter 2.

2

The Deep State Presides: Military, Presidency, and Intelligence Services

The monarchial legacy inherited by the new Republic in 1952 was more favorable than it was portrayed as being by Nasser and his colleagues. Although King Faruq was an ineffective dissolute, the state over which he presided was among the most impressive in what was about to be dubbed the "Third World." Its executive, legislative, and judicial institutions were the most developed in the Arab world. The economy was buoyant, as reflected by the fact that the Egyptian pound appreciated after World War II to the point where it was worth more than the British pound upon which it had been based. A growing industrial sector was being financed by profits from agriculture, which was benefitting from the application of advanced technology learned by Egyptians who studied abroad and returned to take up positons in the Ministry of Agriculture. The financial sector included not only profitable branches of leading western banks, but locally owned ones as well, to say nothing of a dynamic stock market. Physical infrastructure—which included an extensive, well-run railway system; one of, if not the most sophisticated irrigation networks in the world; the Suez Canal, then the world's most strategically vital waterway; and urban amenities that included well run tramways, sewer and water systems, to say nothing of vibrant, attractive commercial centers—was comparable to that in much of southern Europe. Human capital was similarly well developed, as reflected by the high standards of Cairo

University, then one of the leading institutions of higher learning in the Third World, on a par with many in the West. Egypt's performing artists led the Arab world, with its cinema industry more or less equivalent to what Bollywood later became. Egyptian archeology set standards for the newly emerging field elsewhere in the world. Monarchial Egypt, in sum, had constructed a reasonably impressive state that had in turn built up the country's stock of physical and human capital.

The military rulers who inherited that legacy squandered it. This only became widely apparent, however, as global competition intensified, first as a result of the definitive end of colonialism in the 1960s, then further accelerated by the globalization that began to gather pace in the 1980s. As other states in the region and the one-time Third World began to pass Egypt by, its underperformance became ever more visible, both at home and abroad. One measure of that decline is the exchange rate of the Egyptian pound, which slid from $3 in 1960 to less than $0.30 thirty years later, and to some $0.06 by 2016.[1] Until the mid-1960s, however, and at various times after that, it seemed that Egypt was on the verge of a widely hoped for economic take-off, much promised by its leaders. Indeed, within the broad, continuous decline of the state and economy, a recurrent, cyclical pattern of optimism and hope, giving way to pessimism and despair, characterizes the Nasser, Sadat, Mubarak, and now the Sisi regime.

These recurrent cycles included interwoven political and economic dimensions. Nasser commenced his regime with promises of rapid economic growth combined not with political liberalization, but with the liberation of Egyptians from colonialism, imperialism, and local lackeys thereof. By the mid-1960s much of the monarchial capital accumulation had been dissipated, as reflected by the steady depreciation of the currency and the erosion of foreign currency reserves. The final years of the Nasser era were characterized by increasing economic hardship for the nation and its peoples, combined with growing political discontent as manifested in widespread grumbling and demonstrations of students and workers. In the absence of rapid economic growth and political freedom, the anti-colonial rhetoric had worn thin.

The trajectories of the polity and economy under Sadat were similar. On coming to power with his May 1971 "Corrective Revolution," Sadat promised to rein in the "midnight visitors" from the security services who had terrorized the population under his predecessor, and to build a "state of institutions." He orchestrated the emergence of a multi-party or, more accurately, one-party-dominant system, to replace Nasser's single party, the Arab Socialist Union, and endowed the newly created Supreme Constitutional Court with the power of judicial review, including of the freshly drafted, relatively liberal constitution. In the wake of the semi-successful 1973 October War, he declared an economic *infitah*, or opening, in which Egypt was to be reintegrated into the global economy and its private sector reinvigorated. By the time of his assassination eight years later, however, the political and economic openings had fizzled out, despite the temporary enrichment resulting from the decade-long oil boom that commenced in late 1973. Two months prior to his killing he had ordered mass arrests of his critics, while both foreign and domestic private sector interests, other than those closely associated with Sadat himself, had run up against what they increasingly deemed to be insurmountable barriers of state control of their activities.

The cycle was repeated yet again under Mubarak. His first moves as president were to liberalize the polity, reaching out even to those his predecessor had arrested, while allowing reasonably free and fair elections that produced the most sizeable and coherent opposition in the Egyptian parliament since the days of King Faruq. This initial political liberalization ran out of steam once Mubarak's power had been consolidated by the early 1990s, but was succeeded by a second phase that responded to global pressure for democratization orchestrated primarily from Washington. This phase was brought to a close, as noted in Chapter 1, some five years before Mubarak was overthrown. The economic liberalization to which the regime committed as part of an IMF package in the late 1980s—and which received a shot in the arm with the forgiveness of half the country's substantial foreign debt in 1991–2 for its support of western intervention to throw

Iraqi troops out of Kuwait—paralleled the decline of political freedom in the final years of the regime. Mubarak's cronies, many of whom were connected with son Gamal and his efforts to succeed his father, had by the early twenty-first century gained control of the most profitable sectors of the economy, closing off access to new entrants.

So far the Sisi regime seems to be aping its predecessors, and in more condensed fashion. At the time of the July 2013 coup, Sisi promised to lift the threatening hand of the Brotherhood over both the polity and the economy, for which he received widespread applause. Yet once the Brothers had been dispatched, the regime moved quickly to close down any and all channels of independent political expression, simultaneously extending the military's control over virtually all sectors of the economy, displacing civilian actors in both the public and private sectors.

As these gyrations back and forth between economic and political openings and closings have occurred, state capacities have steadily declined, albeit with a few ups and downs, while the rate of capital accumulation, as measured by the investment in and performance of the physical and human infrastructure, has slowed almost to a standstill. This begs the questions of why each regime has seemed about ready to break out of the mold imposed by closed political and economic orders, but then backtracked, re-imposing controls on both; and what the relation might be between this repeated cycle of frustrated hopes for openings and the country's decline.

Fortunately these questions have been taken up more broadly and by scholars from different disciplines. By borrowing concepts they have generated, it is possible to explain these dynamics in terms of something more than just the personal preferences of the five military officers and one hapless Muslim Brother who rose to be presidents of Egypt.

A Limited Access Order

In seeking to explain why some economies develop more rapidly than others, institutional economics, led by Douglass North, has emphasized the nature of economic orders established by political elites. What they term *limited access orders* are those in which political elites grant themselves "privileged control over parts of the economy, each getting some share of the rents...Stability of the rents and thus of the social order requires limiting access and competition." The rents concerned are generated from such arrangements as "government contracts, land rights, monopolies on business activities, and entry to restricted job markets." By contrast, *open access orders* are those in which political elites reduce the possibilities of state breakdown and the dissolution of political community by providing open access and competition. In these orders, "all citizens have the right to form contractual organizations," with this open access sustaining "both economic and political competition as well as an active civil society." Attempts to accelerate economic development by transplanting institutions from open to limited access orders generally fail, in North's view, because the institutions necessarily operate differently in the two settings.[2]

Recent empirical investigations in Egypt of "deep insider-outsider divides" bear out the theoretical proposition that they distort and hinder economic growth.[3] Those within the limited access order reap the benefits of it being closed to competition, as reflected in a World Bank finding that Egypt's "connected firms had average net profits *13 times* higher than the profits of remaining firms."[4] Insider businesses in the Mubarak era also received twice the level of non-tariff protection from imports as outsiders.[5] Among other negative consequences of the disproportion of benefits accruing to those inside the "order" are that "these cost advantages lead to market structures that suppress sector productivity and, therefore, aggregate economic growth."[6]

The Egyptian Republic was founded as and has remained a limited access order (hereafter, LAO). This was not a pre-ordained outcome. Monarchial Egypt had been an at least partially open access order (hereafter, OAO). The choice to impose an LAO as opposed to preserving the OAO, which had traditionally favored non-Egyptians but which was steadily opening up to Egyptians, was at the core of the two-year

power struggle between Colonel Nasser and General Muhammad Naguib, the latter originally chosen by Nasser's Free
Officers as their figurehead leader and then named first President of the Republic when it was declared in June, 1953. In
November of the following year Naguib was overthrown by
Nasser, the core issue in the struggle between them being how
much of the old monarchial order should be preserved. Naguib
favored the preservation of parliamentary democracy coupled
with liberal capitalism, whereas Nasser preferred a military
dictatorship that would extend its control over the economy.

Nasser and his supporters' preference for an LAO over
which they would preside was based on several calculations,
the consequences of which reverberate to this day. First, the
military officers did not trust one another and feared inter-
necine warfare within their ranks. Nasser's first priority was,
therefore, to establish a network of spies who would keep
tabs on his fellow officers. Military Intelligence was assigned
the priority role for this task, one which it still performs today.
Nasser's primary competitor, Abd al Hakim Amer, set up
competitive intelligence services over which Nasser was unable
to assert direct control until finally liquidating Amer in 1967.
So from the outset the heart of the LAO was the top leader
and his most trusted intelligence service, which has generally
been Military Intelligence.

Nasser's second concern was to thwart opposition by non-
military actors, both foreign and domestic. As for the former,
he opened communications with American intelligence as early
as 1949 for the purpose of securing US support against possible counter-moves against the Free Officer coup by the British
or others. His success in reaching out to Washington was
reflected by President Truman's welcoming of the coup and
warning to the British not to intervene.[7] The CIA, duped by
Nasser, committed itself to his defense through the critical
early years of the Republic, before finally realizing that his
and America's interests were fundamentally contradictory. As
for his domestic enemies, Nasser was most worried by the
Muslim Brotherhood and by leftists entrenched in the trade
union movement. The latter were the weaker of the two, so
he struck at them first, jailing scores of leftists and ordering

that leaders of a strike at the Kafr al Dawar textile plant in August 1952 be hung to deter possible emulators. The cat-and-mouse game between Nasser and the Muslim Brotherhood played out for almost two more years before he felt strong enough to pounce, dissolving the organization and executing six of its leaders, jailing 20,000 of its members and chasing thousands of others into exile.[8] For this tough handling of left and right civilian opponents, he relied primarily on his newly established security organs, just as he did in his competition with fellow officers, thereby further reinforcing these agencies' key role in the newly emerging LAO.

The third potential threat Nasser and his officer comrades faced was from those with significant capital. The royal family had been dispossessed immediately after the coup, but this left both a wealthy upper class of landowners, industrialists, financiers, merchants, and others, as well as an upper middle class comprised principally of high-ranking civil servants, professionals, businesspeople, and medium-sized landowners. Under the monarchy, people from a wide range of backgrounds had acquired substantial capital. It was possible they would seek through various means, ranging from expatriating their wealth to enticing foreign interests to intervene, to defend their interests against the feared depredations of the officers.

The fatal weakness which Nasser cleverly exploited was their diversity. In addition to the horizontal cleavages based on their comparative wealth, the upper and upper middle classes were divided by national, ethnic, and religious differences into basically four different groups. The most vulnerable were foreigners, including Italians, Greeks, Armenians, French, and others, as well as some of the Jewish community, many of whom were products of families resident in Egypt for generations but who had chosen not to take Egyptian citizenship as many of their number did under the terms of the 1923 nationality law. Almost as vulnerable were the *mutamassirun*, "Egyptianized" foreigners, including especially Turks, some other Jews, and Syro-Lebanese, who, although of foreign roots, had become Egyptian in nationality, language, custom, friendships, and self-identification, the last with some qualifications.

The third group were well off native Muslim Egyptians, the majority of whom had originally acquired wealth from agriculture and continued to have local roots in rural communities even if they had long ago urbanized and entered business or the professions. Wealthy Copts comprised the final group, and, like their fellow Muslim Egyptians, the richest among them had originally acquired their wealth through land ownership, in this case, primarily in the form of large estates in Upper Egypt.

Toward this potential source of opposition Nasser took two lines of attack. One was to accuse just about all of them of holding back Egypt's progress by refusing to invest—by being backward-looking, self-indulgent feudalists. The implication was that the military was entitled to confiscate their underutilized assets to build the new nation that would emerge under its guidance. The second, more destructive and lasting attack—in that it became part of the regime's, indeed the country's, DNA—was that these wealthy folks, other than the native Muslims, even if they had thoroughly Egyptianized, were not "real" Egyptians. Because they were foreigners, or of foreign extraction, however distant, and because they were not Muslims with roots in the countryside, they could not be truly Egyptian. Copts were left in limbo by this line of argumentation, which did not apply directly to them since they date back to Pharaonic Egypt, so have longer claims to residence along the Nile than Muslim Egyptians. Other Christians and Jews were particularly vulnerable to this charge, and indeed, their assets were much more subject to confiscation than their Muslim counterparts of equal wealth.

So from the outset of the Republic those deemed to be insufficiently Egyptian were vilified. Religious/ethnic credentials became a minimal threshold for access to the emerging LAO. Having been discredited as essentially foreign "feudalists," the upper and upper middle classes were displaced from the economy. Virtually all foreigners and most of the *mutamassirun* fled the country, having to leave much if not most of their wealth behind. Copts were made aware that their futures would never again be as bright as they had been under the monarchy.[9] Encouraging suspicion of anyone and anything less than 100 percent Egyptian was thus institutionalized as a weapon in the armory of the regime. It remains in use today.

The costs of this approach to national development both then and now have been profound. Ill-prepared military officers and those connected to them replaced skilled and experienced foreign, native, and *mutamassirun* businessmen, financiers, and professionals, frequently moving into their "nationalized" apartments, villas, and *izbas* (farms). The entrepreneurial dynamism and cosmopolitanism of the reasonably open order of the monarchy, in which those of many different backgrounds, including the rapidly rising class of native Muslim Egyptians, cooperated and competed in the economy and polity, died away. It was replaced by a stultifying LAO in which state control of both polity and economy, justified largely on chauvinist, nationalist grounds, obviated the possibility of Egypt ever again achieving rates of economic growth envied by most other developing countries, as it had under the monarchy.

The Egyptian version of the LAO was particularly pernicious both because its rationale was founded on a religious/ nationalist chauvinism and because its gatekeepers were men with guns, having experience with them and little else. The term "deep state," coined originally to describe the Turkish government and then broadened out to include governments in other Middle Eastern countries, refers to how the governmental component of the LAO is structured, hence who the gatekeepers of that LAO are. Those in the Egyptian deep state have from the outset been drawn from the triangle of the leader (president) and his immediate entourage, the military, and the security services. This limited core of the deep state has ensured not only that the barriers between the LAO and the remainder of the state and of society remain high, thus preventing access by those with other skills, talents, and outlooks, but also that those at the heart of the deep state are preoccupied with security issues and preserving, by violence if necessary, the LAO over which they preside. Economic development is necessarily subordinate for them to security, so access to the order over which they preside is determined far more by security implications than by potentially positive impacts on development. Real politics are then limited to the struggles for power within and between these three pillars of the deep state, for it is only they who have a chance of determining who gets what, when and how. How those struggles are played out is the subject of the remainder of this chapter. In Chapter 3 the ways and means by which the deep state penetrates and seeks to control the superstructure of governmental institutions will be investigated.

Despotic not Infrastructural Power: A Fierce but Brittle State

The historical sociologist Michael Mann has long been concerned with how states exercise power. His review of the historical record and of the behavior of contemporary states has led him to conclude there are two types of state power—despotic and infrastructural.[10] As the term suggests, despotic power, characteristic of most historical states, including those of the Pharaohs but also many contemporary ones, is the virtually unlimited, autonomous power of the ruler "to do as he wishe[s] with any individual or group in his domain."[11] Compliance in a state based on despotic power rests on fear of retribution and on coercion, rather than on the knowledge that the state has detailed, comprehensive information which could be presented in, say, a court of law to render a decision. Infrastructural power, by contrast, is "the capacity of the state actually to penetrate civil society and to implement logistically political decisions throughout the realm."[12] Despotic power is that exercised by the ruling elite *over* civil society, whereas infrastructural power refers to the ability of elites to "penetrate and centrally coordinate the activities of civil society through its own infrastructure."[13]

Tax collection illustrates the differences between the two types of power. The despotic state lacks the means to gather and utilize reliable, precise data as the basis for levying and collecting taxes. So it operates on the basis of general assumptions, outright guesses, and by threatening taxpayers so they disgorge funds to avoid draconian penalties. A state with infrastructural power, by contrast, has the capacity to track flows of funds, asset transactions, and basically all relevant financial matters down to the level of every citizen, each of whom is required to pay taxes on the basis of established rates and methods. Infrastructural power thus reinforces the state's legitimacy, whereas despotic power militates against it.

The Egyptian state operates with despotic rather than infrastructural power, as its tax collection methods suggest. The only reliable data on salaries possessed by the tax authorities is that for civil servants, who are taxed at source. Otherwise personal income tax is hit and miss, with the vast majority of citizens not filing returns. Total tax revenues from lawyers amounted in 2015 to LE74 million (less than $5 million), and taxes from all professionals to just 1 percent of total tax revenues in that year.[14] Tax collectors visit individuals and businesses to collect taxes, which typically involves bargaining and a side payment to reduce the official assessment. Businesses as a matter of course keep two sets of books to prepare for this contingency. Falsification of documents is widespread among importers and exporters, as taxation on the movement of goods is easier for a state wielding despotic power than is collecting personal and business income taxes. Indirect taxes in the form of customs duties and sales taxes have since 1990 accounted for about two thirds of tax revenue, approximately double their share in OECD economies, which rely much more heavily on direct personal and corporate income taxes.[15] Total taxes as a percentage of GDP were 13 percent in 2015, compared to 27 percent in the US and 35 percent in the UK.[16] Policing is similar. Criminal investigations based on infrastructural power require careful procedures, including gathering of forensic and other evidence and presentation of it before an independent court. In Egypt policing is based on intimidation, a key form of which is beatings, even torture, in local police stations as the initial and frequently only investigatory procedure.

Reliance on inefficient despotic rather than more efficient infrastructural power results to some degree from the broader context of underdevelopment. In a country such as Egypt— with relatively high rates of illiteracy, "informal" housing (built without title deed or permits and typically lacking a registered address), informal employment in micro enterprises, reliance upon cash rather than checks or credit/debit cards for transactions, and a vastly overstaffed but undertrained civil service—there are simply too many obstacles to govern through infrastructural power, which requires a substantial capacity to gather and process accurate information. Only 10 percent of Egyptians deal with banks, already an inflated percentage because it includes those whose dealings are limited to cashing their paychecks.[17] So the state rules by intimidating and coercing, to which the citizenry responds by obfuscating and cheating, hoping to avoid or at least minimize interactions with the government, especially those involving extraction of resources.

But there is a second reason for Egypt failing to shift from despotic to infrastructural power, as many countries in the developing world that were less developed in 1952 have done since then. It is that infrastructural power ultimately has to rest on a relationship of reciprocity between citizens and their government. A mutual, minimum level of trust is required, trust that in turn requires accountability based on regularized legal and political procedures. From the outset, the military government in Cairo rejected the very notion that it would be subject to the rule of law, be held accountable by citizens, or in any way be placed on their level and be a government of, for, and by the people. The military simply assigned itself the right to rule and adjudged any other actors as unfit and unable to do so.

The cost of that choice was that the government could not easily then interfere in citizens' daily lives, lest it provoke a political backlash. In essence a tacit deal was struck whereby the government would leave citizens alone to conduct their private affairs, winking at their transgressions such as tax avoidance. For their part the citizens would reciprocate the favor, essentially leaving the government to make decisions. The only real alternative for the military government was to try to impose a totalitarian, as opposed to authoritarian, order, but it had neither the will, coherence, nor capacity to do so. From the outset then, an implicit "social contract" defined the roles of both the governed and those governing, the former receiving material benefits coupled with considerable slack in applying laws and regulations, thus opening up the possibility of making side payments to regulatory officials; the latter being left alone to run the country. This political bargain left the government with the intermittent and largely unpredictable application of despotic power as the only means by which it could extract resources from and in other ways deal with its citizens.

This was a fierce but brittle state that could not fine-tune governance, so encountered difficulty in such matters as collecting revenue, enforcing civil and criminal law, and in managing the economy. The brittle state has never had the political or administrative capacity to balance the books as it could not easily extract resources from citizens, instead having to cut them a lot of financial slack lest they call the social contract into question. It is this shortcoming of their state and broader political system that Egyptian political economists have increasingly focused upon as the cause of their country's persisting underdevelopment.

Caught in a Socio-Fiscal Trap

Building on the work of Samer Soliman, Amr Adly has explained Egypt's failed economic transformation as the result of a "socio-fiscal trap."[18] This refers to both state revenues, which are too few in type and amount, and expenditures, which are over-committed to recurrent ones to sustain the ever-shrinking political base, and under-committed to investment in physical and human infrastructure.

As just noted, the inherently narrow political base of the LAO founded by the military, combined with the use of inefficient despotic over more efficient infrastructural power as the primary means of governing, have since 1952 rendered the task of raising adequate governmental revenue difficult. That task became virtually impossible with the advent of economic liberalization in the late 1980s. The revenue shortfall then intensified in tandem with the growth of the private sector's share of GDP, which is now about 70 percent, as compared to somewhat less than half in Nasser's economy, which was more heavily socialized than many Soviet satellite economies in Eastern Europe. Privatization, which commenced under Sadat and accelerated under Mubarak, has made it increasingly difficult for the government—long used to direct ownership of much of the means of production, and hence able to extract resources directly by virtue of that ownership— to substitute taxes on private actors as its primary source of revenue. Government revenue as a percentage of GDP began to fall in the 1980s, more or less in direct proportion to the private sector's growing share. With a few ups and downs revenue has continued to decline since then, with the total tax take as a percentage of GDP falling to some 12.5 percent in the wake of the coup-volution. In Denmark the ratio is a whopping 51 percent, but even in two MENA comparator countries it is also considerably higher, with Turkey's being 32.5 percent and Morocco's 22.3 percent.[19]

The government is caught in a socio-fiscal trap, being asked to do more with less. Capital investment in physical and human infrastructure has been crowded out by recurrent expenditures for government wages, subsidies, and interest on the ever growing national debt, which exceeded 100 percent of GDP in 2016 for the first time since 1991. From an average of around 30 percent for most of the 1975–85 decade, capital investment as a percentage of GDP fell to 22 percent in 1987. A decade later it had fallen to some 15 percent. Since 2004 it has averaged around 12 percent.[20] Recurrent expenditures have taken priority, according to Adly, because the regime has had to "mitigate the negative impacts of economic liberalization and privatization by attempting to uphold the old state-dependent coalition of public sector workers, civil servants and state-dependent urban middle classes," through wages and subsidies. Yet, according to Adly, these tactics subjected the old coalition to steady attrition as "the standards of living of state-dependent workers and employees kept declining."[21]

Had Egypt been truly in transition to a private sector led, capitalist economy, private investment would have begun to substitute for the drop in governmental investment. This, however, was not the case, with domestic private investment reaching the rather low peak of $35.8 billion in 2008–9 before commencing a slide that took it to less than half that by 2011–12, from which it has not rebounded. Moreover, at least 54 percent of this reduced investment was in the hydrocarbon or real estate sectors, with another almost 20 percent in transport and communications, leaving only about one quarter of the $18 billion invested in 2011–12, or some $4.5 billion, to all other sectors, which translates into $50 invested annually in industry, agriculture, health care, and various other sectors per Egyptian resident in the country. So the private sector has certainly not picked up the slack left by declining public sector investment, and indeed its contribution would be laughable were the consequences not so dire.[22]

Had the Mubarak regime been able to substitute for the old public sector rooted political base it inherited a new one comprised principally of beneficiaries of private sector growth, it might have survived. It was unable to make this transition for two reasons. First, underinvestment in physical and human resources militated against productivity growth, so Egypt became less competitive as globalization proceeded, generating proportionately ever fewer well-paid jobs. As Adly puts it, the socio-fiscal trap left the regime with too few "supporters of market reforms amid a general inability to create sizable strata of skilled and educated workers…or small and middle entrepreneurs, especially youth, in formal, secure and productive jobs."[23] Underinvestment in physical resources similarly undermined the prospects for productivity growth as Egyptian infrastructure failed to keep pace with that of competitors, in many cases declining to truly deplorable states, as we shall investigate in Chapter 5.

The second, associated problem of trying to substitute a new, private sector support base for the old public sector one was the limited number of beneficiaries from the private sector growth that did occur. Crony capitalism flourished under Mubarak, with the "whales of the Nile," as big businessmen were not so affectionately called, capturing a vastly disproportionate share of newly generated private wealth.[24] Their

conspicuous consumption, ranging from construction of sprawling villas in gated communities sprouting in the desert around
Cairo, to lavish weddings on the scale of *One Thousand and
One Nights*, to high-numbered Mercedes and BMWs, discredited not only themselves and the regime off which they
fed, but the very principle of private sector led growth. That
growth in fact was retarded by their rent-seeking, which among
other measures took the form of protection for their oligopolies
and monopolies. In those sectors of the economy dominated
by cronies, non-tariff barriers to imports were twice as high
as in more competitive sectors.[25] Not being able to go back
to a public sector based supportive coalition, nor forward to
a new, private sector based one, the Mubarak regime simply
collapsed, leaving the military to pick up the pieces and try
yet again.

Now ruling in their own right without having to share
power with the president, his family and their cronies, who
they allowed the mobs to overthrow, or with the Brotherhood,
which they then overthrew, the officers in the high command
led by General Sisi decided that they could dispense with any
broad political support base. Like its predecessor the new
regime could not afford to sustain the old public sector base,
nor was it willing, as had been Sadat and more so Mubarak,
to allocate noticeable economic and political roles to the private
sector, to say nothing of investing at least some capital to
assist its growth. So Sisi and his officer colleagues set out on
a high-wire political act, convinced that their dazzling performance would gain them public acceptance.

That these officers could even contemplate such a risky
approach is testament to their blind faith in the LAO their
predecessors had constructed some three generations ago. How
these new rulers could almost casually dismiss virtually all of
civilian Egypt as being of little economic or political relevance
bears witness to their hubris, their confidence in the durability
of the LAO, and the dilapidated state of the civilian order.
The officers must believe that the deep state at the core of the
LAO is strong enough to govern the country without significant organized popular support or respected, effective execu-

tive, legislative, or judicial institutions. Whether it is or not is the vital question, which can only be answered by a closer investigation of what that deep state is and how it operates.

The Deep State Tripod

The deep state initially erected by Nasser has always rested on three legs of unequal strength, the strongest being the military, followed by the president, with the intelligence services being the weakest. This distribution of power was not preordained. It resulted from power struggles between the Free Officers. It can be contrasted to deep states of other authoritarian regimes. Russia's, for example, rests primarily on the intelligence services which date back to the Czarist era, key of which since have been Stalin's NKVD, followed after World War II by the KGB, and then after the fall of the Soviet Union by Putin's FSB.[26] Russia has been a police state in the true meaning of the term since Czarist times, whereas Egypt has had a military state, or "military society" as it was dubbed almost half a century ago by the Egyptian leftist Anouar Abdel-Malek.[27] While Russia publicly celebrates its intelligence services and their heroes with museums, songs, and names of streets, Egypt does the same with its military, not with its spies.

Neither Nasser, Sadat, nor Mubarak had absolute, direct personal control of the military. None could afford to devote the time and energy to that task once they assumed the burden of presiding over the state. But all three were keenly aware of the threat of being overthrown by their armies. Their coup-proofing strategies relied heavily upon bolstering the intelligence services. This resulted in the steady growth of those services, such that by the end of the Mubarak era their total personnel were approximately double those serving in the military. The Central Security Force (CSF) alone, comprised of barracked units whose weaponry has been steadily militarized, was purposely placed by Nasser under the minister of interior to counterbalance armed forces under the then minister of war (who became the minister of defense after the 1973 War).

The CSF grew from a few tens of thousands in the late 1960s, then deemed ample to control demonstrating students and workers, to some 350,000 by the Mubarak era. Each president preferred to rely upon it for crowd control, counter-insurgency and counter-terrorism activities rather than entrust the military with these responsibilities. They feared that if the military were the key line of defense between them and the people, the military would ultimately dispense with their services, as indeed it did in 2011.

In addition to bolstering the intelligence services as counterweights to the military, each president also devised his own method of asserting as much top-down control over the military as possible. At the outset of his rule Nasser charged his once trusted friend and co-conspirator, Abd al Hakim Amer, with the task of keeping the army in check. This proved to be an almost fatal mistake. Once in command Amer refused to share or relinquish control, despite repeated attempts by Nasser to induce him to do so. The final showdown came in the wake of the June 1967 war. Fearing that Nasser was finally going to move against him, Amer summoned loyal officers to his villa, where they were assaulted by troops loyal to Nasser. Amer was captured, imprisoned, and then allegedly poisoned to death. For the final three years of his rule Nasser relied heavily on Soviet advisors to run his military, which was bent to the task of recapturing the Sinai.

Having observed first-hand the peril of entrusting even one's closest friend with unfettered control over the military, Sadat rotated his ministers of defense (of whom there were seven during his period in office), chiefs of staff, and commanders of the vital second and third armies in windmill-like fashion, regularly purging, exiling, and maybe even having some killed during his eleven-year rule.[28] All of Sadat's prime ministers were civilians, whereas all of Nasser's had been officers. Interestingly, Sadat, who served only briefly in the military, wore his uniform frequently and was wearing it when assassinated, whereas Nasser shed his in June 1956, never to wear it again.[29] Mubarak initially committed the Nasser error of entrusting one officer, Abd al Halim Abu Ghazala, to run his military for several years. As that minister of defense's ambitions and stature rose, Mubarak became increasingly wary, finally purging him in 1989, and placing him under house arrest until his death in 2008. The lesson Mubarak learned from this episode was somewhat different than Sadat's takeaway from Nasser's mistake. Mubarak decided never again to choose a minister of defense who was popular with the troops, or who had a reputation for competence either on the battlefield or in the political arena. He wanted a weak, not a strong man to run the military. He settled on the lackluster General Muhammad Husayn Tantawi, promoted him to Field Marshal, and let him preside over the Ministry of Defense longer than any other person in the country's history. To further ensure that the Amer and Abu Ghazala scenarios did not play out again, he diverted Tantawi's attentions from military matters to business affairs, ordering him to expand the military economy, thereby insuring against a coup. Among other consequences, this diversion from defending the nation undermined Tantawi's popularity with professional, devoted officers, who resented the repurposing and corrupting of the military. But those officers were marginalized, denied promotions and appointments to key units, so were unable to challenge the status quo. Most officers were content to sit back and relax, knowing that their material interests would be served in return for loyalty, not performance.

Sisi's coup-proofing strategy is novel in the sense that he has remained more in the bosom of the military than any of his predecessors. Rather than leaving the military he has extended its direct control over the polity, economy, and society. He remains in daily contact with his old army buddies, who are now handling the sprawling affairs of state. His confidence is reflected in the fact that instead of reinforcing the independence of the intelligence services from the military, he has subordinated those formerly under the Ministry of Interior or presidency more directly to the military's control than did any of his predecessors. Always important, Military Intelligence under Sisi has reached new heights, essentially coordinating and overseeing the work of all the other intelligence agencies. Being from that very branch of the military and securing its control through his sons, in-laws, and closest colleagues, Sisi is obviously confident that his command of the intelligence services is secure and that they in turn can keep a close eye on the operational military. But even these two lines of defense—remaining in daily contact with the military while converting Military Intelligence into his own omnibus intelligence service—he deems insufficient coup-proofing. The final measure is that, like Sadat, he jealously prevents his officer colleagues from sharing the limelight. He keeps his old classmate and now minister of defense, Sidky Subhi, in the shadows, letting him appear in public only infrequently. Also like Sadat, he has churned officers through the operational commands and even the key post of head of Military Intelligence. He keeps those in the high command off balance, worried about their futures and no doubt frightened of their leader. Lest he present an easy target to fellow officers or others, he has no known permanent home address.

This then is the tripod which forms the deep state, in Arabic *al dawla al amiqa*, upon which all the remaining governmental and political superstructure rests. Since these three legs are so absolutely vital to determining who gets what, when and how in Egypt, we need to investigate each in its turn.

The Military

The size, state penetration, and economic/social/political powers of the Egyptian military are unequalled in the Middle East and North Africa and possibly the world. It is the largest military in the MENA and the eleventh largest globally.[30] Its overall strength is ranked twelfth in the world, just behind Germany, Italy, and South Korea, countries whose GDPs per capita are at least twelve times greater than Egypt's.[31] In 2017 its navy was assessed by Global Firepower as the world's sixth strongest.[32] The "officer republic" it has configured over the years, by placing active duty and retired officers into virtually all areas of the state's administration, is without parallel.[33] Egypt's "Military Inc.," which consists of a wide range of business enterprises providing goods and services, is proportionately larger and growing more rapidly than that of any other MENA country, and maybe globally.[34] The Egyptian military's soft power over society, whether in ideational or material forms, is similarly almost without regional or even global parallel, as reflected in its consistent approval ratings among the Egyptian public of above 80 percent.[35] Finally, its direct political power in the form of occupying key political positions or controlling access to them has since the coup of 2013 been akin to the pre-eminent position it occupied from 1952 to 1967, when officers dominated the political life of the country.[36]

The rising power of the military over almost the last century can be traced through its constitutional standing. The only reference to it in the first constitution of independent Egypt, that of 1923, was that the king was commander-in-chief, with the power to declare war. The power to recruit, promote, and dismiss officers was placed in his hands, a power that in the event King Faruq did not use wisely, although, he, like his father, did appoint some civilians as ministers of defense, whereas all nineteen subsequent such ministers have been officers. In all the constitutions of Republican Egypt the powers of the military have been expanded at the expense of civilian actors and institutions, such that the present constitution, that of 2014, written under direct military tutelage, places the military above the law in all meaningful regards. It incorporates and adds to all the military-related clauses of the 2012 constitution, which vested dramatically more powers in the armed forces than did any of its predecessors as a result of the Muslim Brotherhood's intent to solidify its "condominium" rule with the military by rendering it constitutionally autonomous. The president is named the Supreme Commander of the Armed Forces, but his power to declare war is shared with the military by virtue of the provision that he must consult with the military-dominated National Defense Council and the parliament before so doing. If a parliament is not sitting, which was the case between 2012 and 2015, for example, this provision "gives the military the final say."[37] Presidential power is further diluted to the benefit of the military by the minister of defense being specified as the commander-in-chief and the requirement that he be a serving officer. The

National Defense Council, originally created by Nasser in 1969 and chaired by the president so as to dilute the power of the minister of defense, was briefly revitalized by Sadat in 1971 for the same reason, but immediately became a dead letter due to the military's resistance. It was revived by the military just before Mursi became president, only this time it was intended to curtail presidential power. The 2014 constitution vested supervisory power over the military budget in the Council. It also mentions for the first time the Supreme Council of the Armed Forces, which dates back to 1954 when it was established as a coordinating body between the chiefs of the various services and chaired by the president. The 2014 constitution transfers the chairmanship from the president to the minister of defense. The jurisdiction of military courts over civilians in cases concerning "military security," first given constitutional status in 2012, was retained in the 2014 constitution. Similarly conscription, incorporated into the 2012 constitution for the first time, was retained in that of 2014 in Article 86, which states that "defense of the nation and protecting its land is an honor and sacred duty. Military service is mandatory according to law." The real purpose of the clause was to guarantee a flow of cheap conscript labor to military-owned production facilities. Florence Gaub, a specialist on Arab militaries, notes that Egypt is "a country where civilians have been formally almost entirely removed from oversight of the defence sector."[38]

Zeinab Abul-Magd's *Militarizing the Nation* portrays the Egyptian military's enduring success as resulting from it being self-serving, more concerned with preserving and expanding its power and rewards than with the nation's well-being. It has been chameleon-like, tailoring its ideology, alliances, and practices to suit prevailing conditions. Having justified its domestic pre-eminence under Nasser on the basis of Arab nationalism, anti-Americanism, socialism, and economic autarchy, under Sadat it commenced a rightward shift that saw it become by the end of the Mubarak era a champion of US-led, neoliberal globalizing development.[39] Accompanying the rhetorical shift were changes in the military's economic and political alliances. Ties to state-owned enterprise and the socialist political infrastructure associated with that sector, including the then single party, the Arab Socialist Union, were abandoned in favor of alliances with domestic and international entrepreneurs and enterprises. Similarly, goods and services produced by "Military Inc.," which under Nasser were intended almost entirely for military consumption, were first extended under Sadat to serve mass needs, such as for basic foodstuffs and physical infrastructure, then subsequently under Mubarak and now Sisi to bourgeois consumption items ranging from personal computers to resort holidays to luxury automobiles. From being a champion of the poor, the military evolved into a bastion of privilege, paralleling and indeed underpinning the country's drift to the right, all the while reinforcing its power with steadily greater control over the state's administrative structures and the broader economy.

The military's powers to influence domestic politics are best viewed on a continuum ranging from soft to hard. At the former end are its capacities to influence both elite actors and the population as a whole. Those capacities in turn rest on both ideational and material resources. The former include media presentations, song writing, educational curricula, sports and recreation facilities and teams, and various means to shape the historiography of the armed forces.[40] A recent example of this historiographical power demonstrates its broader manifestations. In April 2016, as Sisi's and the military's popularity were visibly sagging, the minister of antiquities in the newly formed cabinet, Khalid al Inany, announced "a major project to retell the country's military history from the ancient Egyptian era to the present day through the opening of several historical sites to tourists as well as the setting up of new museum displays." The minister went on to provide some details, such as the building of a panorama "displaying Egypt's military history" in the area between the original Suez Canal and its recently dug second channel.[41] That its chain of museums is intended more to burnish the military's credentials than to provide reliable historical material to the public was suggested by the gaffes of General Nigm al Din Mahmud, the director of those museums. He was asked in September, 2016, to elaborate on the great historical victories of the Egyptian army, which are, as the reporter noted, "drilled into the minds of Egyptians since primary school."[42] Among other mistakes he misidentified Salah al Din's twelfth-century battle of Hattin against the Crusaders as Ramses III's (in reality it was Ramses II's) victory over the Hittites more than two millennia earlier, causing much satirical comment on social media.[43] Under Sisi the military has assumed managerial roles within the media, as reflected by the appointment in January 2017 of General Muhammad Samir, then the official spokesperson for the armed forces, as Director General of the al Assema Television Network.[44] Soft power also flows from material rewards, which likewise have been expanded under Sisi. The military's role in the economy has widened as its penetration of the state has deepened, thus providing more goods and services to consumers and more jobs for those ranging from draftees to corporate executives. Cradle-to-grave goods and services are pitched to the socioeconomic level of recipients. For the poor the army bakes bread, manufactures pasta, grows fruits and vegetables, builds cheap housing, and rents out inexpensive wedding venues. For the better off the range expands to include bottled water, poultry and meat, fuel for automobiles, the autos themselves, household appliances, holidays in seaside resorts, access to sports facilities, computers and various other consumer items typically, but not always, competitive in price and quality with those offered by the civilian private sector.[45] The Egyptian population has become more dependent upon the military for goods and services than any other single vendor, a fact which the military trumpets when it deems it in its interest to do so, such as when it supplies bread to the underserviced subsidized market. The military thus can and does present itself as the benefactor of the nation, providing it with goods and services while relieving taxpayers of the financial burden of paying for a military depicted as costing the nation comparatively little.

Employment provides the military with more useful soft power because job allocation can be targeted to beneficiaries. At the top, retired colonels and generals are pensioned off into military-owned companies, public sector enterprises, the civil service, and increasingly even into privately owned com panies, whose owners are keen to subcontract to the military. Since these appointments are at the discretion of the high command, they constitute a key incentive for loyalty during and after active service. At the bottom, the some 300,000 conscripts serving at any one time have a roof over their head, a small income, and the opportunity to learn a skill which might provide employment after their discharge, an increasingly wane hope for most young Egyptians. The total personnel of the armed forces is some 450,000. Another 350,000 serve in the Central Security Forces, to which lower quality draftees are directed and which is for all intents and purposes an extension of the army, now that the Ministry of Interior is fully subordinate to the military. More or less the same can be said about the relationship between the military, on one hand, and General Intelligence and National Security, on the other, which between them employ at least 200,000 uniformed and plainclothes personnel. This suggests that the grand total of officers and men directly or indirectly under the high command is about 1 million. This does not include the 350,000 policemen or the 35,000 officers under the Ministry of Interior.[46] If those employed in "Military Inc." are added to the military's figure, then it probably approaches 2 million, although since no definitive information is provided on the military economy this must remain a guesstimate. Egypt's labor force is some 28 million, including those serving in the military and the unemployed, meaning that those actually working outside the military number somewhat less than 24 million. So the armed forces directly and indirectly account for about 8 percent of all the jobs in the country, with civilian public employment of 7 million accounting for another some 30 percent of those holding jobs.

In sum, the government provides about two out of every five jobs in Egypt, a source of enormous material leverage over the population, especially considering the multiplier effect of dependents supported by each such employee. The military-dominated government thus literally has the fate of not much less than half the population of some 90 million citizens resident in Egypt directly in its hands. Such dependency is bound to give pause to those enmeshed in it were they to contemplate

THE DEEP STATE PRESIDES

taking visible, tangible steps against military rule. The military's soft power, in sum, provides both ideational and material justification and bases for its rule.

But it is the armed forces' hard power that sustains it against potential challengers, as the cases of all presidents before Sisi suggest. Each desired to subordinate the military to himself, but none succeeded in doing so in lasting, institutionalized fashion. Blood has been shed in these struggles, as it has been on the streets when the military has confronted challenges from demonstrators, strikers, student activists, and indeed anyone since 1952 who seriously sought to challenge it. The hard power that can be deployed against challengers arising from within the state or from civil society has been steadily enhanced since the Nasser era.

Following the peace agreement with Israel the military no longer had an enemy against which to defend the nation, so gave itself over to expanding the soft and hard power by which it rules and now directly governs. The 2011 uprising did not come close to dislodging the military. Indeed, its reformist nature effectively limited its demand to removing Mubarak rather than the entirety of the deep state. Had subordination of the military and security forces to civilian control been the protesters' objective, Egypt might have dissolved into civil war, possibly with the military fracturing in the process, much as it did in Libya, Yemen, and Syria. But the present combination of seductive soft power backed by the threat of force is sufficient to deter all but the most diehard opponents of military rule, so long as some hope for a better future remains alive.

Intelligence Services

Since 1952 Military Intelligence has been responsible not just for gathering and analyzing information related to foreign military threats, but for spying on the Egyptian military itself and indeed, the whole of society. It has served as a primary coup-proofing tool for all of Egypt's officer presidents. Several ministers of defense, including Ahmad Ismail and Kamal Hassan

Aly under Sadat, served immediately prior to their promotion into the cabinet as heads of Military Intelligence, as indeed did General Sisi. As for Nasser, immediately after leading the 1952 coup he placed his close confidant, Zakarkiya Muhyi al Din, in charge of Military Intelligence, from which position and subsequently as minister of interior he constructed an overlapping military and civilian intelligence network loyal to the president that was intended to counterbalance the then minister of war, Abd al Hakim Amer.[47]

Over the following six decades the centrality of Military Intelligence to control of the military and broader society has varied, but it has always been substantial. Sadat and Mubarak both used State Security Investigations, under the Ministry of Interior, as well as General Intelligence, directly under the presidency, as counterweights to Military Intelligence, precisely because they were not from the heart of the military themselves (Sadat served on active duty in the military for less than five years, whereas Mubarak was an air force, not army officer). They could not, therefore, place all of their trust in Military Intelligence, as it is potentially subjected to cross-cutting military loyalties. Umar Sulaiman, who served Mubarak as an enforcer in much the same way as Zakariya Muhyi al Din had been Nasser's tough guy, was pulled out of Military Intelligence, where he had served as deputy director and then director from 1986 to 1993, to head General Intelligence, from which he was promoted to vice-president in the last ten days of the Mubarak era.

Sisi used Military Intelligence to overthrow President Mursi and then to serve as the primary instrument of his regime, both as watchdog on the military and as ringmaster of the political arena. While serving under Mursi as minister of defense from August 2012, he charged Military Intelligence with the task of recruiting a civilian opposition to the Brothers modeled on that which had overthrown Mubarak. Supported by the Ministry of Interior, Military Intelligence organized the ostensible volunteer youth movement, Tamarrud, which in turn coordinated the petition allegedly signed by 22 million Egyptians demanding Mursi's resignation, presented during the mass demonstrations of June 28 to July 1, 2013.[48]

Sisi's control of Military Intelligence is highly personal. Two of his sons have served in it. He appointed as his successor there his daughter's father-in-law, to say nothing of sprinkling his friends and allies in key positions within that and other key commands, including Muhammad Farid al Tuhamy, his old boss from Military Intelligence, as head of General Intelligence.[49] Military Intelligence's role as coup-proofer was evident in the spring of 2015, when it claimed credit for sniffing out an Islamist coup attempt against Sisi.[50] Simultaneously it has performed its duty of arranging civilian window-dressing to cover the military regime. In the lead up to parliamentary elections in 2015 it organized two political parties which when combined won a substantial majority and went on to form a government in early 2016.[51] It also appears that Military Intelligence has taken on a more direct role than previously in subduing real and imagined opposition, as suggested by allegations of its torturing detainees in its network of secret prisons.[52]

Sisi's methods echo Nasser's in the handling of broader civilian political life. In early 1953 Nasser, profoundly contemptuous of party politics, issued law 179 dissolving the existing parties and confiscating their assets, simultaneously ordering Military Intelligence to create the Liberation Rally, a proto-party designed by Nasser to occupy the civilian political vacuum his coup had created and thereby deter independent political organization. Nine years later, when Nasser created his single political party, the Arab Socialist Union, as a counterbalance to the military, then loyal to Abd al Hakim Amer, he appointed the former deputy director of State Security Investigations as its head, supported by a Secretary General who had been the first commander of the Presidential Guard.

Sisi has adopted a virtually identical strategy, the one difference being that he created two equivalents to Nasser's Liberation Rally—one version for seniors and another for juniors. The first, For the Love of Egypt, the name of which was subsequently changed to Support Egypt, was intended to attract the type of influential and opportunistic elements that had flocked to Nasser's Liberation Rally. Samih Saif al Yazal, ultimately charged with organizing the new party by Sisi, had served in Military Intelligence before being transferred to General Intelligence. After the overthrow of the Brotherhood, he and Murad Muwafi, a former head of Military Intelligence who had been removed by Mursi in August 2012, worked together to organize the contemporary equivalent of Nasser's Liberation Rally. Saif al Yazal soon replaced Muwafi, who lost Sisi's confidence possibly because he posed a challenge to him, and successfully steered Support Egypt to victory in the 2015 parliamentary elections, where it won 120 seats to become the largest bloc in that body, with him at the head.

Sisi also mandated a previously little known twenty-four-year-old, Muhammad Badran— who in April 2013 had been elected as president of the Egyptian student union, presumably with the backing of Military Intelligence—to organize the Nation's Future Party, a junior version of the Liberation Rally intended to draw youth into the regime's embrace and away from the opposition. It won fifty-three seats in the 2015 parliamentary elections, the second highest number.[53] This convenient electoral outcome respecting the senior/junior division of political responsibility was presumably arranged by Military Intelligence, which played the key role for the regime in orchestrating the elections. Kamal Amir, a former Military Intelligence officer and the leader of the Guardians of the Nation Party, a component of the Support Egypt bloc, was in April 2016 elected chair of the parliament's Defense and National Security Committee, which has primary responsibility within parliament for overseeing the military.

Military Intelligence has thus come full circle, back to the role created for it by Nasser in defending his rule against his fellow army officers and the military's rule from civilian challenges and oversight. But Sisi has even more direct control of it than Nasser did, who placed it under the authority of Zakariya Muhya al Din. Moreover, Military Intelligence has under Sisi consolidated more control over rival intelligence agencies—including the presidency's General Intelligence and the Ministry of Interior's State Security and State Security Investigations, the latter renamed National Security after the coup-volution—than under any previous president.[54] This reflects Sisi's background in the high command in general and

Military Intelligence in particular, his commensurate disinterest in civilian politics and institutions, and his preference for more direct military rule.

The Presidency

Although the nuances of presidential control of the military and the deep state within which it is the strongest component have varied—as has personal political style, such as how the president would present his family to the public—there has been no great variance in the thrust of presidential rule. Although the professed ideology changed from Arab nationalism and Arab socialism to Egyptian nationalism coupled with a guarded embrace of private economic activity, presidential preoccupations remain the preservation of the LAO and the president's pre-eminence within it. While the gatekeepers of the LAO have changed, with Mubarak, for example, delegating to his son Gamal influence over the choice of whom in the business community to provide access to, the principle of political entry being a prerequisite for substantial economic gain has never varied. Nor was any effort made to change the regime's political base from one resting ultimately on the state and its allocations to one rooted in an autonomous civil society. Although lip service was paid, especially by Sadat, to building institutions and the rule of law, and by all to democracy, Egypt's institutions are weaker now than when Nasser seized power. The country is further from democracy than at any time since then.

A key reason for persistence of authoritarian rule is that all presidents have sought to ensure that they are the focal point of the entire system. One small indicator of that is that deciding the layout of the front page of government-owned dailies has, since Nasser's time, been the prerogative of the Office of the Presidency, whose concern is how the page presents the president, especially visually. Similarly, that Office is the keeper of presidential archives, none of which have ever been made accessible to the public. The presidency itself is the equivalent of a substantial ministry, staffed at the higher levels by military officers. Egypt, in other words, is one of the world's most institutionalized and longest surviving presidential dictatorships, now in its seventh decade. Since the successive dictators have been the orchestrators of the entire system, starting with the deep state, extending upward into the state infrastructure, and then finally reaching out into political and civil society, it is important to illustrate how they have played the role of conductor. We shall do so by comparing Sisi's rule to that of Nasser's and Mubarak's.

Paradoxically, although the content of Sisi's rule is closer to that of Sadat's or Mubarak's, his tactics are more reminiscent of those of the founder of Republican Egypt. His appeal is less to the poor and downtrodden than to those fearful of them higher up in the social order. He seems to be turning his back on the 7 million strong civil service, the core of the new middle class essentially created by Nasser and then pampered by Sadat, Mubarak, and Mursi.[55] He has rehabilitated disgraced cronies of the Mubaraks, poured scarce funds into mega-projects of dubious economic value, and presided over a precipitate decline in public services, especially health care and education—all steps, with the possible exception of the mega-projects, that belie Nasser's legacy.[56] Sisi now desists from even paying lip service to Arab nationalism, the cornerstone of Nasser's foreign policy and a key ingredient in his domestic appeal. He has substituted for it strong relations with Israel, combined with attempts to court Iran, while retaining US support.[57] The Egyptian public, having anticipated "Sisi-ism" to be an updated, re-energized Nasserism, including social support for the needy and a projection of Egyptian power into the region, are increasingly mystified and disenchanted, if nevertheless clinging to the hope that their savior-president will ultimately deliver.

Tactically, however, it appears that Sisi has copied pages from the Nasser playbook, including in his methods of dealing with the Brothers. As spokesperson for the SCAF and the most manifestly religious of its some eighteen officer members, from the spring of 2011 he cultivated the Brothers while serving as liaison between them and the military. Like Nasser, he succeeded in convincing the Supreme Guide and others on the Guidance Council that he was a fellow traveler. So when the Brothers made their first move against the high command in August 2012, by removing the minister of defense Tantawi, they turned to Sisi not only to replace his boss, but to reconfigure the high command, including its most sensitive posts— among them the commanders of the Republican Guard, created by Nasser in 1953 to defend himself against his fellow officers and upgraded out of the same motive by Sadat in the late 1970s with US-supplied tanks and other heavy equipment, and the Central Command which guards Cairo. Tantawi, in short, played Naguib while Sisi acted out Nasser's role. Sisi then appeared to cooperate with the Brothers for several months, before cautiously distancing himself from their increasingly unpopular rule. In the meantime he charged Military Intelligence with the task of mobilizing civilian opposition to the Brothers modeled on that which had overthrown Mubarak two years previously.[58] Sisi, again like Nasser, then portrayed the July 3 coup as the military responding to the national will to replace an unpopular government. He followed this up in August with a crackdown on the Brothers even more draconian than Nasser's had been, with mass killings in two of Cairo's main squares followed by arrests of thousands of members and a declaration of the Brotherhood as a terrorist organization. By 2014, Sisi's regime had dispatched to prison some 40,000 Egyptians, the majority of whom were Brothers, a figure approximately double the number of those incarcerated by Nasser in the wake of his 1954 purge.[59] Despite repeated mediation efforts by both Egyptians and foreigners, Nasser and the Brotherhood never reconciled, the latter's leadership remaining in exile in the Gulf and Europe. Similar such efforts have yet to bridge the gap between Sisi and the Brothers, whose leadership is now largely resident in Turkey.

As for political opposition other than the Brothers, again Sisi's approach seems a copy of Nasser's, if even more repressive. Mention has already been made of political prisoners, with Sisi's tally double that of Nasser. Nasser's "midnight visitors" spirited away to prison and torture thousands of Egyptians suspected of opposition. In just over one year Sisi's operatives "disappeared" over 500 young Egyptians, while his torturers have been working overtime in the sprawling network of prisons, which includes numerous unregistered institutions.[60] Workers and students have been special targets, as they were for Nasser, who, as mentioned earlier, sent troops to Kafr al Dawar in August 1952 to put down a strike by shooting demonstrators and hanging its alleged organizers. Sisi's forces have likewise engaged in strike breaking. A decree outlawing strikes was issued in 2015, while military courts have been given jurisdiction over violators of this and other labor legislation, including that which outlaws independent labor unions. Nasser's regime sought to tightly control university students, and when they demonstrated in the wake of the 1967 defeat, troops opened fire, killing twenty-one and injuring more than 700, while more than 1,000 were jailed.[61] Sisi's hand-picked university presidents have invited private security forces onto campuses and have raised no public objections to security services "disappearing" students, some taken directly from their campuses.[62] The Ministry of Higher Education overturned the result of the 2015 student union elections in which a candidate independent from the government won the presidency. Governmental media under Sisi are restricted to the same cheerleading role they had under Nasser. The private media, which did not exist in Nasser's Egypt, has been more or less successfully throttled in Sisi's.[63] Non-governmental organizations, of which there were very few performing political advocacy roles under Nasser, have been brought to heel by Sisi.[64] As in Nasser's regime, in Sisi's acquiescence is rewarded and any form of opposition punished. Parliaments in both were dominated by regime-created parties, and most civilian cabinet members, including the prime minister, are officers or technocrats without political background or appeal. Both presidents, in sum, have sought to restrict political space for the opposition to as close to zero as possible.

Given the similarities of their approaches to governing it is not surprising that Nasser's and Sisi's world views seem based on shared beliefs, in particular the conviction that they know better than anyone else, especially the public, what is best for Egypt. Hazem Kandil notes that Nasser was an avid reader of Machiavelli, much impressed by his assertion that

"People are by nature inconstant...you have to force them to believe."[65] Sisi not only shares Nasser's contempt for public opinion, but grounds his disdain in an exalted, rather weird view of himself. Shortly before assuming the presidency he stated in a TV interview: "I'm not leaving a chance for people to act on their own. My program will be mandatory."[66] In a leaked conversation during the election campaign he asked the rhetorical questions, "You want to be a first-class nation? Will you bear it if I make you walk on your own feet? When I wake you up at 5 in the morning every day?"[67] In another leaked recording, from December 2013, he described himself and the military as being "like the very big brother, the very big father who has a son who is a bit of a failure and does not understand the facts. Does the father kill the son? Or does he always shelter him and say, 'I'll be patient until my son understands'?"[68] Sisi's exalted, semi-mystical view of himself was reflected in an interview that same month in which he declared: "I have a long history with visions. For example, I once saw myself carrying a sword with 'No God but Allah' engraved on it in red...In another, I saw President Sadat, and he told me that he knew he would be President of Egypt, so I responded that I know I will be President too."[69] Addressing Egyptian expatriates in Germany in June 2015, he claimed that "God made me a doctor to diagnose the problem, he made me like this so I could see and understand the problems. It is a blessing from God."[70] During a December 2016 speech at the opening of a military-owned factory he broke down and cried when a soldier yelled out, "We love you President. We are with you!"[71]

Nasser's and Sisi's intolerance of others, seemingly deeply embedded in their world views and personalities, also conveniently reinforced their appeal to foreign patrons. For Nasser the primary bogeymen were the communists, whose threat to Egypt he portrayed to the US government as being mortal. He did so initially to secure Washington's backing for his coup, thereafter to obtain the CIA's support in reorganizing and rearming his security and intelligence services.[72] For Sisi the designated evil has been Islamists, a category he does not subdivide. Lumping them all together rhetorically and even legally—in the sense that he decreed the Brotherhood to be a terrorist organization, thereby putting it on an equal basis with the Sinai branch of the Syrian/Iraqi Islamic State—he has managed to enlist US and European support for his politically more vital campaign against the Brothers. Out of their fear of Islamist extremism, both within Egypt and projected from it, western powers have been willing to indulge Sisi's crackdown on the Brothers and, indeed, all political opposition, showering him with new weapons and intelligence support despite their reservations about human rights violations and the claim that the Brothers are terrorists. Just as Washington was willing to ignore Nasser's excesses out of the (mis)calculation that he shared their anti-communist commitments, so it and the West more generally are now supporting Sisi as a necessary evil to be indulged out of fear of a greater one. When it subsequently suited Nasser's interests to rehabilitate his domestic communists and ally with Moscow, he did so. Possibly that precedent will be copied at some later stage by Sisi, who is devoutly religious and differs from moderate Islamists out of political competition with them, not because of any root and branch rejection of their views.[73]

Sisi's mode of rule differs from that of his immediate predecessor. Mubarak's path to the presidency, for example, did not lie through a free and fair election, whereas Sisi's did, albeit with the ground having been well prepared by the coup d'état of July 2013. Never truly popular, Mubarak at best enjoyed a grudging, resigned acceptance. By contrast, Sisi was already the most popular political figure in Egypt when serving as minister of defense under his predecessor, President Mursi. That popularity soared following Mursi's overthrow, with his approval rating remaining in the 80–90 percent range until the second half of 2016, then falling from 82 percent in August to 68 percent in October. Those saying they would vote for him in a presidential election fell from 85 percent to 59 percent over the same period.[74]

Sisi's having been elected and possessing voter appeal, at least for the first three years of his public life, are not the only differences with his predecessor. Mubarak presided over the National Democratic Party (NDP), the lineal descendant of the ruling party first founded by Nasser. Sisi ran for the presidency without partisan identification and subsequently refused to anoint the two most successful parties in the parliamentary elections as his offspring, as it were, despite the fact that his Military Intelligence organization had created them. His presumed motive was that an official regime party would remind voters of Mubarak's much abhorred National Democratic Party, a motive that by late 2016 was giving way to the need for just such a patronage party to offset his declining popularity in the face of the scheduled 2018 election.[75]

Paradoxically, Egypt is more authoritarian under Sisi than it was under Mubarak, despite Sisi's greater popularity, his having been voted into office in a relatively free and fair election, and his refusal thus far to establish a dominant party. The Economist Intelligence Unit differentiates between full democracies, flawed democracies, hybrid regimes, and authoritarian regimes based on scores along five dimensions—electoral processes, governmental functioning, political participation, political culture, and civil liberties. By these measures Egypt under Mubarak bounced between hybrid and authoritarian status.[76] Sisi's Egypt, classified as authoritarian, has sunk yet lower in the rankings, being placed in 2015–16 138th out of 167 countries.[77] How then can one account for this paradox?

A possible resolution is to draw upon the notion of "delegative democracy," a term coined in the 1990s by Guillermo O'Donell and applied primarily to Latin American states that by then seemed no longer to be surging forward on the "third wave" of democratization that had first welled up in Portugal in 1974 and then globalized. Contrasted to representative democracy, delegative democracy was identified as a stalled phase of democratic institution building in which an elected president feels "entitled to govern as he or she sees fit, constrained only by the hard facts of existing power relations and by a constitutionally limited term of office."[78] In these systems "horizontal accountability"—imposed by "a network of relatively autonomous powers (i.e., other institutions) that can call into question, and eventually punish, improper ways of discharging the responsibilities of a given official"—is missing, so the only constraint on the executive is "vertical accountability," imposed by voters through the ballot box.[79] The voters delegate their authority to the president, who rules unconstrained by a balance of institutional powers.

This of course begs the question of whether Egypt under Sisi is analogous to, say, Argentina under Carlos Menim, in the vital sense of whether Egyptian voters could really remove Sisi in a future election. Unable to answer that question definitively, but assuming the answer is likely to be "no," it seems appropriate to strip out "democracy" from O'Donell's term, leaving "delegative" as the adjective to be applied to Sisi's authoritarianism. Indeed, O'Donell himself notes that the characteristics of delegative democracy are also those of "authoritarianism under such names as caesarism, bonapartism, *caudillismo*, populism, and the like."[80] What then are these characteristics, and do they accurately describe "Sisi-ism"?

The primary features of delegative authoritarianism are those of its key figure, the president, who, O'Donell notes, is "the embodiment of the nation and the main custodian and definer of its interests." Because the body politic is in disarray, the "delegative" president has the right and the duty to administer "unpleasant medicines that will restore the health of the nation."[81] How then does Sisi propose to restore the health of Egypt? Consistent with O'Donell's delegative prototype, he provided few specifics in his campaign, but asserted that it is his business alone, i.e., the doctor knows best. To start with, according to O'Donell, the president's "policies...need bear no resemblance to the promises of his campaign—has not the president been authorized to govern as he (or she) thinks best?"[82] Urged by his advisors to declare some specific economic and foreign policies, Sisi avoided doing so for most of the campaign. One exception was his relatively early commitment to invest $40 billion in "social housing," a campaign promise that had enormous appeal among Egypt's poor.[83] As president, Sisi has made few references to the plan, leaving it to his subordinates to accuse the original Emirati partner, Muhammad Alabbar, of reneging on a deal that apparently underpinned the project. Several days before the election Sisi appeared to respond to mounting criticism of his lack of any specific policies by offering a color-coded "Map of the Future," which he claimed would guide his administration, "achieve unprecedented rates of development and effect a quantum leap in the Egyptian economy."[84] The Map called for construction in the desert of forty-eight new cities, eight new airports, fish farms, and renewable energy projects to generate 10,000 megawatts of power, at a total cost of $140 billion, of which $120 billion would be provided by Egyptians living abroad, according to the presidential candidate. As it transpired, a far smaller version of the Map had been presented by its designer, Faruq al Baz, to President Mubarak in 1985, who rejected it as too costly and unworkable. Apparently lacking any other clear plan to present to the electorate, Sisi had dusted this old one off, multiplied the figures, and claimed it as his own.[85] This pledge sank deeper into oblivion after the election than even the promise to build 1 million social housing units. But Sisi's infatuation with the grandiose intensified once he became president. On Coptic Christmas 2017, he announced that the largest mosque and largest church in Egypt would be built in the heart of the $45 billion new capital city being constructed in the desert between Cairo and the Gulf of Suez, and that he would be the first to donate money for the two buildings.[86]

Other similarities between the O'Donell prototype and Sisi are similarly striking. "Resistance—be it from congress, political parties, interest groups, or crowds in the streets—has to be ignored" by the delegative authoritarian, according to O'Donell. In addition, "The President isolates himself from most political institutions and organized interests, and bears sole responsibility for the successes and failures of 'his' policies."[87] And indeed, Sisi has consistently denigrated (even labelling them as terrorism) any resistance to his initiatives, for which he has sought no organized support. Major policy initiatives—such as reduction of energy subsidies, importation of gas from Israel, imposition of capital gains taxes on share transactions, prohibition of importation of short staple cotton—and in many cases their abrupt modification or cancellation, are suddenly announced, typically by relatively low-ranking officials, thereby veiling their presidential origins. Never has the president or a spokesperson for him offered an explanation of the reasoning behind a decree, named those involved in its formulation, specified the time period in which it is to be in effect, or supplied any other information that would suggest engagement between the presidency and the various constituencies impacted by the decree, to say nothing of the institutional context in which it was formulated. What is offered instead is consistent with O'Donell's description of a delegative regime as one in which "only the head really knows: the president and his most trusted advisors are the alpha and the omega of politics." The nation's problems "can only be solved by highly technical criteria," which are understood only by *tecnicos* recruited and shielded by the president.[88] The Sisi regime is just such an anonymous, apolitical entity, in that the identities of his close advisors remain unknown while inputs from public political actors, who do not have access to channels of participation, are rare to non-existent. In sum, Sisi's Egypt appears to be an authoritarian version of O'Donell's delegative democracy, insofar as it manifests key characteristics of the type, except that Egyptian voters probably do not have the power to remove their president through the ballot box, were they to want to do so.

According to O'Donell, the inevitable degeneration of delegative systems should "naturally" be terminated by coups d'état, but typically they are not.[89] Indeed, he notes that in Latin America these systems demonstrate a "remarkable capacity for endurance," where, with the partial exception of Peru, no coups have taken place.[90] He explains this paradox with reference both to the assistance provided by the international system, which seeks to prevent breakdown and disorder even at the cost of sustaining one-man rule, and to some sectors of the population being willing to continue to indulge the delegative president. Only in cases where such systems had previously been democratic can they be put back on the path to democracy—Uruguay and Chile in his Latin American sample. In those countries, institutions gradually came back to life and asserted themselves against the delegative president. But where there is little or no legacy of effective institutions, "the arduous task of institutionalization" is rendered yet more difficult, if not altogether impossible, by economic crisis. So states with little democratic heritage stumble on under ineffective presidents from whom their populations become ever more estranged, if nevertheless still accepting. Whether or not Egypt is likely to follow the Latin American model will be considered in the final chapter.

Conclusion

Nasser established a limited access order to subordinate his enemies, real and imagined, to his will. That LAO, which dissipated much of the country's accumulated human and physical capital, remains in place more than six decades later. It is the primary obstacle to the country's development. It has from the outset lacked both the capacity and the political will to shift from despotic to infrastructural power as the means by which to govern the country. One of the consequences of reliance on inefficient despotic power, alongside globalization and the privatization of the economy, is a socio-fiscal trap. The state cannot extract sufficient resources to both service its eroding state-centric political base and simultaneously invest adequate capital in the human and physical infrastructure required to create growth and a potential new political base that would make possible the opening up of the LAO. Hence that closed order continues to rest on its original tripod comprised of the military, presidency, and the security/intelligence services.

Recurrent cycles of limited political and economic liberalizations initiated by incoming presidents have been just that—cycles that return to the point of departure without lasting impact. Possibly each president launched them only as a tool with which to consolidate power, or maybe one or more of them had genuine intent until it became apparent that liberalization would undermine their personal power and probably the entire regime as well. So no political development or even major change has occurred. Power has shifted marginally between the three legs of the tripod over the last sixty-plus years, but the tripod itself has remained remarkably stable. The declining resource base, however, renders the task of ruling ever more challenging. President Sisi has responded to the financial squeeze by foregoing any effort to reinvigorate or even sustain the old public sector regime base, or to build a new support coalition with the beneficiaries of private sector growth. Instead he is performing a political high-wire act, presumably based on the hope that he can mesmerize enough of the population to maintain his perch. This shaky act is bolstered by repression reminiscent of, if tougher than, that meted out by Nasser. The hybrid or soft authoritarianism of Sadat and Mubarak is gone, replaced by the unadulterated variety. The regime, in other words, has come full circle, back to the point where the military first seized power and established an LAO to subdue its enemies. It has succeeded in that, but at the cost of enormous collateral damage to the polity and economy, leaving neither capable of contributing effectively to the development of the country.

3 | Under the Thumb: Bureaucrats, Judges, and Parliamentarians

The deep state at the heart of Egypt's limited access order utilizes "superstructural" governmental institutions to control specific constituencies and to serve as gatekeepers assisting the deep state in regulating access to the LAO. Governmental institutions thus have limited autonomy from that deep state. Performance of the institution's or organization's nominal function—say, implementing policy for the agricultural or industrial sectors—is undermined by its serving control and gatekeeping functions for the deep state, a veritable elephant in the rooms of those institutions. Its hulking presence is officially recognized by none, known to all, and accommodated by just about everyone. It sits atop these institutions, crushing effective performance of governmental functions. We shall examine how these control mechanisms operate within governmental institutions and then in the broader polity, in this and the following chapter, respectively. We shall then explore in Chapter 5 the consequences for the country's economy, human and physical resources, and its foreign relations.

Executive Branch

The sprawling executive branch consists of ministries, agencies, and various bodies that in total employ around 7 million civil servants, more than half the formally employed labor force. The executive is vital to the deep state because of its administrative, control, and political support functions. It is the principal arm through which "despotic power" is asserted in managing the day to day affairs of the state. Through its routine administration it imposes the first layer of political control over the population, simultaneously regulating initial access to higher levels in the state and economy. It is also the regime's largest political base, albeit, as noted above, an eroding one. The deep state must, therefore, ensure its absolute control of the executive and that branch's dominance over other superstructural institutions and organizations. It does so by penetrating, dividing, and centralizing it.

Penetration by the deep state

Each of the three legs of the deep state penetrates the executive, but not in a carefully planned, coordinated, or cooperative fashion. Indeed, the executive is an arena for power struggles between the military, security/intelligence services, and the presidency. The military's methods are the most direct, obvious, and crude. Yezid Sayigh has chronicled the rise of the "officer republic," by which he means the tens of thousands of retired or seconded officers serving almost everywhere in the executive branch. Their appointments cluster in areas of greatest interest to the military, primarily for reasons of control and accessing state resources. So, for example, the administration of "local government"—as it is euphemistically called, because in reality it is the mechanism for central government control throughout the country—is dominated by military officers. A majority of the governors of the country's now twenty-seven provinces are former military generals, another handful were police generals, and a still smaller number had prior careers as civilians. This pattern dates back to the earliest days of the Republic, with ebbs and flows between the three types of recruits into governorships determined by relations between the military and security/intelligence forces at any given time, as well as variation in presidential interest in civilian window-dressing for the regime, of which Sadat's was the greatest. Yet despite being the primary pool from which governors and their assistants and subordinates are recruited, the military does not have exclusive control over the sprawling local administration. The Ministry of Local Administration is heavily staffed by former security/intelligence officers, as is the Secretariat which reports to it. Moreover, while governors have cabinet-level rank, they report to the minister of interior. So the military and security agencies share domination of "local" government, the former mainly by virtue of connections between ex-officers working in it, the latter by being in control of the formal hierarchy. This duopoly reflects presidential intent to balance off the two primary coercive elements of the deep state, thereby assuring that neither gains absolute, direct control over local administration.

Other administrative domains penetrated by the officer republic are those with responsibilities connected to the military's economic interests, including regulatory agencies charged officially with financial oversight. So executive agencies with responsibility for transport and communications, for example—such as the Suez Canal Authority; the River Transport Authority; Alexandria Ports and Harbour Authority; virtually all administration of civil aviation, including the national airline Egypt Air; and bodies regulating electronic communications—are heavily staffed by former or seconded military officers. The distinction between state-owned enterprises (SOEs), such as Egypt Air, and the executive administration is artificial in that both are part of the public bureaucracy and subordinate to the deep state. Former officers are also disproportionately represented in SOEs working in the most lucrative sectors, key of which are oil and gas.

Since regulatory agencies pose a potential threat to the deep state in general and the military in particular, the two key ones, the General Organization for Administration and the Central Agency for Auditing and Accounting, have former officers among their staff and are in general closely supervised by the military. So, for example, when the civilian head of the latter, Hisham Ginaina, challenged the military in 2015 by revealing startling amounts of corruption within the government it controlled, he was illegally and peremptorily dismissed, charged with criminal offenses, and in 2016 sentenced to a year in jail. The officer republic is thus a network based on its penetration of elements of the public administration and public sector that are central to the military's core interests, namely: security (hence local government); capitalizing economically on its institutional strengths, such as transportation, communication, control of land and natural resources; and ensuring that it not be subjected to civilian oversight and control (hence the regulatory and auditing agencies).

Security/intelligence organizations penetrate the state differently because they are not connected to an equivalent of the centrally owned and organized military economy. The minister of interior does not preside over a sprawling conglomerate of economic enterprises akin to those over which his cabinet colleague, the minister of defense, asserts control. Penetration of the executive *is* the actual job of security/intelligence, whereas for the military that penetration is primarily for the purpose of benefitting the military and its officers, thereby ensuring their loyalty. So whereas the officer republic is essentially parasitic in its relation to the executive branch, capturing resources from it, security/intelligence directly influences the executive's operations in the name of security. The executive can thus be seen more as an extension of the security and intelligence services than of the military.

The public administration is nevertheless also exploited by security/intelligence officers for material gain, albeit in more subterranean, "entrepreneurial" fashion than is typically the case for military officers. Russia's *siloviki*, agents of the KGB and then its successor, the FSB, are similar to Egypt's security and intelligence operatives. Having penetrated the Soviet bureaucracy and public sector, their insider knowledge and connections enabled them to capture state assets and consolidate their networks of power and privilege in the transition to the Russian Republic. *Siloviki*, the most well-known example of whom is Vladimir Putin, now run Russia. Unlike their Egyptian counterparts, Russian *siloviki* have not had to contend with a competitive military, which in the Soviet Union was subordinated to the Communist Party and the intelligence agencies closely connected to it. Indeed, former and active duty military officers serving in Egypt's public administration, public sector, and military economy are more akin in terms of their collective power to Russia's *siloviki* than are Egyptian security/intelligence agents similarly employed, simply because Egyptian civilian intelligence agencies are weaker than the military. Intelligence operatives in Egypt cannot hope to take over their country in the way their equivalents did in Russia, or in the way in which the military under Sisi has done in Egypt, although from the top down rather than bottom up. So Egyptian intelligence agents essentially "moonlight," performing their day duties of monitoring and controlling civil servants and public sector employees, while simultaneously accumulating and utilizing networks and information for personal gain, usually but not always following retirement.

The Egyptian security agencies' partial degeneration into *siloviki*-style corruption was a cause of their weakness in the face of the 2011 uprising. The opportunities for personal gain were such that the agencies had trouble retaining intelligence officers, who after a decade or so in the job would be tempted to take advantage of the business opportunities their service had provided. The then minister of interior had complained of this very problem in 2010 to a western ambassador. The increasing case load on his agents resulting from the ever harsher crackdown in the final years of the Mubarak era had resulted in them being subjected to frequent twelve-hour shifts, without commensurate compensation. Preferring shorter hours and higher pay in direct employment in the economic sectors they had spied upon for government wages, they jumped ship.

An example of the triangulation strategy of an Egyptian *siloviki*, aptly described by Sarah Smierciak, illustrates their modus operandi.[1] Prior to his retirement Mansur Muhammad (pseudonym) had served as director of the economic section of General Intelligence. His primary responsibility was monitoring the business elite, a task which put him in regular contact with Mubarak's top cronies. He parlayed his spying job into that of serving as middleman between these cronies and various governmental agencies and departments, assisting them to obtain permits and in general facilitating their business interests, including at a policy level. Even prior to retirement he had established several companies to produce ready-made garments for export, one of the sectors in which Mubarak cronies had heavily invested, partly as a result of having received foreign public assistance which Muhammad's behind-the-scenes maneuverings apparently facilitated. Five years after retirement he was living in a large apartment in Heliopolis, happy to reminisce about his friendships with those he had formerly spied on and about his contribution to advancing the Egyptian economy, at least as he saw it. Like many of his colleagues, Muhammad had successfully triangulated between his own intelligence agency, the government more broadly, and businessmen.

In various positions I held in Egypt from 1965 I encountered the phenomenon of penetration of the executive branch by military officers and security agents. Working at the front desk of a five-star hotel owned by the Egyptian government but operated by a prominent international hotelier, I was made aware of both military and civilian intelligence officers among my colleagues, surprisingly in some cases because they would reveal their identities, while in others colleagues would report on them. This office was a virtual nest of spies, with Military Intelligence having the upper hand, among other activities running the eavesdropping system that operated in every room of the hotel. Our socializing outside working hours was carefully planned to either include or exclude agents, with everyone knowing which situation prevailed so what subjects could and could not be discussed.

Some years later I was researching a biography of the Speaker of parliament, a prominent political figure whose son was married to President Sadat's daughter and who was himself a close confidant of the president. Some months into my research, conducted primarily with him and his family members, but also in parliament, the Speaker warned me that intelligence operatives housed in his very office were keeping a close eye on me and that I had better be careful. Shortly thereafter I was called in to State Security Investigations (SSI), interrogated, and ordered to leave the country. I contacted the Speaker, thinking he would be able to overturn the decision. Alas, he confessed that he had no power over SSI, including the unit operating out of his office.

A couple of years later I was invited by the minister of state for foreign affairs, who was not aware I had been expelled from Egypt, to lecture at the Foreign Ministry. I accepted, wondering if his ministry would be able to obtain a visa for me. In the event it could not, with an embarrassed Egyptian diplomat explaining to me that the Foreign Ministry had no power over State Security. I then turned to a former Military Intelligence officer and friend who had been forced to flee the country for siding with Abd al Hakim Amer against Nasser in the summer of 1967. Since he remained well connected to his old colleagues, who had either shifted to SSI, had friends there, or had power over it, a few hundred dollars and two weeks were sufficient for the visa. The minister of state for foreign affairs was intrigued.

About a decade later I was director of an organization that mediated between the Egyptian government and American scholars and academic institutions, as well as undertaking preservation of Egypt's material cultural heritage, the latter financed principally by grants from the United States Agency for International Development. Discharge of the former function involved among other things obtaining permission for American scholars to conduct research, which was granted by a ten-member committee within the Ministry of Higher Education. That committee's decisions were unpredictable, the explanations for them generally making little if any sense. In trying to get to the bottom of the matter we learned that as many as eight of the ten members on the committee were in fact from SSI. They had little if any idea about the intended subjects of research, or indeed about academic research in general. Their reactions were to what they considered to be key words in research proposals.

My cultural heritage preservation work also revealed penetration by the military, security, and presidency of the various parts of the executive branch involved in that work. All three legs of the deep state had at least indirect pecuniary interests in preserving the nation's material heritage, typically in the form of competing companies controlled by their colleagues or favorites. The minister of culture, a client of the First Lady, looked after her interests, while military and security officers worked through that and other ministries involved in granting permits, and through local government. The technical difficulties involved in preserving the country's crumbling material cultural heritage were in some cases easier to overcome than the political ones resulting from struggles between bureaucratic actors and companies serving the interests of those elements of the deep state by which they were penetrated or controlled. While restoring the Bait al Razzaz, a badly dilapidated Mamluk townhouse that dated to the fourteenth century, our organization became caught up in a power struggle between two contracting companies, one connected to the military and the other to the Ministry of Interior, both of which were seeking to displace us and take over the restoration contract from the Ministry of Culture.

As we were working on this matter an old friend was recruited into the cabinet as minister of agriculture. Having been closely involved with that ministry over the years I was aware that it housed a significant security presence, the purpose of which was to utilize the ministry to watch over rural politics and to channel patronage to preferred clients. One of the new minister's predecessors, Yusuf Wali, was in fact a security agent himself, having risen politically through the Vanguard Organization, the intelligence wing of Nasser's Arab Socialist Union. Despite being aware of this longstanding security presence in the ministry, I was astounded to be informed by my friend that of his eighty or so undersecretaries, about half were working in various capacities for intelligence. He complained that the ministry was for the most part given over to performing political/security functions related to rural Egypt, so was unable to effectively formulate or implement agricultural policies. This minister was sentenced after a brief trial to two years in prison in the wake of the coup-volution. It was widely believed his real transgression was not corruption, but having been less than completely cooperative with security while serving as minister.

The executive branch, in sum, resembles a Swiss cheese, full of holes in which those with military or security backgrounds or connected to the presidency are lurking, nibbling away at the cheese. If one had a three-dimensional model of the executive that revealed the presence of these penetrators, presumably they would cluster in different parts of it, although, as suggested above, with overlap and competition in many areas. So the coherence and performance of the executive branch is undermined by the presence within it of powerful forces pursuing other agendas. Aggravating the incoherence of the executive is its purposeful division, or "stove-piping," into a host of parallel vertical units which also compete with one another, as we shall now discuss.

Divided and ruled

Many public administrations suffer from "stove-piping," referring to their sharp division into separate ministries, departments, agencies, and so on, existing in grand isolation from one another, lacking horizontal channels of communication and coordination. A standard objective of administrative reform is to create a "whole of government approach" to forming and implementing public policies. Egypt's "balkanized" government, to use Nathan Brown's apt synonym, may therefore be just another example of poorly integrated executive branches, the standard cure for which is administrative reform.[2] The phenomenon is so pronounced in Egypt, however, that it does raise the questions whether it might be qualitatively rather than just quantitatively different, what the cause of such extreme "balkanization" might be, and whether its cure might require stronger medicine than simply administrative reorganization.

Stove-piping is manifested and reinforced in Egypt by several factors. Most career trajectories are within a single "stove-pipe," slowly rising up it, rarely shifting laterally to another. The mono-track career trajectory typically commences even before the initial appointment into the civil service, at the point when the then student enters a university faculty. A large cohort of graduates go on to the relevant ministry, say from a faculty of economics to the Ministry of Finance. Among other consequences are strong personal loyalties as cohorts of classmates move upward together virtually in lock-step toward retirement. The importance of graduating classes is reflected by the fact that most employees know exactly in which year one of their colleagues graduated. The same is true in the military and security services, with graduating classes being key determinants of intra-service personal relations, in part because promotion there is also based primarily upon seniority.

Living metaphorically in a bureaucratic enclave, the administrator may also physically live in close proximity to colleagues, with many ministries having gated second-home communities, typically on a beach. The military's common residential space includes not only such resort-style facilities, but also primary residences in the militarized community spreading from Nasr City to Cairo Airport and beyond on Cairo's outskirts. In the case of the military, housing and resorts are organized by units, such as infantry, mechanized, air defense, supply, and so on. Yet another sign and cause of the balkanization of the bureaucracy is that many ministries operate their own retail outlets for staff. The Ministry of Agriculture, for example, operates shops that sell food products to employees. Being a civil servant is a cradle-to-grave experience which creates strong loyalties, keen competition, and, in some cases, powerful animosities.

Much of the competition and most of the animosity, however, occurs between, not within the stove-pipes. The cabinet is a gathering of grandees who head the various ministerial fiefdoms, each seeking to defend and expand turf, with few held together by common membership in a political party, or even shared political views. This has contributed to the decline in importance of the body itself, as reflected by the fact that 425 ministers served in it between 2011 and 2017 and that the Sisi government has found it increasingly difficult to entice highly qualified recruits into it.[3] Cabinet discord though is a constant of government in Egypt. Various ministries have long-established jurisdictional disputes, typically driven by a desire to control and extract resources. The Ministries of Agriculture and Supply, for example, compete for control over wheat, the country's most basic foodstuff. The former is charged with producing it locally, the latter with distributing it. Since the bulk of both domestically produced and imported wheat is

purchased by the government, then sold to consumers at subsidized prices, any price gap between locally grown and
imported wheat provides opportunity for illegal arbitrage. In
2015–16 the price gap widened such that the former was
almost double the price of the latter, thereby making it possible for those involved in the wheat trade to extract profits
by selling the government imported wheat mislabeled as having
been domestically produced. Among the profiteers were high-
ranking officials in the Ministry of Supply, including the minister, who along with several of his staff was removed and
indicted on corruption charges in 2016, a few months after
the then minister of agriculture, Salah Hilal, had been arrested
on separate corruption charges. The Ministry of Agriculture
had played a role in the downfall of their competitors in the
Ministry of Supply by seeking to disrupt wheat importation
by declaring several shipments as unfit because of high levels
of ergot, a common wheat fungus which in small proportions
is harmless and had never before been the cause of wheat
shipments being rejected. But the victory of the Ministry of
Agriculture was short-lived. President Sisi nominated a fellow
general as the new minister of supply, the first time it had
been headed by an officer since the ministry's founding during
World War II, raising the question of whether Sisi and the
military were seeking to prevent or benefit from corruption
in the wheat trade.

The Ministry of Finance is generally resented by line ministries because of the financial control it seeks to assert over
them. One method by which ministries fend off Finance is
for them to create their own "special accounts," into which
funds garnered from their various activities are directly depos-
ited rather than being paid into the Ministry of Finance's,
hence general government's, accounts. These special accounts
were estimated in 2016 to contain as much as $14 billion, a
sum then almost equivalent to the entire foreign currency
holdings of the Central Bank.[4] The noted economist Hazem
Beblawi, who served as minister of finance under the SCAF
in 2011 and then as prime minister in the immediate wake
of the July 3, 2013 coup, complained that the existence of
these special accounts made it impossible for him to know

the precise state of the nation's finances.[5] Total funds held in these special accounts appeared to increase as the financial situation steadily deteriorated after the coup-volution, possibly suggesting that the military's motive in permitting this growth was to justify its own special funds, which are far and away the best endowed. Such accounts naturally render corruption difficult to detect and punish, presumably one of the reasons they are allowed to flourish, as they help cement the loyalty of the executive branch to the deep state.

Excessive stove-piping of the civil service could be interpreted as a specific case of the general rigidity of all institutions in Egypt. It does indeed characterize other institutions, such as universities, hospitals, and even large private businesses as well. But variability in the degree of stove-piping of the executive branch seems to suggest a more direct cause. It expanded in the wake of the 1952 coup and then, after a flat trajectory, grew again in tandem with the rise of the military's power from 2011, as reflected for example in various constitutional clauses, especially in the 2014 constitution, that Nathan Brown interprets as purposefully providing the basis for further governmental balkanization.[6]

The relationship between stove-piping and the direct assertion of military power over the government suggests intent by the military. Robert Bianchi, one of several observers of Nasser's Egypt who saw similarities to fascism in what he referred to as the "corporatism" of Egyptian sociopolitical-administrative life, accounted for it as an organizational manifestation of fascist ideology.[7] Vertically organized "corporations," including those within the government itself, were advocated by fascists as a counter to the Marxist interpretation of society as being horizontally divided into classes. While Egyptian military officers have never been close students of fascism, they along with other Egyptian political forces active in the 1930s and 1940s, such as the Young Egypt political party and the Muslim Brotherhood, both of which were major influences on the officers, were aware of and favorably impressed by at least the organizational structures of the fascist movement, and sought to emulate them. The Brotherhood's organizational model, for example, is a hybrid cross between Sufi orders, the Boy Scouts, and fascist political parties.[8]

In the case of the military, this ideologically influenced preference for corporatizing/balkanizing/stove-piping the executive and the country as a whole has been reinforced by a natural preference for a command and control structure akin to that of the military itself. They extended the military model into civilian government, a step which has the additional advantage of subordinating it to their control. As just noted, the cabinet does not serve to integrate the many stove-pipes, and in fact reinforces them. Virtually the only horizontal linkages in the sprawling executive branch are those provided by the deep state that underpins it, so by military and intelligence officers and those connected to the presidency. The deep state has an overall view of the executive branch, but those within it do not. Unless the deep state deems it to be within its interest to secure cooperation and coordination within the executive, which it rarely does, the executive remains fragmented and discordant, unable to effectively make or implement public policy.

Those in the deep state paradoxically blame the civil service for its poor performance, generally holding it in contempt. President Sisi himself does little to hide his personal disdain, as reflected in various statements about the civil service associated with his declaration of a new civil service law in early 2015, one of the 342 laws he and his predecessor, interim President Adly Mansour, decreed before the new parliament had been elected. This law was widely viewed primarily as an attack on pay and conditions within the executive, only secondarily as a tool to reform it. When finally convened, the parliament was constitutionally empowered and required to pass on all presidentially decreed pieces of legislation. In the event it was only the civil service law that was not immediately approved, it finally being ratified in October 2016, after much debate, two amendments, and numerous demonstrations by civil servants. That the president was willing to attack, even if mildly, the core of his own regime's fragile civilian political base is reflective of the general contempt he and his fellow officers have for the civil service, ignoring their own contribution to its dysfunctionality.

Hyper centralization

In addition to being penetrated and divided by their masters in the deep state, the civil service is profoundly centralized, thus cutting it off from any potential independent, local political base. All civil servants report to higher levels of government that culminate in the capital, not to any local interests, including voters. Local elections, which is to say those at the provincial, regional, and city/town/village level, have since the Sadat era been for so-called Popular Councils. Even the narrow political space represented by them has been further constricted by a combination of factors. First, the majority of their members are civil servants, thereby eroding the distinction between Popular and Executive Councils. Second, the majority of seats in local council elections are uncontested, victors being declared by acclamation as a result of prior negotiations between heads of locally prominent families and security and party officials at the respective levels. Third, elections are held irregularly, the last being conducted in 2008. In 2011 all councils were disbanded and although in February 2016 the regime promised a new local government law and elections within a year, neither have so far materialized. Fourth, the powers of Popular Councils are extremely curtailed, with virtually no powers of the purse, so few if any resources to accumulate or distribute. Fifth, no political parties other than the Muslim Brotherhood have substantial local bases, so Popular Councils are not arenas for party competition or recruitment. Finally, successive regimes have tolerated corruption at the local level, primarily to secure acquiescence by civil servants and local notables. A secondary motive might be to tarnish the image of local government, rendering it unable to attract those seeking to establish a base of power autonomous from the central government or to be the focus of a political reform campaign. Indeed, even the political opposition under Mubarak opposed decentralization on the grounds that it would simply place more resources in the hands of corrupt officials.

Nevertheless, some of those mobilized into politics by the dramatic events of 2011 believed that decentralization would facilitate reform and democratization, so they strongly advocated it. Chief among their demands was for governors to be elected, a demand that was originally dismissed outright by the military, which, as noted above, has generally filled these key positions from its own ranks. Some other, less significant demands were ultimately incorporated into the 2014 constitution. It contains a chapter on local administration that affirms the state's commitment to supporting financial, administrative, and economic decentralization within five years, to be preceded by elections to Popular Councils. It also tilts the balance of power away from Executive toward Popular Councils and requires membership of the latter to be one quarter women and one quarter youths under thirty-five. And it references the possibility that governors might in future be elected. Implementation of these clauses, however, depends on the issuing of a new local administration law, which may or may not happen and may or may not accurately translate the intent and principles embodied in these clauses into law.

In sum, the executive branch is structured by the deep state to serve as an instrument of broader control, as an arena for competition between the three actors in the deep state, as a counterbalance to the other branches of government, and as a political base for the regime.

The deep state seeks simultaneously to ensure that the executive neither becomes rooted in the civilian population nor provides a channel for articulation of popular demands and political mobilization. These objectives have more or less been met throughout the history of Republican Egypt, although the emphasis on control combined with ever declining resources have steadily undermined the value of the executive as a political base for the regime, to the point that the military is arrogating to itself many of the executive's functions, thus further eroding its status and rewards. Having used and abused the civil service, such that it is now incapable of effectively implementing public policy, the deep state audaciously blames the victim for failings that are the direct consequence of it having penetrated, divided, and overly centralized it.

Judicial Branch

It seems paradoxical that a country lacking the rule of law has such a comparatively large, to say nothing of long-established, even well-regarded, judiciary. Egypt, with a population of some 90 million, has more than 13,000 judges. The UK's 64 million citizens are served by about 3,200 judges. Egypt's judge-to-population ratio is thus roughly three times that of the UK, the veritable progenitor of the rule of law.[9] Desire for an efficient legal-judicial system cannot account for Egypt having such a high ratio of judges to population. Egypt ranks 155th out of 189 countries on the "contract enforcement" indicator of the World Bank's Ease of Doing Business Index, compared to the UK's 33rd position on that scale. Of the eleven indicators that make up the Index, Egypt's lowest score is on contract enforcement, the most direct measure of the efficiency of the civil court system.[10] On the World Justice Project's 2016 Rule of Law Index, Egypt ranks 110th overall out of 113 countries evaluated. On the civil justice sub-index, it ranks 104th, with the lowest scores on the six indicators that make up that sub-index being for "no unreasonable delay" and "effective enforcement."[11] It appears that the more judges there are, the slower they reach decisions and apply them.

One obvious explanation for the poor performance of the judicial branch is that there are too many judges, just as there are too many civil servants and, as we shall see below, too many parliamentarians.[12] All three branches are overstaffed, begging the question of why. The simple, if incomplete answer, is that public employment serves as a labor sponge to absorb excess numbers of the nominally qualified, thereby heading off youthful opposition while bolstering the regime's sagging political base. A more complete explanation must include reference to the control strategy of the deep state. An excess of employees not only enhances opportunities for patronage, it also dilutes solidarities within the respective branches, solidarities further undermined by stove-piping. And as with the executive, the judiciary's performance is undermined not just because it is overstaffed—an outcome of some benefit to the deep state—but also by it serving gatekeeping and control functions for the limited access order underpinned by the deep state.

The relationship between the deep state and the judiciary, however, is not exactly analogous to the former's relation with the executive, which is primarily a hierarchical one of command and control. Because the legal-judicial system is central to the legitimation of the regime and its acts, the deep state has to grant it some autonomy. Public belief in the independence of the judiciary is vital if its decisions are to effectively contribute to compliance and legitimacy. The plea by the two major protest movements for the military to overthrow Mursi in early July 2013, for example, was based on the claim that the president had lost legitimacy because he "violated the laws, the constitution, *the judiciary* [emphasis added] and the freedom of the media."[13] The judiciary, like the parliament, can serve as a shock absorber between ruler and ruled, but only if it can plausibly be presented as at least semi-independent of the regime. The judiciary has thus enjoyed some political space in which to operate, rather more in fact than the parliament, the real independence of which would pose a greater threat to the deep state because as an elected body it could claim to truly represent the people. The judiciary, by contrast, can serve to protect the peoples' rights, but not to represent them. It can contribute to, but not lead a revolution.

The history of the judiciary in Republican Egypt is thus akin to that of a pendulum, swinging back and forth between greater and lesser autonomy from the deep state. The extreme of the arc was at the outset, when Nasser chose to bypass the judiciary by creating revolutionary courts to implement his new government's will, Anwar al Sadat being among the officers who dispensed rough and ready revolutionary justice. But this was only a temporary measure as even the powerful and charismatic Nasser could not replace the legitimation and adjudication functions performed by the Arab world's oldest, most prestigious modern legal-judicial system, upon which most others came to be modeled. Accommodation between judges, naturally conservative by virtue of their profession and the high social status typical of their backgrounds, on the one hand, and Nasser's regime, on the other, was nevertheless uneasy. In 1966, Law 25 curtailed the jurisdiction of civilian courts on various matters by extending that of military courts. When Nasser's political grip was loosened by defeat in the June 1967 war with Israel, the judiciary, among other forces, began to assert independence. But by August 1969, Nasser had regained firm control after having subdued students, workers, and others who had raised their voices against him. He then perpetrated what came to be called the "massacre of the judges." He dissolved the board of the prestigious Judges' Club, founded in 1939, which along with the bar association that dates to the turn of the century is the most prestigious of the many syndicates that represent professionals such as journalists, engineers, teachers, actors, and so on. Appointing replacement board members, Nasser went on to purge some 200 judges from the bench and to directly subordinate the judiciary to the executive.

Among the measures taken by Sadat in the "Corrective Revolution" he launched in the wake of his May 1971 purge of Ali Sabry and other opponents in the residual Nasserist elite, were steps to bolster the status and autonomy of the judiciary. The Judges' Club was permitted again to elect its own board members; the Supreme Judicial Council, which manages the judiciary, was made more accountable to judges than to the executive; and, most importantly for politics, a new Supreme Constitutional Court (SCC) was established and empowered to rule on the constitutionality of legislation, a step given added importance by virtue of the ratification of the new, more liberal "permanent" constitution of 1971, which provided for the SCC.[14] In 1974 administrative courts were granted increased autonomy.

Hopes that the judiciary might play a key role in reestablishing the rule of law that Nasser had undermined did not, however, come to fruition. Under political pressure during the last three years of his presidency as a result of his opening to Israel, a flagging economy, and his reneging on promised reforms, Sadat reeled back freedoms he had granted earlier in his presidency, including several related to the executive control of the judiciary. Like Nasser he also utilized Law 25 of 1966 to transfer civilian cases to military courts.

The swing of the pendulum of judicial autonomy was repeated again under Mubarak, although over a larger arc and with some secondary oscillations. Like Sadat before him, Mubarak initially presented himself as a liberalizer. Once he had consolidated power he rescinded many reforms, only later to reinstate some as a result of economic stress and pressure from Washington. Once these endogenous pressures abated as the US became bogged down in Iraq, the Egyptian economy improved as a result of a dramatic increase in the production of natural gas from 2002, and as the threat to Mubarak's rule increased as a result of his earlier reforms, he began in 2006–7 to reel those reforms in yet again, only this time with more vigor and no letting up before he was overthrown.

The judiciary, including the courts and the Judges' Club, were swung back and forth by these political gyrations. Until 2000 the Supreme Constitutional Court, headed by the crusading Justice Awad al Murr, and lower-level administrative and even state security courts, were permitted to issue rulings that challenged the regime. The SCC struck down election laws in 1986 and 1990, thus dissolving sitting parliaments. It issued a series of rulings that extended rights for political and civil society activists and their organizations, although it shied away from direct challenges to the Mubarak government on high-stakes issues, such as its increasing use of military courts. Rulings by administrative courts in favor of plaintiffs seeking redress from governmental actions stimulated a dramatic increase in case filings, which increased six-fold from 1995 to 2008.[15] Even state security courts, authorized by the notorious Emergency Law, in effect for virtually the entirety of Mubarak's presidency, demonstrated some independence from the executive. In 1987 one such security court acquitted defendants employed by the national railway authority of a charge of violating the labor law that prohibited strikes. Six years later another security court acquitted twenty-seven defendants of the charge of assassinating the Speaker of parliament, on the grounds that evidence from them had been extracted by torture.[16]

But the tide began to turn against judicial independence in 2000, when the SCC ruled that the constitutional provision requiring judicial supervision of elections required a judge to be physically present in each and every polling station. This interpretation posed a clear and present danger to institution-alized ballot-box stuffing, hence to presidential control of parliament. Mubarak immediately took steps to subordinate the judiciary, steps further intensified after the 2005 election in which a record high of eighty-eight Brothers were elected to parliament. In March 2007, the regime amended Article 88 of the constitution to remove judicial oversight of elections. In that year it also rescinded the judiciary's control over recruit-ment onto the bench and packed the SCC, doubling its size by adding hand-picked, compliant justices. It also appointed police officers as judges on other courts. Mubarak finished bringing the SCC to heel in 2009, when he appointed as Chief Justice Faruq Sultan, a primary court judge whose judicial experience had been on military and state security courts, so he had no direct familiarity with constitutional law.

The regime coupled its attack on this and other courts with a reassertion of its control over the Judges' Club. In 2002 a slate of independent candidates for the board defeated the government-backed slate, then initiated a campaign for par-liamentary and presidential elections to be made free from executive interference and for a new law for judicial indepen-dence focused on powers over budgets, promotions, second-ments, and disciplinary procedures. Prominent leaders of the Club released reports during and immediately after the 2005 parliamentary elections that graphically detailed regime-backed electoral fraud. The government's response was to censure two of the Club's leaders for "unprofessional engagement in politics," and to begin a behind-the-scenes campaign to divide the Club and secure victory for a pro-government slate of candidates for its board. This it accomplished with the elec-tion in 2009 of a slate led by Ahmad al Zind, a staunchly pro-government judge and outspoken critic of judicial activ-ism. By the December 2010 parliamentary elections, the courts had been brought firmly under executive control and the organizational voice of the judiciary silenced. Paralleling growing executive control of the judiciary was an increasing reliance on Article 6 of the Military Judiciary Law, which Mubarak drew upon to transfer some 12,000 cases from civilian to military courts.[17]

The judiciary's roller-coaster ride in the wake of the coupvolution reveals the deep internal tensions between pro- and anti-government judges and demonstrates both the political importance of the courts to the deep state and the ways and means by which it subordinates judges. The contours of the judiciary's ups and downs started at a high point. Many of its members sought to support and broaden the "Tahrir Revolution," such as by legalizing the Wasat Party, dissolving Mubarak's ruling National Democratic Party, fining Mubarak and many of his ministers, and supporting a suit intended to force the government to pay pensions to those injured during the uprising. But the judiciary was quickly pulled down from those lofty heights as the SCAF gathered more powers into its hands from the spring of 2011. It sought to prevent judicial weight from consolidating behind secular reformers such as those associated with the April 6 movement or Muhammad al Baradei, and to prepare the ground for using the courts against the Muslim Brotherhood. The judiciary was sent further downward once the Brotherhood gained control of the presidency. President Mursi purged judges in revenge for their support of the SCAF, ordering as many as 3,000 into retirement, and simultaneously moving to bring the judiciary under direct control.

This rough ride ended in the wake of the July 2013 coup with the hard core of conservative pro-government judges in the ascendency. They cemented their relationship with the military by serving as its accomplice in crushing first the Brotherhood, then political dissent more generally. The military rewarded its loyal faction within the judiciary by promoting the Chief Justice, Adly Mansour, to the role of acting president, who returned the favor by keeping that seat warm for almost a year for the president in waiting, General and then Field Marshal Abd al Fattah al Sisi, faithfully decreeing legislation concocted by the military in the interim. At the end of this bumpy ride the judiciary was left exhausted, reduced to a secondary, subordinate role to the military similar to that of the Nasser era.

Some of the lowlights of this tumultuous period illustrate the judiciary's political utility to the deep state. The SCC, bowing to pressure from the SCAF which feared the Brotherhood's simultaneous control of parliament and the presidency, issued a ruling in June 2012, two days prior to the presidential election which Mursi was anticipated to win, that dissolved the lower house of parliament in which the Brothers and Salafi parties had won three quarters of the seats in elections six months previously. Beginning a year later, the judiciary, in flagrant disregard of due legal process, handed down *en masse* hundreds of death sentences, primarily against Brothers, but also against virtually any opponent of the regime, with scant regard for the actual type of opposition, peaceful, legal, or otherwise. Journalists and academics were convicted on trumped-up charges in what amounted to show trials, with fifty-eight of the former imprisoned in the wake of the July coup.[18] These politically inspired convictions were meted out alongside acquittals of security and police officials accused of killing demonstrators, torturing political prisoners, and other abuses. Five years after the coup-volution not a single member of the military or security forces that had killed thousands of demonstrators had been convicted, whereas a reported 40,000 political prisoners languished in overcrowded jails, thanks to much if not most of the judiciary being either forced or choosing to side with the executive.

The relationship between the deep state and the judiciary is thus more mutable, complex, and political than that between the former and the executive. Deep-state influence is exercised with varying severity, as its historical oscillations reflect. As a consequence, the judiciary serves as a barometer of the overall political climate. High and low levels of judicial independence within the courts and the Judges' Club are readily discerned indicators of liberalization and de-liberalization periods, respectively. These variations result from quantitative rather than qualitative changes in the deep state's control methods—subordination, isolation, and restriction. They have been applied with greater or lesser vigor over the years, but have never fundamentally changed and have certainly not been abandoned.

Nominal autonomy and the carrot and the stick

The most direct means by which the deep state asserts itself over the judiciary are both official and routinized, including constitutional/legal provisions and administrative structures and practices, as well as unofficial and irregular, principally the manipulating of personnel through rewards and punishments. Various constitutional clauses, especially those in the 2014 version, appear to guarantee judicial independence, including control over the vital matters of finance and personnel, as well as key roles for judges in appointing the head of the SCC and the public prosecutor. In practice, however, judicial autonomy is curtailed by law and by administrative procedures supplemented by informal practices. The minister of justice, not the judiciary, appoints the heads of the highest courts other than the SCC. The Supreme Judicial Council (SJC), nominally independent of the executive and with substantial powers over remuneration, promotion, and postings, is in reality heavily influenced by the president and minister of justice. Approval of one or the other is required for each judge appointed or promoted by the SJC. They also directly interfere in this vital body, "ensuring those promoted to the SJC are either regime loyalists or predictably uncritical of the state."[19] Although the SJC has the authority to reject decisions by the minister of justice over many appointments and secondments, "it rarely does so for fear of retaliation."[20]

Whereas the SJC enjoys limited autonomy from the executive, the Department of Judicial Inspection has none. According to Article 78 of the judicial authority law, it is placed squarely under the Ministry of Justice. Its encompassing mandate is "to inspect the work of judges and presidents of courts of first instance," meaning it has direct power over members of the Office of Public Prosecution and all judges beneath the presidents of courts of first instance.[21] In 1991 the Judges' Club passed a resolution in its general assembly calling on the government to transfer the Department of Judicial Inspection from the Ministry of Justice to the Supreme Judicial Council, but the resolution was ignored.

Unofficial but virtually standardized manipulation of individual judges supplements the legal and administrative means of subordinating the profession as a whole. Sahar Aziz, an expert on the judiciary, has chronicled the use of carrots and sticks. The latter include transferring "judges whose rulings are constantly unfavorable to the regime" to remote areas in Upper Egypt; filing baseless charges of ethical or legal violations against judges to force them off the bench; and passing over such judges when they are up for promotion. Carrots doled out include lucrative secondments to the Ministry of Justice, to international organizations, and elsewhere. Aziz adds that "the judiciary is wrought with nepotism," providing the example of the executive-friendly head of the main court in the Delta city of Tanta, who has twenty-one sons and nephews employed as judges or prosecutors despite their academic records not meeting required standards.[22] The complex legal, administrative, and personnel means by which the executive subordinates the judiciary attest to its apprehension of being challenged by it, as well as its desire to at least partially camouflage its control in order to maintain the myth of judicial independence and thereby legitimate its rulings and, by implication, the regime.

Institutionally isolated with restricted jurisdictions

Granting the judiciary greater autonomy than the executive, the deep state has to guard the periphery around it lest it coalesce with other actors and/or provide a legal umbrella for potential challengers to the deep state. The possible coalition of greatest threat would be with a parliament that aspired to break free from deep-state control. These two institutions acting in concert, as to some extent they did in the early and mid-Mubarak era, the heydays of Chief Justice Awad al Murr and the SCC, could achieve significant political reform, each lending support to the other's struggle for independence from the deep state. Judicial supervision of elections, rulings on election laws and outcomes, legislation governing the judi-

ciary, and parliamentary interpolations of ministers inter-
fering with the judiciary, are just some examples of areas
and types of tactical cooperation possible between the two
institutions.[23]

Fear of such a coalition reinforces the deep state's natural
propensity to stove-pipe all of the state superstructure. The
result is the isolation of the judiciary from the institutional
context in which it is nominally embedded. This is achieved
by elevating the judiciary above other institutional contenders
and, indeed, above society as a whole. By playing to judges'
egos and material desires and cultivating the sense of their
own exceptionalism, the deep state causes the judiciary to be
inward looking and generally obedient, rather than searching
for institutional allies to curtail the powers of the deep state.

The SCAF and its military successor, the Sisi government,
being politically vulnerable and having need of support from
the judiciary, have gone further than preceding rulers in their
efforts to isolate the judiciary by elevating it. As Nathan Brown
notes, from the first interim constitution under the SCAF's
authority, followed by the 2012 and 2014 constitutions, initial
drafting was "dominated by judges nominated by their colleagues and law professors." Only after that "were political
actors to have their say and the people be allowed to vote."[24]
The drafting judges were given free rein to proclaim the excep-
tional character of the judiciary, which they did in remarkable
fashion. In the final iteration of the post-coup-volution constitutions, that of 2014, explicit reference was made to "the
regular judiciary, administrative courts, public prosecution,
administrative prosecution, state cases authority, Supreme
Constitutional Court, military courts, judicial experts, other
court personnel and even the legal profession."[25] Judges
were exempted from financial disclosure requirements mandatory for other public officials. It is as if a major purpose of
the constitution was to celebrate the judiciary and its
status, to say nothing of rewarding them materially. Brown
compares this to other countries, where judicial independence
is sought through a "multiplicity of appointing bodies and
procedures to ensure that the judiciary reflects broad social
consensus rather than partisan interests." In Egypt, however,

"the judiciary has sought to anchor its independence not so much in general political and social consensus as in professionalism and complete autonomy."[26] The deep state's management of the judiciary is thus an interesting case of political judo. It gives way to judicial momentum in search of status and independence, which elevates it above the rest of the state's institutional infrastructure and actors in political and civil society. Rather than reinforcing the potential for the judiciary to join coalitions with these other actors, it undermines it.

Coupled with the isolation of the judiciary is the restriction of its jurisdiction. This is accomplished through parallel court systems, including state security, military, and "special circuit" courts, and by the deep state circumventing the legal-judicial system altogether by empowering security forces and the military to engage in extra-judicial killings, detention without charge or notification of next of kin, torture, and the autonomous operation of military and security prisons, the existence of which is not officially acknowledged, nor visits to which are allowed. In July 2016, Amnesty International reported a rapidly growing "trend which has seen hundreds of students, political activists and protesters, including children as young as 14, vanish without trace at the hands of the state. On average three to four people per day are seized...held for months at a time and often kept blindfolded and handcuffed for the entire period."[27] In 2015, 137 political detainees died in officially recognized prisons, an unknown number in the others.[28] The judiciary's jurisdiction, in other words, has been dramatically narrowed so as to exclude cases that involve real or perceived challenges to the deep state, with which it now deals directly in extra-legal, brutal fashion.

This process, originated by Nasser and continued intermittently by Sadat before being hastened by Mubarak, has been dramatically accelerating since the coup-volution. In 2011, 12,000 civilians were tried in military courts. The number then declined until the passage in October 2014 of Law 136, which extended the jurisdiction of military courts to any alleged crimes "occurring on public land, including electric towers and stations, gas pipelines, roads, bridges, and other undefined public facilities."[29] In the following two years, 7,000 civilians were tried in military courts. In August 2016, parliament extended Law 136 for five years, until 2021. Article 204 of the 2014 constitution prohibits civilians from being tried in military courts, "except for crimes that represent a direct assault" against anything under military authority. That "anything" has been expanded under Sisi to indeed include just about anything, ranging from alleged crimes in gas stations, on public roads, and in one case, in the Alexandria Shipyard, where workers were striking. Judges serving on military courts are themselves military officers guaranteed autonomy by Article 204. But in practice and according to Article 1 of the Military Judicial Law, they report to an administrative body within the Ministry of Defense.[30] In the wake of Mursi's ouster the new military-backed government—anxious to prosecute its high-profile opponents as rapidly as possible and not having access to security courts because the Emergency Law had lapsed—established so-called "special circuits" midway between criminal and military courts. Headed by hand-picked judges appointed by the regime-friendly Supreme Judicial Council, these circuits churned through cases against dissidents at breakneck speed.[31]

By early 2017 it appeared that the venerable Egyptian judiciary had been fully tamed by the deep state. It seemed to have subordinated it by legalistic and personalistic means, isolated it from other institutional and organizational actors, and progressively restricted its jurisdiction. But suddenly a case exploded onto the national scene that suggested that pockets of the judiciary remained independent, or perhaps sensed that Sisi was weakening and that it was now possible to signal a desire for reassertion of judicial autonomy. That case involved the promise made by Sisi to the Saudis in April 2016 to hand over the islands of Tiran and Sanafir, at the head of the Gulf of Aqaba. Immediately faced with the unanticipated strong domestic challenge, including the most intense demonstrations against him since becoming president, he reacted in knee-jerk fashion, ordering the arrest and imprisonment of demonstrators, who he referred to as "evil people," while pledging to proceed with the transfer of sovereignty. Sisi presumably calculated that the merits of the case were at least sufficiently mixed that a bit of executive leverage on the courts would be sufficient to produce the outcome he desired.

But Sisi's ill thought-out plan began to come apart in June, when on the 21st Judge Yahia al-Dakrury of the Court of Administrative Justice ruled that Prime Minister Sharif Ismail had violated the constitution by signing the agreement and that its legal substance would have to be ruled on by the Supreme Administrative Court. This kicked off an ever-intensifying struggle between Sisi and key elements of the judiciary that he sought to bend to his will. Not only was the issue of Tiran and Sanafir at stake for Sisi, but so too was that of a possible increase in the independence of the judiciary, virtually the only actor left within or outside of the state with any meaningful autonomy from the executive.

The focus of the struggle was the administrative court system, within which several battles were fought. Judge Dakrury, who had not only demonstrated his willingness to cross the president but was also a candidate to become head of the Maglis al Dawla, or State Council, at the end of June 2017, was a threat Sisi could not ignore. If Dakrury were to assume the latter position he would head the Supreme Administrative Court, which presides over the administrative judicial structure and which handed down the Tiran and Sanafir ruling. So Sisi instructed his Ministry of Justice to draft a law that would transfer power from the senior judiciary to himself to make that appointment.

At the end of December, when Sisi must have calculated that the court would overrule his decision, and when the Judges' Club was considering how to rebuff his efforts to take control of judicial appointments, the pressure was ramped up in dramatic, chilling fashion. Gamal al Din Labban, the head of procurement for the State Council and the son of its former supreme judge, was arrested on corruption charges, with state television broadcasting pictures of bags of cash allegedly found in his apartment. Immediately thereafter Wail Shalaby, Secretary General of Administrative Courts, was also hauled in, but before he could be charged he was found hanged in his cell. The coroner immediately declared it suicide, which Shalaby's father hotly contested.[32]

During that same fateful week, the cabinet, obviously acting on direct, urgent instructions from the president (since Prime Minister Sharif Ismail did not sign the document as required by administrative procedure), reapproved the decision to hand over the islands to Saudi Arabia and sent it to parliament for approval. This brazen attempt to pre-empt the impending court ruling divided parliament itself, with the small opposition, joined even by a few typical supporters of the government, protesting that it would be unconstitutional for parliament to interfere prior to the court ruling. In the event parliament did not have time to act, possibly because the court accelerated its decision making to ensure that its ruling would be issued prior to parliament's approval. In sum, the judiciary, apparently sensing Sisi's weakening despite the growing intensity of his crackdown on all forms of opposition, appeared to have chosen the highly charged issue of Egypt's sovereignty, as represented in those two small, uninhabited islands, to challenge executive power. A judge may have paid with his life for that. An absolutely clear indication that the executive intended to redouble its pressure on the judiciary was the banning on January 9, 2017, by the Supreme Judicial Council of all judges from "publishing any news or comments related to cases under their supervision or other judicial affairs on social media platforms under any circumstances."[33]

Parliament

As with the judiciary, the legislative branch offers benefits and poses threats to the deep state, although the balance tilts more in the latter direction than it does in the case of the judiciary. In its cost-benefit analysis, the deep state fears the threat more than it covets the benefit, so it interferes even more directly in the parliament than it does in the judiciary. As the only national elected body, parliament could come to represent the will of the people and embody national sovereignty. In a democracy no unelected body can exercise power over an elected one. As Philippe Schmitter and Terry Karl observe, "Popularly elected officials must be able to exercise their constitutional powers without being subjected to overriding (albeit informal) opposition from unelected officials. Democracy is in jeopardy if military officers, entrenched civil servants or state managers retain the capacity to act independently of elected officials or even veto decisions made by the people's representative."[34] The democratic relationship of elected officials holding power over unelected ones is inverted in authoritarian Egypt, so democratization threatens to turn the established order upside down.

As with the judiciary, a benefit bestowed on the deep state by parliament performing one of its duties, in this case legislating, contributes directly to the acceptance of, hence compliance with the law, and indirectly to regime legitimacy. Other official functions, such as overseeing the executive or representing the people, would provide even greater legitimacy for the regime, but are too threatening to be allowed to be effectively performed. The unofficial function of serving as channels for the distribution of patronage, hence reinforcing the personal political bases of members and that of the regime more generally, is, by contrast, encouraged and supported by the deep state. The control mechanisms it employs are similar to those applied to the judiciary, although gatekeeping access to the legislature plays a more central role than does the recruitment of judges.

Parliamentary elections ratify choices either made outright by the deep state or profoundly influenced by it. As such, it is more accurate to speak of the *selection* of deputies than of their election. Since the first parliamentary election in Republican Egypt in July 1957, only one and a half have been reasonably free and fair. The half was the first of the two rounds of the 2005 election. Gamal Mubarak, who had grossly overestimated the degree of support for him and his political allies and encouraged his father to permit reasonably free balloting to help prepare his path to the presidency, was brushed aside when first-round voting produced eighty-eight Muslim Brother winners. President Mubarak ordered an about turn, with security taking direct control of the second stage, physically preventing voters from reaching polling stations, stuffing ballot boxes and forging results. No Brother prevailed in the second stage. The only complete election deemed free and fair, although not by the international community which the SCAF banned from official monitoring, was that of 2011–12, won overwhelmingly by the Brothers and their Salafi allies. The lower house of parliament produced by that election was prorogued less than six months later by the SCAF through a decision of the SCC, which on dubious grounds deemed the 2011 electoral law to be unconstitutional. The upper house was dissolved in the immediate wake of the July 2013 coup. That the deep state had to adjourn the two houses *sine die* attests to the vital role of its selection of entrants to parliament, normally a sufficient measure to ensure its control of the legislative branch.

Selection not election

Selection is implemented through election laws and procedures, regime manipulation of which has become more pervasive and effective as a result of greater experience gained from the increased number and political importance of elections since the mid Sadat era. The deep state has learned the tradeoff between the two. An election law virtually guaranteed to produce a quiescent parliament reduces the need for the deep state to select individual candidates and interfere in voting processes. Appreciation of this tradeoff is illustrated by the 2015 election.

Because the 2011 election law had been ruled unconstitutional, a new law had to be drafted in the wake of ratification of the 2014 constitution, which mandated that procedures commence in July of that year for the new, single house parliament, the Maglis al Nuwwab, or Chamber of Deputies, evoking memories of Egypt's earliest parliaments, which bore the same name.[35] The military-dominated government drafted the law itself, which specified both the size of the parliament and the means by which its members were to be elected. As noted with regard to the executive and judicial branches, large numbers militate against effectiveness, a relationship of which the newly entrenched government of President Sisi seemed well aware. The law it produced called for 596 members of the new unicameral parliament, the largest in the country's history, more than 100 members larger than the parliament it was to replace. The primary role of a legislative body is for its members to reach decisions. Typically the more there are, the more difficult that task and the less likely the body can be effective—precisely the outcome intended by the Sisi government. In fact it was initially proposed that there be 630 members.[36] Further undermining the body's effectiveness was the large turnover of its members, with 415 of the 596 MPs elected in 2015 having had no previous parliamentary experience.

More controversial than the parliament's size was the means by which its members would be elected. Political activists with even the slightest degree of independence from the regime sought a list system that would favor representation of political parties. Seats won through contests between individual candidates would "likely be dominated by wealthy independents and local bosses with ties to Egypt's security forces, tribes, and Mubarak's former National Democratic Party." Such candidates have "the money to finance their campaigns and the networks to turn out voters."[37] In the event the law specified 448 seats for individual candidacies in 205 constituencies, as compared to 120 to be elected through winner-take-all party lists, that number in effect to be further reduced by the requirement that those lists have quotas for youth, women, Christians, and workers. Moreover, the lists would compete in four huge constituencies: Cairo and the south and middle Delta (45 seats); middle and upper Egypt (45 seats); the eastern Delta (15 seats); and the western Delta (15 seats), meaning that small opposition parties would have virtually no chance, an outcome made yet more likely by the provision that all the seats in each constituency would go to the list that secured a majority. Indeed, in the Fall 2015 election, the regime-supported For the Love of Egypt won all 120 seats allotted for party lists, the other eight lists emerging empty handed. 5,420 candidates were approved to compete for the 448 independent seats, the sheer number swamping the prospects that nascent opposition parties could enter parliament through that route. The balance of members was made up of twenty-eight presidential appointees. The highly restrictive voting law was a contributing factor to the scanty turnout in the election, in which the government claimed 28.3 percent of registered voters participated, probably an overstatement but still just half the proportion achieved in the 2011–12 election.

The regime's artfully crafted electoral law thus produced a politically supine parliament, obviating the need for direct interference in the voting process, although vote-buying was widespread.[38] The US Department of State expressed several concerns about the election, but observed that overall it was conducted "professionally and in accordance with Egyptian laws."[39] So the potential cost to the deep state of having to wrestle with a politically active and independent-minded parliament in which newly founded opposition political parties might begin to mature was avoided, at the price of that body being deemed by most Egyptians to be a rubber stamp that provided them little if any representation, so adding no legitimacy to the regime.

Lurking behind the benches: subordination to the deep state

Subordination of the legislative to the executive branch, hence to the deep state, is achieved through the constitutional/legal framework that defines its roles and responsibilities, and through official procedures and unofficial practices within the parliament. Regarding the former, the 2014 constitution slightly upgraded the nominal comparative standing of the Maglis al Nuwwab, reflecting the regime's confidence that it could filter out politically problematic candidates, and its desire to appease a public that had vocally endorsed the empowerment of parliament. It granted to parliament the power to hold a referendum on whether the president should be dismissed, to hold a vote of no-confidence against the government, and to approve the president's choice for prime minister (if it disapproves, then the president must accept the choice of the party or alliance that holds the majority). But these nominal powers are in reality tightly circumscribed, primarily thanks to the selection process.[40] In the unlikely event that parliament were to confront the executive, Article 137 of the 2014 constitution grants the president the power to dissolve it. Scott Williamson and Nathan Brown conclude that parliamentary powers "assume an independence and coherence to the House that is unlikely to materialize, and even then the constitution's balance of power still favors the president by a wide margin."[41] As for the power of the purse, the 2014 constitution restricts it further than previously by removing even nominal oversight over the military budget, which is to be presented in one number to the parliament. The state budget as a whole includes not much more useful information than that, as reflected in Egypt's ranking on the Open Budget Index, which in 2015 was 16th from the bottom of 88 ranked countries. On the sub-index of budget oversight by the legislature, it scored zero.[42] Parliament has no say whatsoever over the dispersal of public foreign assistance monies.

The heavy hand of the executive is exerted through the leadership of the parliament, which is loyal to it, not the body over which it presides. That leadership consists of the chairs of standing committees, of which in the parliament convened in January 2016 there were twenty-five, up from the previous eighteen, as well as the Secretary General and the Speaker, in ascending order of importance. Committee chairpersons and their two deputies are elected by committee members, with the overwhelming number of chairs and deputy chairs being drawn from those in or allied to the ruling party, committed to implementing its will in their committees. An exception proves the rule. Muhammad Anwar Ismat al Sadat, nephew of President Sadat and founder and head of the Reform and Development Party, has been a member of all parliaments since 2005, although he was stripped of his parliamentary membership two weeks after the opening session of the 2007 parliament for expressing views deemed to be too independent by the Mubarak regime. His brother, Talaat, also an MP under Mubarak, was similarly ejected from parliament and then jailed for a year on the grounds of showing contempt for the military by claiming it had shown complacency in protecting his uncle on October 6, 1981. The Sadat brothers, in short, are political mavericks, whose name virtually guarantees them some stature in Egyptian political life, but does not protect them from retribution by the deep state. And indeed, some seven months after his election as chair of the human rights committee at the commencement of the 2016 parliamentary session, Muhammad Ismat al Sadat's political isolation caused him to resign his post. The proximate cause of that isolation, which was orchestrated by the Speaker within the parliament and the media, was that he had attended an international meeting on human rights in Geneva without receiving prior approval from parliament, one of several pro-human rights initiatives he had taken and which had exhausted the leadership's patience. Collaboration between the executive branch and the leadership of parliament in dealing with Sadat was revealed in November 2016, when the minister of social solidarity, Ghada Waly, lodged a complaint to the General Committee of the Maglis al Nuwwab, accusing Sadat of "leaking the government-drafted NGO law to a number of foreign embassies in Cairo."[43] The General Committee, formed of the Speaker, his two deputies and all twenty-five committee chairs, is the veritable embodiment of the executive's power in parliament. Sadat's response to the charge was: "I did not leak the draft copy of the law because it has never been sent to parliament."[44]

Sadat was replaced in the new session that commenced in October 2016 by Alaa Abid, the parliamentary leader of the Free Egyptians Party, a junior partner in the ruling coalition. Abid, a former police officer, owed his election to the stacking of the human rights committee by his party followers, twenty-six of its sixty-five MPs joining the committee and taking its membership from thirty-eight to sixty-four. Abid commenced his chairmanship by attacking his predecessor for "attending conferences by human rights groups which are hostile to Egypt." He noted that this was a mistake "we will not repeat." When asked if the committee would continue its efforts to undertake surprise visits to prisons, he replied, "There is no such thing as a surprise visit. There is a series of procedures that must be followed before committee members can visit prison cells."

He concluded by blaming the Muslim Brotherhood for "spreading false reports about the human rights situation in Egypt," and specifying the responsibility of his committee to be "defending the image of Egypt against malicious reports."[45] Chosen as Abid's deputy chair was Muhammad al Ghul, also a former police officer. The leader of the Conservative Party in parliament, Akmal Qurtam, resigned in protest against the stacking of the committee and Abid's alleged torture of detainees when serving as a police officer.[46] In February 2017 Sadat was expelled from the parliament.

Sadat's case, which is atypical as he has been the most outspoken, independent-minded committee chair in the history of Republican Egypt, thus illustrates the narrow limits imposed on committee heads by a parliamentary leadership which takes its cues from the executive. Most committee chairs are drawn from state institutions that correspond to the subject of the committee, or are prominent figures in that area. The National Security Affairs Committee, for example, is habitually headed by a military general. In the second session of the 2016 parliament the Labor Committee was chaired by the head of the state-controlled Egyptian Federation of Trade Unions, the Media Committee by a former minister of information, the Religious Affairs Committee by the president of al Azhar University, and the Housing and Public Utilities committee by a construction magnate. Nineteen of the twenty-five committee chairs in that session were taken by members of the pro-Sisi Support Egypt bloc, three by members of the Wafd Party, which has hovered between allying with that bloc and being formally independent, two by members of the moderate leftist "25-30" bloc, and one by an "independent," a Mubarak-era minister of social solidarity—a remarkably misleading title for a ministry charged with controlling civil society organizations. Other than Sadat, no committee chair could be said to be an opponent or indeed even critical of President Sisi.

The administrative head of parliament is the Secretary General, a post with exceptionally low turnover. During the long Mubarak era only two persons held the post. Nominally appointed by the Speaker, the Secretary General is in fact the executive's man. He is in charge of rewarding and punishing

MPs through his administrative powers over financial matters, office assignments, travel arrangements, etc. While parliament was in abeyance and after he was elected president, Sisi personally appointed a military officer to this post, the first time in the history of the Egyptian parliament, which dates back to 1866, it had not been held by a civilian. As this caused political discomfort even among the regime's supporters, this Secretary General was replaced once the parliament convened. His successor, named by the new Speaker, was a former police officer, who in turn appointed as Deputy Secretary General yet another former police officer. Never before had police officers occupied these two posts.

At the apex of the executive's control system operating in parliament is the Speaker, a constitutionally and politically prominent position. Changes in the type of person holding this key position and his operating style illustrate the ebb and flow of soft and hard authoritarianism over more than half a century, with the flow to the hard end more pronounced under Sisi than at any time in the 150-year history of the body. Ali Abd al Aal, a former public prosecutor and law professor who taught at the police academy and military college, was elected Speaker in January 2016, thanks to the backing of the For the Love of Egypt bloc, the military's surrogate in parliament. Previously he had played a key role in drafting the parliamentary electoral law that produced the overwhelming victory for pro-Sisi forces. He has ruled over parliament with an iron fist, reshaping the vital role of Speaker. He has instructed deputies that their duty is one of "cooperation rather than confrontation" with the executive.[47] He pledged to use "all of his strength" to prevent criticism of the government, because "in tough times there is no individual legislative or executive authority—rather, all of them should act as a single authority."[48] Following an uproar on the floor of the Council on the very first day of the session, he banned further live television coverage of plenaries. He orchestrated the expulsion from parliament of Tawfiq Ukasha, al Aal's primary opposition challenger for the post of Speaker. In May, al Aal threatened to report to the Ethics Committee any member who criticized the government's monetary policy, simultane-

ously warning deputies not to speak to the media on this
sensitive subject. He followed up that threat with an accusa-
tion that efforts to train parliamentarians, even when conducted
by Egyptian organizations, such as the prestigious Al Ahram
Strategic Studies Center, constituted "a systematic campaign
to destroy the country's constitutional institutions."[49] It is
worth noting that al Aal himself has received support for his
travels and other activities from the international Inter-
Parliamentary Union. Sauce for the goose is in his view not
sauce for the gander. To those deputies who complained that
his dictates violated their freedom of expression, he responded
that "freedom of expression should be responsible, and harming
the state's interests is not considered freedom of expression."[50]
When it was revealed in February 2017 that al Aal had ordered
the purchase of a fleet of new cars for the parliament's leadership, in apparent violation of a recent government ban on
such acquisitions, he responded by urging the parliament to
declare its budget secret on grounds of national security.[51]

Egypt's new Speaker of parliament, in sum, is President
Sisi's watchdog over that body. Barking at those who might
be so bold as to try to learn how to be better deputies, and
biting those, such as Tawfiq Ukasha, who openly challenge
him, al Aal has a novel interpretation of his new role. Trained
as a prosecutor, nurtured by forces within the Ministry of
Defense and the Ministry of Interior, it is not surprising that
he sees his job as intimidating the negligible opposition, using
threats and worse to cow it into absolute submission. This
represents a departure from long-established parliamentary
tradition, according to which the Speaker has played a less
malignant role.

From the first parliament of independent Egypt in 1923
until the last of the monarchial era before it was prorogued
by the military in 1952, the Speaker was a semi-neutral figure.
One of his implicit tasks was to mediate between government
and opposition, typically seeking to induce compliance of the
latter to the former with both carrots and sticks. Interestingly,
even in Nasser's parliaments a vestige of that mediating role
remained, especially when occupied by Anwar al Sadat, the
longest serving Speaker of that era. He was tasked by Nasser

to use his role as a bridge to conservative, rural elements represented in parliament, whom Nasser distrusted but did not want to completely alienate.

The same logic and practice prevailed to an even greater degree in the Sadat era prior to 1978, when the relative autonomy of the Speaker was eroded as the regime slid toward ever greater authoritarianism. At the height of the "infitah" (opening), which followed the 1973 war and ended with Sadat's November 1977 trip to Jerusalem, Sayed Marei, whose son married Sadat's daughter, served for almost four years as Speaker. Marei was a consummate politician. His conception of the role of Speaker was that of a shock absorber between the opposition in parliament, on the one hand, and the executive and its supporters in that body on the other. He was invariably polite in dealings with members on both sides of the aisle. He took care when handing out "carrots," such as trips abroad, to ensure that even critics of Sadat were not entirely excluded. Although closely connected to Sadat personally and politically, he did not see his role as being that of the president's watchdog, barking at and biting the opposition. It was rather the reverse in fact, for he deemed his job to be one of monitoring the pulse of the opposition and reporting it to the president.

Not since that time has a Speaker enjoyed so much prestige and influence, but those who served under Mubarak were men of independent standing with considerable political intelligence. Rifat al Mahgub was assassinated by extremists in 1990 in part because he was an outspoken critic of them, while Fathi Surur, the longest serving Speaker in the history of Egypt's parliament, took care like Marei to cultivate the opposition by, for example, giving some among them access to the sorts of training programs that al Aal has recently identified as being subversive. Surur, in fact, was a strong advocate of such programs, believing that deputies skilled in parliamentary practice would be an asset, rather than a threat, as al Aal obviously thinks.

Even the Muslim Brothers' Speaker who nominally served during the year in which they held power, Saad Katatni, was by the standards of that organization a liberal. Having sat

for several years in parliament, he was the primary interlocu-
tor between the Brothers and diplomatic missions, as American
and many European diplomats could avoid self-imposed restrictions on contacts with Brothers by meeting Katatni as a deputy
rather than as a Brother. Like Surur, he was an advocate of
parliamentary development through training and education,
so sought to encourage his fellow Brother MPs to participate
in US and other countries' programs. Of the leading members
of the Brothers he was the most open minded, willing to
engage in substantive debates with others. This did not spare
him from the military's wrath, however, which has had him
incarcerated since the coup.

The role of parliamentary speaker provides a useful barometer of the political climate. The less autonomy granted by
the president to the Speaker, the greater the political pressure
the regime seeks to apply to the opposition. Al Aal, who
enjoys zero degrees of freedom from Sisi and the military, is
a political cipher, with no independent reputation and no
reputation for independence. He has discredited himself and
the parliament he heads, thereby eroding what has previously
been an important institutional link between the regime and
the political class, even occasionally the country as whole. Al
Aal's presence reflects the ever growing isolation of the Sisi
regime and the mediocrity of those associated with it. It also
tarnishes the reputation of the oldest legislature in the Arab
world and by so doing, the country's once proud standing as
the leading Arab state.

Isolated and ungrounded: parliament cut off at the feet

Embeddedness in the government and political centrality are
prerequisites for the assertion of parliamentary power. If MPs
and their institution are to gain political leverage, they must
at a minimum be able to access the executive for information,
indeed, compel it to provide it. In democracies, legislatures
not only obtain information from the executive branch, they
oversee it and seek to bend it to their will. In the US, for
example, the president and Congress struggle for control over
the federal administration, most importantly through person-

nel appointments. The Congress, in other words, is thoroughly embedded within the broader US government.

Political centrality refers to the degree to which parliament serves as the arena in which contending political forces fight out their battles and how much those battles captivate national political attention. Centrality is a product of constitutional and political contexts, for which the media can serve as a surrogate measure since it is through the media that the public is informed about parliament. The degree to which the business of parliament is a matter of public concern is simultaneously a measure of the relative power of the legislative versus the executive branch.

Isolating parliament from government and the political system is thus key to the deep state's control of it. It determines which MPs are able to obtain information, to say nothing of favors, from the executive branch. Administrative access is vital to MPs serving their constituents, hence to building political support bases. Not surprisingly, opposition MPs have traditionally complained that they are selectively denied access to the executive branch as they seek information or other services. By contrast, the regime cultivates loyalties from MPs it wants on board by providing them such access so they can in turn serve their constituents' personal interests, such as by obtaining permits. The deep state even gatekeeps access to local government because it is at that level that the bulk of constituent requests can be fulfilled. The deep state, in other words, cuts parliament off at the feet, preventing it from becoming institutionally grounded, embedded in the state. By providing administrative access selectively to its MP supporters, it vitiates parliament's institutional powers and capacities. It also works to marginalize parliament from the political system, with the media playing an important role in this regard. Access to the media through which the parliament could achieve greater political centrality is closely regulated by the regime, typically through the Speaker. He decides when, how, and by whom plenary sessions are broadcast. Committee meetings are closed not just to the media, but to citizens. Only the state-owned media can afford to have full-time parliamentary reporters, whose articles are typically bland and on their papers' back pages. The executive further isolates the parliament by restricting even its constitutionally mandated duties, especially when those duties would intrude into politically sensitive policy areas. Article 127 of the 2014 constitution, for example, stipulates that "The executive authority may not contract a loan, obtain funding, or commit itself to a project that is not listed in the approved state budget entailing expenditure from the state treasury…except with the approval of the House of Representatives." As government indebtedness steadily mounted after Sisi was elected president and the issue of borrowing from international sources became increasingly sensitive, so did the government refer ever fewer loans to parliament for its approval, whether individually or as included in the annual budget. By late 2016 one source calculated that at a minimum over the preceding two years $40 billion in loans had been obtained by the government which had not been approved by parliament.[52] That this was not just a simple oversight was suggested by the treatment of two MPs who questioned why the government had not sought parliament's approval for a currency-swap loan from China and the $12 billion IMF loan agreed in November 2016. Proceedings were initiated against both deputies which could result in their expulsion from parliament. In the case of MP Haitham al Hariri, son of the former presidential candidate Abul Izz al Hariri and head of the small but increasingly vocal leftist 25-30 bloc, the Alexandria Prosecution Office applied to parliament for his immunity to be lifted so he could be investigated for receiving a salary from a company while serving in parliament. Al Hariri denied the charge, saying it had been lodged because of his demand that the government of Prime Minister Sharif Ismail be dismissed because it had violated the constitution by accepting loans without parliament's approval.[53]

The parliament is a stove-pipe of its own, more or less like the judiciary, purposefully isolated from other institutional and political actors with which it could form common cause against the deep state. That it is unable to effectively assert itself against the executive and the deep state is reflected in the score assigned to "limits by the legislature" on the subindex of "constraints on government powers" of the World Justice Project's 2016 Rule of Law Index. The score of .21, which places it at the bottom of the third decile of overall rankings, is the seventh lowest score on the forty-four indicators that make up the Index. On the sub-index that ranks relative corruption in the executive, judiciary, police/military, and the legislature, the Egyptian parliament is deemed to be the most corrupt, which is saying quite a lot given the company it is in.[54]

Possibly a more revealing measure of parliament's subordination to the executive is its desire, or at least willingness, to appear more royalist than the king by taking restrictive measures that would stimulate a backlash against the executive were it to introduce them itself. A case in point is the bill approved in November 2016 to regulate non-governmental organizations (NGOs). For more than two years the government had been working on similar legislation, but apparently ultimately deemed it preferable to have parliament take the lead. Two-hundred-and-four MPs signed on as sponsors of the bill, the eighty-nine provisions of which would ban any NGO not registered with the Ministry of Social Solidarity; restrict NGO activity to "developmental and social work" and impose jail terms of up to five years for non-compliance; prohibit conducting fieldwork or public opinion polls; require foreign NGOs to be supervised by a new regulatory agency staffed by representatives of the military, General Intelligence, and the Ministry of Interior; and render illegal "cooperating in any way with any international body without the necessary approval." Human rights activists decried the legislation, noting that leaked drafts of the government's proposal revealed it to be "liberal compared to this bill."[55] Possibly the government had second thoughts about the content of the bill because after its passage on November 29 it more or less disappeared, neither being signed by the president nor returned to the parliament within thirty days, as required by Article 123 of the constitution. Sisi himself claimed not to have received the proposed law from parliament, presumably because it was being held in the Speaker's office on his orders. Attempts by independent MPs to determine the fate of the legislation were unsuccessful.[56]

The executive also uses parliament to intimidate critics. On December 19, 2016, the parliamentary session was devoted to an attack on prominent TV host Ibrahim Aissa, a former strong supporter of Sisi turned skeptic. On January 1, 2017, his show was taken off the air, apparently as a result of businessman Tariq Nur, owner of the station hosting the program, being informed by the government that his long-planned, expensive exhibition of Egyptian furniture would not proceed unless and until Aissa was removed.[57] In the following month Speaker al Aal orchestrated a majority vote in favor of referring Aissa to the Prosecutor General to investigate the charge that he had "insulted parliament."

Conclusion

The three branches of government form a perimeter around the deep state, protecting it from challengers while serving various of its interests. The depth of that perimeter expands and contracts as the deep state asserts greater and lesser control over it. With the rise to power of the military in the wake of the coup-volution, the perimeter has retreated as the power of the military has grown. Hobbled by greater penetration and control than at any time since the early days of Republican Egypt, the executive, judicial, and legislative branches are unable effectively to perform their nominal functions, to say nothing of their implicit political one of legitimating the regime by encouraging the belief among citizens that they have some access to their government which pays at least some attention to their interests. The cost to the deep state of asserting such thoroughgoing control over government institutions is that as the quality of governance declines, compliance comes to depend more on coercion, actual or threatened, than on satisfaction. Republican Egypt is as close to this tipping point as it has ever been. An ever greater proportion of the population is profoundly dissatisfied with the quality of governance and its consequences. The three branches of government are providing an ever thinner layer of defense for the deep state, which has responded by doubling down on its control of them and thus the population, rather than by seeking to open up the limited access order over which it presides.

4 Political and Civil Society: Little Room to Breathe

The institutions that comprise the state superstructure were characterized in the preceding chapter as schizophrenic. On the one hand their nominal, constitutional functions are related to making, administering, and adjudicating law. On the other hand, the deep state compels them to perform functions related to gatekeeping the limited access order and controlling those excluded from it. The inherent conflict in performing these different functions undermines the effectiveness of executive, judicial, and legal institutions in discharging their nominal duties. Collectively, however, the state superstructure does serve as an outer perimeter for the deep state, protecting it from the broader political system, in considerable measure simply by hiding it from view, but if necessary, by more energetic means.

Beyond this perimeter are organizations that constitute the political and civil societies of which the broader political order is constituted. The former refers to organizations with a manifest political purpose, primarily political parties and Islamist "movements," but also informal political collectivities, such as those formed to bring down Mubarak. Civil society is composed of public actors which express views on public policies, such as non-governmental organizations, trade unions and professional syndicates, business associations, religious institutions, media outlets, charities, and so on. In Egypt the line between political and civil society is blurred because some civil society actors, especially advocacy NGOs, more closely resemble small political parties than organizations in civil society devoted to services rather than advocacy. This lack of a clear division reflects the vacuum resulting from most political parties being weak, causing NGOs to be sucked into direct competition with them more or less as surrogate political parties. Since Egyptian political parties do not adequately perform the defining functions of parties, which are those of interest aggregation, political recruitment and representation, civil society organizations assume some of those tasks.

Political and civil society, like the state superstructure, are enfeebled by the deep state's interference in their functioning. It intervenes into political society to secure compliance with its interests, as well as to provide a buffer from and absorb the energies of real or potential political opponents. The immediate costs of such manipulation are reflected in the poor performance of political party functions. They do not aggregate collective interests, such as those expressed by NGOs of similar outlooks, so no party can claim to represent a broad segment of the population. They do not provide channels of recruitment into the political elite, so the elite formed at the outset of each presidency tends to age along with the regime. As for civil society, its key function of articulating views on public policies is severely restricted by limitations imposed by the deep state, typically acting through superstructural institutions.

The broader, systemic cost of the enfeeblement of political and civil society is to further debilitate the country's institutional capacities, which, as was noted in the introduction to Chapter 2, are deemed by Douglass North and other institutional economists to be the key determinant of economic growth. Indra Overland, in investigating the relationship between institutional capacities and effective resource management, especially oil, has found that those capacities, as exemplified in his native Norway, depend heavily on what he terms "public brainpower." Inspired by writings on the public sphere, civil society, and social capital, he defines this concept as a polycentricity that results from "the coexistence of many different public actors each freely expressing their thoughts... The more polycentric a society is, the greater is its brainpower." Public brainpower aids "decision-makers in the governance of society" because the open expression of ideas and contestation between them "constitutes a capacity for thought that narrower elites lack on their own."[1] In other words, institutional capacity is determined by interactions between governmental institutions and actors in political and civil society, not just by features internal to the institutions. The stove-piping of Egyptian government, its isolation from political and civil society, and restrictions on freedoms in the latter are, in other words, antithetical to "public brainpower" and bound to produce poor governance and depress economic growth.[2]

The Prosperity Index for 2016 reflects the impediments to Egyptian public brainpower and their costs. That Index, compiled by the Legatum Institute, measures the prosperity of 149 countries through nine indicators, including the overall economy, growth foundations, economic opportunities, etc. Egypt ranked 117th, below such countries as Ukraine, Tanzania, Malawi, Burkina Faso, Algeria, and Uganda. Its lowest score on the nine indicators was on personal freedom, on which it ranked 146th, surpassing only Yemen, Sudan, and Afghanistan.[3] Personal freedom is of course a prerequisite for building public brainpower. Its near absence in Egypt is the price imposed on the nation by the deep state's jealous guarding of the limited access order which it created and maintains.

The means by which political and civil society are manipulated and controlled by the deep state range from soft to hard, their very complexity attesting to the challenge of the task and the state's preoccupation with it. Moving from the soft toward the hard end are such tactics as co-opting and balancing off organizations and individuals, pre-empting political space with tame organizations, attacking reputations, interdicting information flow combined with disinformation, application of financial incentives and disincentives, imposition of restrictive laws and regulations, and, finally, outright repression, culminating in torture, detention without trial, and extrajudicial killings. Reactions among political and civil society actors range from exit to voice, meaning that some acquiesce and abandon the public arena, while others protest in ways ranging from articulating opposing views, to joining opposition organizations, to participating in peaceful demonstrations, to becoming violent extremists.

The deep state, in sum, is like the mafia boss who makes the offer that cannot be refused, the implied threat intended to secure compliance with the "offer." In the case of Egypt's deep state that offer is to accept the rules of political engagement as presented, or face an escalating range of sanctions. Embodied in those rules of the political game is co-optation of potential opponents and their being balanced off against other actors, some of whom are regime clients intended to pre-empt political space. The application and impacts of these rules of the game will be illustrated with reference to three constituencies—the religious, labor, and youth—within which oppositional political and civil society organizations could pose threats to the deep state.

The Religious

Islam and Christianity are not only central to the identities of their adherents, they provide the doctrinal and social bases upon which much of the organizationally related life of those adherents rests. Belonging to congregations, contributing to religious charities, working within religiously organized NGOs, and, in the direct political realm, joining religiously associated political parties, are manifestations of the extent to which sociopolitical behavior is rooted in religion. The profound degree to which religious identity and thinking shapes views on issues of direct or indirect political importance renders the challenge of managing the relationship between religion and politics a particularly difficult one, including for the deep state. It seeks to benefit from religiosity without allowing authority to pass from its hands into those more manifestly religious, whether by virtue of an official role, such as the head of al Azhar or the Coptic Patriarch, or by virtue of standing in a religiously connected organization, such as the Muslim Brotherhood.

The depth of Islamic identity intensifies the challenge of managing the relationship between religion and public policy. Egyptians are among the world's most devout Muslims, as reflected in the findings of a succession of polls conducted by the Pew Research Center between 2010 and 2016. Seventy-four percent of Muslim Egyptians favor making shari'a the official law, a proportion only exceeded in the Arab world by Iraq, Palestine, and Morocco.[4] Seventy-five percent believe shari'a is the revealed word of God rather than the work of man, only exceeded in the Arab world by Jordan.[5] Three quarters of Egyptian Muslims also believe that the shari'a should apply to Muslims and non-Muslims, the highest ratio in all of the twenty-one countries in which the poll was conducted. Similarly, 95 percent of Egyptian Muslims believe religious judges should decide family and property disputes, again the highest rate in the countries polled. Even more remarkable is that 86 percent of Egyptian Muslims advocate the death penalty for those renouncing their faith, the only other country coming close to that proportion being Afghanistan at 79 percent. Eighty-one percent of Egyptian Muslims support stoning for adultery, the third highest after Pakistanis and Palestinians.[6] That Egyptian Muslims may believe their government is insufficiently devout is implied by the fact that only 39 percent believe their country's laws follow the shari'a somewhat or very closely, the second lowest proportion in the Arab world, with only the Lebanese (for much better reason) more doubtful that their country's laws reflect the shari'a. This finding alone suggests that Egyptian Muslims experience dissonance between their religious beliefs and the semi-secular nature of their state, a dissonance that provides the normative political space within which Islamism, politically mobilized Islam, operates. According to the Arab Political Barometer, 89 percent of Egyptian Muslims would object in some degree to a marriage between a relative and a man or a woman who does not pray.[7]

It is symptomatic of the status of Coptic and other Christians in Egypt that there are no polling data available about their religiosity or other beliefs, including political ones. Even

census data about them is contentious and ambiguous, with
the official if not completely reliable data suggesting that slightly
less than 6 percent of the population is Coptic, while the
church itself, drawing on other demographic data, claims the
true figure is 15 percent.[8] Impressionistic evidence suggests a
Hegelian dialectic is at work within and between the Muslim
and Christian communities, in the sense that the religiosity
of one, especially the former, stimulates religiosity in the latter.
Members of both faiths appear to have become outwardly
more religious since the late 1960s, as measured by clothing,
jewelry, praying, attending places of worship and so on. It is
reasonable to surmise that these public signs of religiosity
reflect inner beliefs, including among Coptic Orthodox Christians, who account for the vast majority of all Egyptian Christians. Other behavioral evidence, including the growing
importance of a Coptic youth movement centered on monasteries and monastic clergy, confirms that hypothesis.

In short, by global standards, Egyptian Muslims and Christians are highly religious. Their intense religiosity, combined
with their very divergent theologies regarding matters of law
and governance—as well as with inter-religious tension and
violence, which have been steadily increasing since the early
Sadat era—indicate that the politics of religion, both within
and between the two faiths, is fraught with peril for those
seeking to ensure they do not destabilize the existing order.

Christians

Since Christians are of a different faith and because they pose
less of a threat, their management by the deep state is more
straightforward and top-down. More intrusive, bottom-up
interference in the Christian community itself would be prob-
lematical for a government officially and deemed by all to be
Muslim. For political purposes the Coptic Orthodox community can be thought of as consisting of 1) the official church
headed since November 2012 by Pope Tawadrus II; 2) disaf-
fected, mainly young secularists who resent the role of the
church in their lives; 3) radical Coptic "nationalists" mostly
based abroad who are highly critical of the Egyptian govern-

ment for discriminating against Copts and of Pope Tawadros
and his predecessor, Pope Shenouda, for doing too little to
combat that discrimination; and 4) the wealthy Sawiris family
along with its various businesses and the Free Egyptians Party,
founded two months after the coup-volution by Naguib Sawiris,
the most politically active of the three sons of the family
patriarch, Onsi Sawiris.

With one brutal exception the deep state has no direct
engagement with either the rebellious secularized Coptic youths
or the expatriate "Coptic nationalist" movement, although it
does have government spokespersons from time to time refute
claims of discrimination against Copts by the latter. The exception is known as the Maspero Massacre, named after the
Maspero television building along the Nile in Cairo in front
of which, on October 9–10, 2011, young, overwhelmingly
Coptic demonstrators protested against the demolition of a
church in Aswan and the confrontations there between Copts
and Salafis, to which in their view the governor's response
had been inadequate. They were attacked by the military,
which killed up to twenty-seven demonstrators and injured
another 300 or so, then denied culpability.

The deep state's primary strategy for maintaining the quiescence of Copts is two-pronged. The first consists of empowering the Pope to preside over his flock, sub-contracting
responsibility to him to keep it in order. His power is indirectly
enshrined in the 2014 constitution, Article 3 of which states,
"The principles of the laws of Egyptian Christians and Jews
are the main source of laws regulating their personal status,
religious affairs, and selection of spiritual leaders." Thus
empowered, the Pope speaks on the community's behalf, as
he did for example when he gave a televised speech in the
wake of the July 3, 2013 coup endorsing the military's removal
of President Mursi. His power is reinforced by the state's
recognition of Coptic family law, which was made yet more
restrictive in 1971 and among other things prohibits divorce.
The clergy plays such an intrusive role in marriage that one
of the most prominent Egyptian human rights organizations,
the Egyptian Initiative for Personal Rights, issued a report in
2016 condemning the interference.[9]

The state's treatment of the "church as the sole representative of the Copts, rather than dealing with members of the community as full citizens in their own right," was reinforced by both the manner of adopting and the content of the 2016 law on church construction, the very first in the country's history. With the removal of President Mursi, longstanding Coptic demands for the process of approval of church building to be regularized resulted in the opening of discussions between the patriarchate and the government on that issue. The resulting draft law was sent to parliament without prior public debate. Parliamentary discussion of the legislation was cut off on the grounds that the church had agreed to the law already. The law's text referred to a "religious sect" rather than "Egyptian Christian citizens." It specified that the size of a proposed church be proportionate to the Christian population in the vicinity and removed a commitment in an earlier draft that an application would be considered approved if not responded to within sixty days. As the observer quoted above noted, "the new law will not likely solve the problem of church building in Egypt."[10] That it is indeed a problem is reflected by the fact that, as noted earlier, in 2016 there were 2,869 churches in Egypt compared with 108,395 mosques, a ratio of about one to forty, compared to the population ratio of about one to ten or twelve.[11] Papal authority is reinforced by patronage networks among the faithful, which in the case of Pope Tawadros' predecessor were presided over by his relatives. The state and the Pope, in other words, are mutual political backscratchers.

The other prong of the regime's strategy of control is intended to offset its economic and political discrimination against Copts, the primary components of which are restricting their numbers in political life and providing them proportionately less access than Muslims to government resources, especially employment, most profoundly in the military and security services. In the armed forces, for example, Mubarak imposed on Copts a glass ceiling at the rank of colonel.[12] The Sawiris business conglomerate and the Free Egyptians Party are used to offset this economic and political discrimination, respectively. The conglomerate was originally built by father

Onsi's Orascom Contracting Company, which was among if not the largest firm building facilities for the military. The sons then branched out, the most profitable endeavor being the Mobilnil cellular phone company over which Naguib presided and which by virtue of being a monopoly service provider initially, and subsequently one of only two for several years, was a license to print money. On various lists of Africa's and the world's most wealthy people over the past two decades, all four Sawiris males have appeared. In 2016, Forbes magazine identified brothers Naguib and Nassif Sawiris as having increased their fortunes more than any other Egyptians, taking their combined holdings to some $9 billion, making them the two richest Egyptians and two of the ten richest Africans.[13] Accumulation of such wealth would have been impossible without support from the deep state. That support was provided primarily out of the calculation that this business empire, known by all to be led by Copts who disproportionately employ their co-religionists, would absorb some of the employment slack resulting from government discrimination against Copts, while also countering some of the reputational damage from that discrimination. Sawiris enterprises and the huge success of the family were repeatedly pointed to by the Mubarak regime as proof that Copts are not discriminated against in Egypt.

The Sisi regime added a political dimension to the associated economic one by fostering the growth of the Sawiris' Free Egyptians Party, which serves as a sponge to absorb Coptic political ambitions. The party has enjoyed remarkable electoral success in its short history. In the 2011–12 parliamentary elections it competed as part of the Egyptian Bloc, which had been formed in August 2011 but was immediately weakened by defections of those alleging it included remnants of the Mubarak regime. The Bloc won thirty-three seats, of which fourteen were taken by the Free Egyptians Party, making it the fourth most successful party in the elections. It endorsed Sisi in the May 2014 presidential election. In 2015 it contested parliamentary elections as a member of the regime-backed For the Love of Egypt bloc, again winning the largest number of any party in the bloc. Its success was due both to regime

backing and to it serving as the vehicle for Coptic representation, the latter support evidenced in a leaked recording of
Bishop Bula of Tanta urging Copts to vote for the party.[14]
But in late 2016 internal dissent erupted among the Free Egyptians, with founder and financial backer Naguib Sawiris launch-
ing a suit against the party's board of directors and its head,
Isam Khalil, who out of their subservience to the regime had
marginalized him. Presumably the combination of his phe-
nomenal wealth, much of which is held outside Egypt, and
the regime's declining popularity among Copts, caused Sawiris
to calculate that for him and the Free Egyptians it was economically possible and politically advisable to appear to be
more, rather than less independent of Sisi. In February 2017,
Khalil and the board expelled Sawiris from the party, but he
took with him a large component of its membership. By early
2017 the success of the regime's two-pronged strategy was
eroding as a result of its failure adequately to defend Copts,
combined with the general decline of its popularity.

The government's management of tension and violence
between Muslims and Christians is intended to reinforce the
power of the official leaderships of the two faiths, to evade
the political wrath of Islamists, and to prevent this issue from
becoming a vehicle for increased demands for the rule of law.
These goals it has attained with reasonable success, at the
cost of failing to deter a deterioration of inter-faith relations.
Studies by individual scholars, human rights and faith (especially Christian) affiliated organizations have charted an increase
in sectarian violence since 2008. Between that year and 2014
incidents of violence occurred on average fifty to sixty times
annually. Since 2014 the rate has escalated to over 200 annually.[15] The various studies all pinpointed the four principal
causes of violence as being church building, romantic relations
between those of different faiths, conversions, and expressions
of opinions about religion. Moreover, they all found that the
single most common intervention by the government into these
conflicts was to seek to mediate them through "customary
reconciliation." Notable in its absence was the use of legal/
judicial means, which would have involved utilizing the police
and courts to determine guilt and innocence, to say nothing

of making public the conflict and those found guilty of perpetrating crimes. By relying on customary mediators, most especially Christian clergy and Muslim *ulama* (religious scholars), the government simultaneously reinforces the power of official religious hierarchies, undercuts the centrality of police and courts to the rule of law, avoids publicity, and prevents extremists on either side from making political capital out of the conflict. The net result has not been to reduce the problem nor to protect Christians, who as much the weaker party are necessarily disadvantaged by this approach as compared to one that would use the full powers of the state to protect them.[16] In sum, the deep state extracts a considerable price from Christians for extending a rather tattered umbrella of protection over them, in good mafia boss style.

Muslims—official Islam

Political activists inspired by Islam pose a far greater danger to the regime than Christians, so the strategy to contain them, although not fundamentally dissimilar, is accordingly more complex and embracing of heavy-handed tactics. The first prong of the two-pronged strategy closely resembles the use of the church and its hierarchy, culminating in the Coptic Orthodox Pope, as a primary religious bastion of the regime. In the case of Islam, Muslim institutions and their respective heads, at the pinnacle of which is the Shaikh of al Azhar, are functional substitutes for the church and the Pope, with one key difference being that the state asserts much more direct control over Muslim than Christian institutions. Another analogy besides the church in the case of al Azhar, the venerable institution of Islamic learning at the heart of Egypt's Muslim institutional order, is the judiciary. Like the judiciary, al Azhar is officially part of the state, its degree of autonomy fluctuating as a result of political considerations. In order to gain legitimacy from it, and to have it occupy political space that might otherwise be taken up by politically driven Islamists, the regime has to grant al Azhar some operational freedom, just as it does the judiciary. The extremes of that continuum of freedom were Nasser's nationalizing of al Azhar University in 1961, not long after he "massacred" the judges and as he commenced his shift to the left, and the period since the 2013 coup, during which the military-backed government has sought to have the Muslim religious establishment shore it up against Islamist retribution, so has granted it greater constitutional and operational freedom.

The Islamic establishment consists of al Azhar headed by its Grand Shaikh, the Ministry of Religious Endowments, the Grand Mufti, and Dar al Ifta (literally "House of Fetwas"), more or less in that order of political importance. In one of his several excellent analyses of al Azhar, Nathan Brown accurately describes it as a "sprawling complex of university faculties, primary and secondary schools, and research bodies," in which literally hundreds of thousands of students are enrolled from the first grade to PhD level. Brown further notes that "Since the time of Muhammad Ali in the 1800s, Egypt's leaders have regarded al-Azhar as an influential tool in shaping and promoting the government's domestic and foreign policies. Accordingly, they have gradually extended their control over the institution."[17] But, as just noted, that control was lessened in the 2014 constitution as a reward for political services performed by the institution and its head, Grand Shaikh Ahmad al Tayyib, during the military's two-year struggle with the Muslim Brotherhood. Article 7 grants al Azhar "exclusive competence over its own affairs," and the promise that "the state shall provide enough financial allocations to achieve its purposes." Its Grand Shaikh is deemed to be "independent and cannot be dismissed," with his appointment being vested in the Council of Senior Scholars—a body of forty *ulama*, recreated by the SCAF in 2012 (Nasser had abolished it in 1961) as a tactic to contain Brotherhood influence—whose members were chosen by the Grand Shaikh himself and who have the additional power to choose the Grand Mufti. The military, in other words, concentrated the power of Islamic institutions in al Azhar and its leader, Shaikh Ahmad al Tayyib, who literally stood by General Sisi, and next to the Coptic Patriarch, on July 3, 2013, when he announced that President Mursi had been deposed and the 2012 constitution suspended.

Al Tayyib can be thought of as analogous to high-ranking judges in being a member of the state-associated establishment, anti-Brotherhood, enamored of the prestige and power of the institution over which he presides and jealous of its prerogatives. He is a graduate of the Sorbonne, a former president of al Azhar University and Mufti, as well as being a leader in Mubarak's National Democratic Party, with a reputation for being politically adroit and ambitious. He presided over a purge of Muslim Brother faculty and students from al Azhar in the wake of the coup, which contributed to him becoming a target of student demonstrators subsequently. While winning some independence for his institution by way of thanks from the military for his support, much in the way that loyalist judges were similarly rewarded, al Tayyib has had to bear the cost of damage to his and al Azhar's reputation. The institution, according to H.A. Hellyer and Nathan Brown, is "derided as politically co-opted and increasingly irrelevant, even by those within its own ranks."[18] Possibly it was the damage to al Azhar's and his own reputation resulting from the overly close association with Sisi that caused al Tayyib to assert greater independence once the general was elected president and sought to utilize al Azhar in his campaign against Brothers and jihadis. Tayyib pushed back against presidential requests to "develop religious discourse which would contribute to the intellectual fight against extremism as another means of support for the ongoing fight against terrorism led by the security apparatus." In referring to what he obviously perceived as Tayyib's obstructionist tactics, Sisi commented to a Cairo newspaper that he "wears me out."[19] So just as in the cases of the judiciary and the Sawiris, al Azhar and its leadership can push back in measured fashion against the executive, especially when they see it weakening.

Of the other three institutions that comprise establishment Islam, the Ministry of Religious Endowments plays the most direct, significant political role. The Grand Mufti, which literally translates as the "principal issuer of fetwas," presides over Dar al Ifta, which is under the authority of the Ministry of Justice, thereby limiting the potential importance of its responsibility to review death sentences to ensure they comply with relevant legal and religious provisions. The Grand Mufti is among other things the representative of official Egyptian Islam abroad and traditionally has been a leading scholar of shari'a and jurisprudence, which in fact is a selection requirement stipulated in the bylaws of al Azhar. Prior to 2013 he was appointed by the president, with Shawki Allam being the first to be chosen by the newly created Council of Senior Religious Scholars in February of that year. The symbolic importance of the Mufti was signified by an assassination attempt on his predecessor, Ali Goma'a, in August 2016. Presumably he was targeted by violent Islamist extremists not only because he is a Sufi known for his liberal, anti-Salafi interpretations of Islam, but also because he was a longstanding critic of the Brotherhood and an ardent supporter of both Mubarak, who appointed him, and Sisi.

Despite being a political lightening rod, the Mufti asserts only moral authority over believers, whereas the Ministry of Religious Endowments is empowered to control not only endowments, which provide it with substantial revenues, but also mosques and Qur'anic schools, which gives it hands-on control of both the physical premises in which believers gather and the content of the messages delivered to them. Within two months of the July 2013 coup, the then minister of religious endowments, Muhammad Mukhtar Goma'a, commenced a move to bring mosques directly under government control, banning prayers in mosques other than those under his ministry and prayers given by any imam other than one qualified at al Azhar. He accompanied this with a purge of several thousand imams, presumably those identified as being members of or sympathetic to the Brotherhood, and a prohibition of collecting alms that "go to those who do not fear God," meaning any organization not approved by the government.[20] These steps commenced an unrelenting campaign to bring as much as possible of the practice of Islam under the ministry's, hence the government's, control. Within three years thousands of mosques had been placed under the ministry's jurisdiction, a move accompanied by the confiscation of "unapproved" books from them. All mosques smaller than 80 square meters were closed, they being the ones that most easily evade governmental control. The magnitude of the task of monitoring mosques is suggested by their sheer number, which in 2012, according to the government, was 11,333 in Cairo and Alexandria alone, as compared to 494 churches in those two cities.[21] In November 2016, the ministry moved against unlicensed Qur'anic primary schools, accusing them of indoctrinating children with radical ideas. According to a spokesman for the ministry, "The drive is aimed at revising the legal status of the schools set up to teach Islam's holy book, the Quran, to children and ensure they are not manipulated into promoting radicalism."[22] There were some 2,400 licensed Qur'anic schools under direct ministerial supervision at that time.

Muslims—Islamist organizations

The second prong of the regime's strategy to control political behavior inspired by Islam is necessarily more complex than its equivalent regarding Christians because of the greater diversity of political organizations among Muslims and their potentially more profound impacts. The strategy addressed to non-official Islam consists of divide-and-rule tactics, including co-opting, balancing, and pre-empting Islamist organizations, and outright repression. Mention has already been made of the use of Copts as counterweights to Islamism, that being but one example of the broader tactic of bolstering political and cultural forces that can check and balance Islamists. Those forces include secular political "partylets" other than the Free Egyptians Party founded by Sawiris. These little, notional parties occupy some seats in parliament and fill a bit of political space. For their troubles these partylets, comprised principally of aging political has-beens, receive subsidies from the government. Counterbalances also include women's organizations and individual women opposed to the Islamists and their discriminatory gender policies. Increasing the proportion of women in parliament and the cabinet, which Sisi has done, is an indicator of the general approach, as is granting women's organizations more scope than they would otherwise have. Artistic expression is also indulged more than might otherwise be the case, as that indulgence highlights the role of the government as protector from narrow- minded Islamists. But these and other tactics of counterbalancing Islamism with non-Islamist forces and actors are of less moment than direct engagement with the Islamists.

Presently Islamist political organizations are of four types, of which the Muslim Brotherhood is among the oldest, having been founded in Ismailiya in 1928, far and away the largest, as its membership has been in the six and possibly seven figures for decades, and the most politically important, in that it is the only non-governmental political organization with a countrywide popular base, as attested to by its winning both the first parliamentary and presidential elections after the coup-volution. Although the fundamentalist movement known as Salafism dates back to Arabia in the eighteenth century, it first appeared in more or less its present form in modern Egypt in 1926, with the founding of Ansar al Sunna al Muhammadiyya (The Supporters of the Prophet's Tradition). But Salafism gained little traction in Egypt until the 1970s, in part because the Brotherhood absorbed much of the Islamist constituency, and in part because its origins in Saudi Wahhabism rendered it discordant with the more liberal indigenous tradition of reformist Islam. As Saudi influence in Egypt spread and as Islamism radicalized, Salafism was essentially reborn out of al Gama'a al Islamiyya (the Islamic Group), itself a radical offshoot of the Muslim Brotherhood, with the founding in Alexandria in 1977 of al Da'wa al Salafiyya (The Salafi Call), which went on to form the Nour Party that along with the Brotherhood won some three quarters of the seats in the 2011–12 parliamentary elections.

The third type of Islamists are violent extremists, who also first appeared in the 1970s, steadily radicalizing thereafter until 1997 when their insurrection, by then largely confined to Upper Egypt, was crushed. Two phoenixes eventually rose out of those ashes. One was comprised of the chastened remnants of Islamic Jihad, which had assassinated Sadat, and the Islamic Group, whose leaders after lengthy prison sentences announced their rejection of violence, were freed and then politically rehabilitated in the wake of the coup-volution, primarily in order to serve as counterbalances to the Brotherhood, to Salafis, and to the other rising phoenix, a new crop of jihadi extremists. The first incarnation of the latter was in the northern Sinai in 2011 in the form of Ansar Bait al Maqdis (Partisans of Jerusalem), whose initial acts were to repeatedly sabotage the gas pipeline linking Egypt and Israel through Sinai. In November 2014 it swore allegiance to the Islamic State headquartered in Raqqa, Syria, renaming itself Wilayet Sinai, or Sinai Province. Since then jihadi extremist organizations have proliferated in Egypt itself as the Sinai has been engulfed in an insurgency that has claimed the lives of thousands of extremists and security personnel and the homes and well-being of tens of thousands of residents. Within Egypt this proliferation has been marked by an increase in violent incidents, most notably assassination attempts on security personnel and figures associated with the regime. In sum, then, the Islamist landscape in Egypt is both dense and variegated, ranging from contemplative, politically quietist Salafis, to hyper-organized and politicized but largely non-violent Brothers, to a range of jihadis seeking to blow up the established order.

Islamism thus poses both a political and a security threat to the regime, which has responded by conflating the two, arguing they are one in the same thing because the Brothers are at best stepping-stones to violent extremism or, at worst, violent extremists themselves. Of the two threats, the political one posed by the Brothers has long been the more important, so that organization necessarily must receive our greatest attention.

Of the myriad studies of the Muslim Brotherhood, two stand out for having focused primarily on its unique organizational structure, the first concentrating on its sources and early development, the second on the evolution of that organization into a cult. Brynjar Lia's *The Society of the Muslim Brothers in Egypt* describes how its founder, Hassan al Banna, was influenced by three models with which he was familiar in 1920s Egypt.[23] As the son of a Sufi Shaikh and a Sufi himself he had first-hand experience of the extreme veneration of and subordination to the head of the order displayed by its members.

He coupled this traditional, religiously inspired model with two modern western ones, the Boy Scouts and fascist political parties, both of which he personally encountered in Egypt. The motto he chose for the Brotherhood was copied from the former's "Be Prepared." This then was from the outset a hierarchical, authoritarian organization suffused with religious piety that reinforced the power of its leaders over its members. Hazem Kandil's *Inside the Brotherhood* reveals how the quasi-religious, quasi-fascist organization degenerated into a cult, replete with totalitarian control of its members' lives, including their marriages, divorces, careers, finances, places of residence, reading, and daily activities. By the time of the coup-volution, the organizational glue of quasi-religious authoritarianism had been strengthened by an elaborate network of kinship and marriage connections that almost literally made the Brotherhood one big, if not altogether happy, family.

It is this unique organizational structure that is vital to understanding the remarkable appeal, persistence, resilience, yet flawed nature of the Brotherhood, and the paradox implied in Kandil's observation: "A reputation established over eight decades collapsed in less than eight months."[24] In his subsequent work Kandil succinctly identifies the cause of that collapse: "Mohamed Morsi and his Muslim Brothers continued to embody the closed and subordinated nature of their organization. Even at the height of power, they mistrusted other political factions and deferred to their past tormentors in the military and security."[25] The Brotherhood's nature, in short, emerged through a dialectical process of engagement with government virtually from its founding. Originally tightly knit and hierarchical, it became ever more so and ultimately cultic as it sought to preserve itself and expand its resources and power, first in monarchial, then in Republican Egypt. Quasi and fully political organizations that were more open, less hierarchical, less cultic in nature, succumbed to regime pressure, with the minor, partial exception of the Wafd Party, the principal vehicle of the nationalist movement from 1919 until the post-war period, then resuscitated under Sadat and limping along to this day. The Brothers hunkered down as successive regimes mowed down other political and semi-political organizations. Their survival strategy came to include not just secrecy, absolute obedience, and commitment, but compromising with authority, indeed, serving rather than challenging it.

On those occasions when the Brotherhood or at least some of its members violated that basic principle and confronted regime power head on, it always lost badly. In November–December 1948, the regime responded to bombings and the assassination of the head of the Court of Appeals by the Brotherhood's "Secret Apparatus" by rounding up its leadership, dissolving the organization, and, in February 1949, by assassinating Hassan al Banna himself in retaliation for the assassination of Prime Minister Mahmud Nuqrashi, who had ordered the crackdown. Within months 4,000 Brothers were imprisoned. This was the basic script that was to be rerun at least three more times. In 1954 the Brothers, having supported Nasser but then turning on him and attempting his assassination, were again decimated through killings, imprisonments, and flight. In the summer of 1965 another failed assassination attempt on Nasser provided the justification for a further crackdown, which included the execution in 1966 of Sayyid Qutb, the secularist scholar turned Islamist ideologue whose call to jihad had been embraced by a substantial portion of Brothers. Sadat's crackdown on the Brotherhood shortly before his death did not run exactly to the same script, as other political activists were also rounded up and the Brothers were not directly responsible for his assassination. But yet another rerun did take place in July–August 2013, when the Brothers under President Mursi ran up against the military with predictable results for those familiar with modern Egyptian history, which the Brothers themselves seemed not to be. History repeating itself includes the present aftermath, with the Brothers having again been outlawed (as under the monarchy and Nasser), declared in December 2013 by Sisi to be a terrorist organization, with its leaders and cadres in jail, in hiding, or on the run, again as in the previous episodes.

So the Brothers have wavered between cozying up to authoritarians and rashly lashing out against them, never reaching a stable midpoint in which they could cooperate with other political forces to form a coherent, unified civilian opposition.

They have in fact been contemptuous of all other political organizations, which is understandable in the sense that none, other than radical jihadis, have been as tightly knit, tough, and enduring as the Brotherhood. After all, these non-Islamist organizations consisted of political activists drawn together primarily or only by shared political opinions, not fellow cult members united by blood, marriage, businesses, etc. But it is this profound schism within the civilian political system, resulting from its repression over decades and the Brothers drawing further in on themselves as a result, that has rendered civilians as a whole unable effectively to stand up to the deep state and the superstructure that rests upon it.

The perfect opportunity for Brothers to escape their political ghetto came in January 2011, when young activists launched the uprising with demonstrations in Midan al Tahrir. The Brothers, who had long shunned street activity as foolish and counterproductive, hesitated for days before throwing their cadres into the breach. Their collaboration with the activists lasted only briefly after the primary objective of removing Mubarak was achieved. At that point the Brotherhood fell back into its default mode, cozying up to the military which, as it had under Nasser, accepted the embrace as a means to divide the potentially unified civilian opposition. The marriage of convenience lasted until again the Brothers thought they were indispensable and even stronger than the military and security forces, so increasingly overplayed their hand before finally, in July–August 2013, being once again brutally removed from the political scene.

If history repeats itself yet another time, the Sisi or a successor regime will rehabilitate the Brotherhood as a counterweight to other civilian political forces. The Brothers will accept that junior role, seeking the material but limited political benefits that come from it. Since none of the previous episodes has caused the organization to learn from experience and reach out to fellow potential oppositionists, to broaden its class appeal from its present base in the middle and lower middle classes, or to moderate its Islamist agenda so it is acceptable to other than true believers, it should not be predicted that it will do so the next time around. More likely it will try to force the regime to cohabit with it yet again, this time by leveraging terrorism and external backing, provided now by Turkey.

The Salafis have proven to be no more politically adroit than the Brothers since their organizational rebirth in the late 1970s. As their traditional political quietude and focus on personal improvement began to be supplemented by political ambition, so did they become easy prey for the deep state seeking counterbalances to the Brotherhood. Stéphane Lacroix has carefully charted the transformation of the Salafi organization under the tutelage of first the Mubarak, then the Sisi regime. Mubarak facilitated its competition with the Brotherhood by granting it broadcasting licenses, with its two main channels becoming "among the most widely watched in Egypt" by 2010.[26] Its leaders were alternatively courted and imprisoned, but "were generally released more promptly than other Islamists."[27] In the wake of the coup-volution they formed the Nour Party, which in alliance with two smaller Salafi parties went on to win 27.8 percent of the votes in the 2011 elections for the lower house of parliament, a proportion second only to the Brothers' Freedom and Justice Party's 37.5 percent and which translated into 123 seats for the Salafis and 235 for the Brothers, with the Wafd Party dragging along in third place with forty-one seats.

But success proved to be the ruination of the Salafis. First, a leadership schism broke out in the wake of the election that was profoundly aggravated by the Nour Party's stance in favor of the July 2013 coup, a position it took out of the calculation that it could replace the Brothers as the regime's right-hand civilian force. But like the Brothers, the Salafis overplayed their hand. The Nour Party actively supported Sisi's campaign for president in May 2014, whereas other Salafis, including al-Watan, a 2013 breakaway faction from the Nour Party, and the Salafi Front, rejected Sisi in favor of loyalty to the Brotherhood. By the parliamentary election of 2015 Sisi and his comrades no longer needed an even semi-independent civilian support base. Accordingly, the Nour Party captured only some 2 percent of the votes, less than a tenth of those it had won in 2011–12. The constitutional provision banning parties based on religion could be invoked at any time against it, so presumably the Nour Party is being kept alive to absorb some Islamists and possibly to be reinvigorated when and if the Brothers are allowed back onto the political stage.

Jihadis

Jihadis are of two types—lapsed and active. The former consist of leaders of Islamic Jihad and the Islamic Group who after long prison sentences renounced their previous ways and condemned violence. As with the Salafis, they enjoyed the blessings of the SCAF out of its calculation to divide the broader Islamist movement. But these lapsed jihadis never gained much political traction, presumably because of their advanced age, because their recanting of previous sins undermined their credibility, and because of the greater appeal of active jihadis in response to the regime's increasingly draconian crackdown in the wake of the 2013 coup.

The two geographic loci of jihadi violence have progressively overlapped. The first to emerge was the insurgency in northern Sinai fired by local discontent over mistreatment by Cairo, formed primarily through tribal alliances, and fueled through connections to Gaza. From 2012 that insurgency began to spill over into Egypt proper in the form of attacks on regime personnel. The 2013 coup initiated a wave of violence in urban Egypt that has subsequently intermingled with the Sinai-based insurgency, such that it is difficult to determine the real loci of operations and affiliations of the groups involved. Sinai Province, which as mentioned above was formerly known as the Partisans of Jerusalem, is the most experienced and deadly of the insurgent organizations. It broadened its attacks on the gas pipeline that commenced in 2011 into killings of security personnel in Sinai in the following year. After the coup it commenced operations elsewhere in Egypt with the dramatic assassination attempt on the minister of interior, Muhammad Ibrahim, in central Cairo in September 2013. It claimed responsibility for downing the Russian Metrojet airliner over the Sinai on October 31, 2015.

Other jihadi organizations have been less durable, possibly because unlike the Sinai Province they don't have a geographic base cum safe haven. Ajnad Misr (Soldiers of Egypt), for example, emerged in Cairo in early 2014, where it conducted a number of attacks with homemade improvised explosive devices, primarily against police officers and security officials responsible for the arrest and/or torture of militants. Its rhetoric suggested it was a Salafi jihadi organization, but not one calling for the establishment of a caliphate, rather one endorsing the ideals of the "2011 revolution." By 2016 it had fallen silent, either because all of its members had been killed or rounded up by security, or because they had drifted off to other organizations. Among those was the Popular Resistance Movement (PRM), a coalition of jihadi groups active in Cairo, Fayum, Bani Suif, and Alexandria, formed more or less simultaneously with Soldiers of Egypt. While hardcore members of the PRM are jihadis, it apparently also includes young men who are not Islamists but self-professed revolutionaries. They initially targeted police stations and security personnel but then began to attack businesses, especially banks and communication companies, apparently to deter foreign investment. In the first half of 2016 the PRM claimed eighty-six attacks, most of which were in Cairo. By then it had been joined by several other organizations, all of which the regime declared to be fronts for the Brotherhood. On its official Facebook page in early November 2016, the Ministry of Interior claimed to have arrested scores of jihadis who confessed to various attacks, including the assassination of the Public Prosecutor, Hisham Barakat, in June 2015, and the failed attempt on the life of Mufti Ali Goma'a two months later. In both cases the ministry said the perpetrators were operating under orders from Brotherhood leaders in Turkey or "the group's Palestinian offshoot Hamas."[28] It listed various organizations, including Hasm (Decisiveness) and Liwaa al Thawra (Revolution Brigade), as "media fronts" intended to "take the blame for the Brotherhood's violent attacks."[29] Still other shadowy organizations, such as the Islamic State in Egypt (as distinct from Sinai Province) and the Murabitun (The Sentinels), also sprang up and claimed various types of attacks, the latter being led by Hisham

Ashmawy, a former special forces officer who defected to al Qaida and is probably based in eastern Libya.

Whatever relations they may or may not have with the Brothers, these shadowy organizations managed during 2016 to scale up their attacks throughout Egypt, during which time their operations also became more sophisticated and deadly, although considerably less so than those undertaken by Sinai Province. On September 29, 2016, for example, Decisiveness claimed responsibility for a car bomb intended to kill the Assistant Attorney General, General Zakariya Abd al Aziz, but which exploded after he had passed, the botched attempt similar to that directed at the Mufti and also very much like the failed effort in November 2016 to blow up judge Ahmad al Futuh, who had sentenced former President Mursi. But Decisiveness did succeed in killing police officers in Sixth of October City, a suburb of Cairo, in Tamiyya, some 65 kilometers south of Cairo, in the port of Dumyat (Damietta) on the Mediterranean, and elsewhere, including in the vicinity of the Pyramids in Cairo where they blew up a police post in December 2016.[30] Another shadowy organization operating in Asyut Governorate led by a person the regime identified only as "Salah A" became the target of attacks by military helicopters, army commandos and interior security forces in early 2017.[31] This uptick in attacks claimed by these organizations ostensibly based in Egypt proper coincided with increased attacks in the Sinai claimed by Sinai Province, which resulted in the deaths of twelve soldiers in one attack in October, at least eight more in another attack in late November, an army colonel in charge of Brigade 102, a key force in the government's counter-insurgency campaign, and a brigadier general based in al Arish with overall responsibilities for that campaign. As the intensity of attacks was increasing, State Security Prosecution referred 292 alleged members of Sinai Province to military court for trial on charges of plotting to assassinate President Sisi, first in 2014 in Mecca, Saudi Arabia, and subsequently in Cairo by trying to blow up a presidential motorcade. The operatives were identified by the prosecution as being a cell in Sinai Province known as the "Bearded Police Officers Group," which had been formed in 2012 as a protest by Islamist police officers against not being allowed to have beards.

Data on violence in Egypt provided by the Tahrir Institute for Middle East Policy suggests that intense counter-terrorism and counter-insurgency campaigns by security forces resulted in a fluctuation of incidents that were in total greater in 2016 than in 2013 or 2014, although less than in 2015.[32] Outside of North Sinai the average number of incidents per quarter in 2013, 2014, and 2016 was about fifty, or slightly more than one every second day. In the second quarter of 2015 they spiked at 267. In North Sinai, on the other hand, the number of improvised explosive device attacks has increased every quarter from 2013. In the first half of 2016 the Sinai Province was conducting attacks at the rate of almost two per day. For its part the government reported having killed 2,529 alleged terrorists in slightly less than a year ending in mid-2016, with 801 reported killed in the second quarter of 2016 alone. In a single battle at Mount Hilal the Third Field Army claimed to have killed 200 militants, which seems rather surprising since most estimates of the total number of members of Sinai Province, including those by the Israeli and US governments, are less than 1,000.[33] To add to this statistical confusion, in February 2017, General Farag al Shahat, head of Military Intelligence, stated that the army had killed 500 militants in the Sinai since 2015.[34] The government declared a state of emergency in northern Sinai in October 2014, which it renewed in May 2016 and again in January 2017. Sisi announced in a television interview in January 2017 that the military currently had 25,000 troops in some forty-one battalions deployed in North Sinai.[35] The Ministry of Interior reported conducting almost 2,000 operations against the Brotherhood in the two years ending in January 2016, resulting in 11,700 arrests, a rate of 511 monthly. All information released by the government on terrorism is, however, suspect, as suggested by an incident in January 2017. The Ministry of Interior announced that it had killed ten terrorists in a firefight on January 13 with those responsible for an attack in al Arish four days previously. It was immediately revealed by the families of six of those identified that they had been in detention for months, so presumably were killed in cold blood by the security forces. North Sinai MPs raised the matter in parliament as demonstrations broke out in al Arish against the Ministry of Interior.[36] That the insurgency was yet to be contained was reflected in May 2016 by the US Department of Defense sending under its Excess Defense Articles grant program (which is separate from the $1.3 billion annual Foreign Military Funding to Egypt) $44 million worth of MRAP (Mine Resistant Ambush Protected) vehicles to the Egyptian military.

In sum, since 2011 Jihadi extremists have sustained a low-level insurgency in northern Sinai and since 2013 a campaign of violence concentrated in Cairo but spreading northward into the Delta to Alexandria and south at least to Asyut. The insurgency and terrorist attacks have corroded the economy, deterred investment, and scared off tourists. Their political effects have been mixed. The regime has trumpeted its success in dealing with the security challenge, only to have such claims quickly belied by a major incident. Such attacks, however, do generate support for the government. Most importantly, the violence provides justification in Egypt and abroad for the indiscriminate application of heavy-handed deterrence so that it impacts not just jihadis, but virtually anyone opposing the regime by peaceful means. The strategy intended to quash dissent includes legal, quasi-legal, and extra-legal means, the mix intended to give a gloss of legitimacy to the crackdown, while simultaneously instilling fear, even terror, because it is evident there are no limits on reprisals against dissent, violent or otherwise.

Indiscriminate deterrence

Against jihadis the regime employs standard methods of counter-insurgency and counter-terrorism, albeit heavy-handed, clumsy ones. Whole villages and city quarters have been bull-dozed in the Sinai, in which a three-to-five mile security belt was created by destroying more than 1,300 homes.[37] Indiscriminate air attacks from fixed-wing aircraft, including US-provided F16s and helicopter gunships, have killed scores of innocent civilians, including Mexican and other tourists. In

January 2017, the government announced that special forces, counter-terrorism units, and military helicopters were attacking jihadi elements in the eastern desert mountain area of Asyut Province.[38] Northern Sinai has been blacked out for news coverage and intermittently even for normal telecommunications since 2013. Police and security personnel throughout Egypt have been given a blank check to round up virtually anyone they want to and treat them any way they please, including killing them.

As the insurgency in Sinai and the campaign of violence elsewhere have persisted despite these methods, and as the regime's and its leader's popularity have declined, so has pressure on the entire population been ratcheted up. President Sisi himself provided justification in an interview with *Der Spiegel* in early 2015, when he stated that "The Muslim Brotherhood is the origin of it all. All these other extremists emanated from them."[39] Whether true or not, his observation implicitly justifies the indiscriminate crackdown if only because the Brotherhood has been active politically for generations, including holding the presidency and plurality in parliament, thereby suggesting at least tacit support for it from millions of Egyptians. Violent and non-violent oppositionists have been lumped together in Sisi's strategy of deterrence, which since July 2013 has resulted in more than 40,000 arrests, 3,000 deaths, and hundreds of "disappeared."[40] Neither prominent Egyptians nor innocent foreigners have been spared. Vice-president Muhammad al Baradei fled Egypt at the time of the massacres of Brothers at Rabaa al Adawiyya and al Nahda Squares, remaining silent in exile until November 2016. He then wrote on Facebook that his hasty departure was due to a direct warning from "organs of the state" that he would be "destroyed" for working toward a peaceful dispersal of the sit-ins in those squares.[41] Baradei was lucky to have escaped, as subsequent events demonstrated. Giulio Regeni, a Cambridge University PhD student researching informal labor unions was, according to the best informed, unbiased accounts, snatched off the street in downtown Cairo by security agents, and brutally tortured to death over a period of several days before his body was dumped on a roadside outside the capital.

The Egyptian government denied all culpability, put forward several preposterous, contradictory explanations, and then just hunkered down, stonewalling efforts by the Italian authorities to discover the truth.[42] Since the security forces seemed to have no qualms about torturing and killing a foreign student from one of the world's most prominent universities, it is hardly surprising that it has felt under even fewer constraints in dealing with its own citizens.

Punishments meted out to deter criticism of the regime reflect the mindset of security and the courts under executive influence. The novelist Ahmad Nagi was sentenced to two years in prison in early 2016 for "undermining public morality" after publishing a chapter of his novel in a magazine. Amr Nuhan, a military conscript, was given three years in jail by a military court for placing Mickey Mouse ears on an image of Sisi, the charge being attempting to overthrow the government. Four Coptic teenagers were convicted in absentia in February 2016 for violating Article 98(f) of the Penal Code which forbids "ridiculing or insulting heavenly religions or inciting sectarian strife."[43] They had produced a 30-second video mocking the Islamic State before fleeing the country. The Penal Code is rife with such phrases as "undermining public morality," or "tarnishing the nation's reputation," or "defaming monotheistic religions." In November 2016, the chairman of the board of the privately owned *Dustur* newspaper, along with the former editor in chief and a journalist were sentenced to three months imprisonment and a LE20,000 fine for "publishing false news," in this case the offending phrase being "the return of the Ministry of Interior's injustice and its practice of offending the dignity of citizens."[44] In 2016 the regime added the tactic of freezing and/or confiscating financial assets to its toolkit of repressive measures. In September it froze the assets of five leading human rights activists and three prominent NGOs, a "pending investigations" qualifier intended as a sword of Damocles to hold over their heads and thereby silence them. If found guilty of the charge of receiving foreign funds to destabilize the country, they could lose all their assets and be sentenced to life in prison. Two months later the Nadeem Center, a human rights organization specialized in treating victims of torture, found that its bank account had been frozen, the bank manager explaining that the Central Bank had ordered the account suspended until the Center registered with the Ministry of Social Solidarity, which would then ban its activities, according to Amnesty International.[45] Not long before its account was frozen the Center had announced that in 2015 there were 137 deaths due to torture in prison. Police padlocked the Center's office in February 2017. In January 2017, the Cairo Criminal Court suddenly announced it had placed 1,538 people on the national terrorists list, including the country's most famous footballer, Muhammad Abu Trika. Human Rights Watch responded with a statement saying that "dumping hundreds of people onto a list of alleged terrorists, with serious ramifications for their freedom and livelihood, and without even telling them, makes a mockery of due process."[46] In early 2017 an investigative report was released that detailed how the government had installed sophisticated monitoring equipment that enabled it to monitor and block all internet traffic entering into and within the country.[47]

Deterrents such as these are the tip of a very nasty iceberg. In June 2016, the Washington-based Project on Middle East Democracy (POMED) issued a report under the title "Egypt Under President Sisi: Even Worse Than Under Mubarak or Morsi."[48] According to the report, in the first six months of that year security forces had committed 754 extra-judicial killings; had abducted and disappeared 204 people in the first three months; held more than 40,000 political prisoners; tried at least 7,420 civilians in military courts and sentenced some 1,700 people to death since October 2014; imprisoned hundreds of protesters without charge; jailed at least twenty-three journalists on such charges as spreading false news and illegally protesting—this number of imprisoned journalists exceeded only by China. If the Arabic Network for Human Rights Information claim that sixty-three journalists were imprisoned in late 2016 is correct, then Egypt actually leads the world with this dubious distinction.[49]

As noted previously, the World Justice Project in 2016 ranked Egypt 110th out of 113 countries on its Rule of Law Index.[50]

This abysmal ranking reflects among other things the network of laws and regulations enacted since the coup in which the regime can entangle essentially anyone it so desires. The November 2013 protest law requires advanced notification of demonstrations, bans gatherings of more than ten persons without prior consent, restricts where protests can be held, and carries penalties of up to five years imprisonment and a LE100,000 fine for participating in even a peaceful demonstration. Law 128 of 2014 is widely mocked as the "law of other things," as it specifies life imprisonment for a citizen and death for a civil servant who accepts money, material, or "any other things" in violation of the law.[51] The anti-terrorism law passed in August 2015 not only employs loose language in defining terrorist "entities," but includes a provision criminalizing dissemination of "false" reports on terrorist attacks, meaning any information that the government itself does not release. A former MP's comments on just one of the 342 laws decreed by the president and then hurriedly passed by the newly seated parliament in 2016 characterizes the legal network as a whole. The "Organization of Lists of Terrorist Entities and Terrorists" law, according to him, "defines acts of terrorism in an extremely broad manner that can be easily manipulated to pursue peaceful dissidents and to punish independent nongovernmental organizations."[52] Relevant phrases include "preventing and impeding public authorities, disturbing public order, harming social peace, and harming national unity and security." It does not restrict its definition of terrorism to violent means but refers to "any means." An individual can be placed on the terrorist list by an opaque procedure conducted by the public prosecution and criminal court in which no documentation is required and against which a defendant has no right of defense. The law also targets organizations against which various measures can be taken even before an appealed verdict has been confirmed, including banning, closing all its offices, freezing funds, preventing members from travelling and seizing their passports, and revoking their constitutional right to run for public office. As if this were not enough, the NGO law passed by parliament in late 2016 added yet more fine mesh in the legal network intended to snare malcontents. It bans any NGO that is not registered with the Ministry of Social Solidarity and any activities other than those for "development and social work," explicitly criminalizing conducting polls and undefined "fieldwork." Violation can attract a five-year prison sentence and a fine of up to LE1 million.

This legal framework constitutes a license to kill for police and security forces, a license of which they have taken advantage. Since Sisi became president the number of incidents of policemen on or off duty wounding or killing citizens for trivial reasons has skyrocketed. With the slightest provocation, even high-ranking police officers have pulled out their guns and shot taxi drivers, fruit and vegetable street vendors, and other law-abiding citizens. As public discontent rose in the face of this murderous conduct, the regime responded by lodging criminal cases against a few perpetrators. In November 2016, for example, a criminal court sentenced a police officer to life in prison for fatally shooting a waiter who refused to give him a free cup of tea.[53] That was the third such case to be brought against a policeman in that year, although Amnesty International noted that "the vast majority of incidents in which security forces have used excessive force have gone without investigation."[54] In August 2016, the government amended the police law to prohibit the use of firearms in circumstances other than those prescribed by law and require policemen to return their firearms at the end of their shifts. Simultaneously, however, the law was also amended to prohibit police from "forming coalitions" or participating in protests or sit-ins, suggesting that appeasing a public enraged by out of control police provided cover for the more important step of subordinating the police to regime diktats. Intermittently since the coup-volution policemen have tried to form unions and protest against their conditions and even the regime itself. In August 2015, for example, security forces were sent to Sharqiya to put down a police riot in which a local police department had been taken over in protest against salaries and working conditions.[55]

Spreading the net against any and all opposition has frayed it at the edges. Police called upon as the first line of defense are taking advantage of their empowerment by abusing citizens, but also by voicing discontent at their own mistreatment by the regime. The legal network is so all encompassing that virtually any even vaguely political act can be deemed illegal, even terroristic. But that network is only a legal nicety. The security forces know it has been put in place as a visible deterrent to head off citizens who might be tempted to voice their political grievances in a peaceful manner. The real work of deterrence is in their own hands to be done in whatever way they deem fit, regardless of the law. Legality is for the law abiding, whereas the muscle of the security forces is for all. Islamists have more to fear than any other grouping, but three other constituencies that the regime fears could destabilize it—youth, labor, and professional syndicates—are also in jeopardy of being subject to heavy-handed tactics, albeit not as severe as those applied to Islamists.

Hobbled Vanguards: Youth and Organized Labor

Youth and organized labor pose management challenges to the deep state. Repeatedly in the history of modern Egypt they have been at the forefront of political protest. Youth, especially students, were a vital component of the nationalist movement, going on to be one of the few categories of citizens brave or foolish enough to challenge Nasser and Sadat on campuses and in the streets, before then sparking the overthrow of Mubarak. The two types of organized labor, unions comprised of "blue-collar" workers, and twenty-four syndicates of professionals ranging from lawyers, doctors and teachers to pharmacists and veterinarians, have been similarly troublesome from rulers' perspectives. The Bar Association, a hotbed of nationalist agitation, was targeted for repression by Kings Fuad and Faruq, before then being quashed by Nasser, revived by Sadat, and then refrozen by Mubarak. Nasser's first significant move in the wake of overthrowing King Faruq was to break a worker's strike in the Delta and hang its leaders, suggesting how aware he was of organized blue-collar labor's potential political power. He subsequently turned to the transport workers union for support in his struggle against Naguib. The political nightmare of all Egyptian presidents has been youth and labor coalescing in opposition against them, as happened in January–February 2011. In the two years prior to the October 1973 war, when workers and students were agitating against his perceived "no war, no peace" paralysis, Sadat strategically interposed his Central Security Force troops between campuses and union facilities to prevent demonstrations of workers and students merging in central Cairo.

Youth and organized labor have resources that make it difficult for the deep state simply to crush them. First, they are numerous and ever more so. By 2016 the some 18 million fifteen to twenty-four-year-olds comprised almost one fifth of the entire population. Ten million of these youths are in secondary or tertiary educational institutions. The Teachers' Syndicate alone has more than 1.2 million members, suggesting total syndicate membership approaches 5 million professionals. According to the Egyptian Trade Union Federation, 7 million Egyptians belonged to its 2,200 constituent unions by 2009, so present membership approaches 8 million workers.[56] While a relatively small percentage of youths, workers, and professionals are committed members of the organizations that nominally represent them, the total pool is huge so the actual number of potential activists is substantial. The very fact of organized collectivities of potentially volatile constituents poses a challenge to the deep state that abhors autonomous organization of any sort. Second, these constituencies and their respective organizations have skills which the state needs, as well as standing in the broader community, thus giving them some voice on public policy matters which the state cannot just silence without paying political costs. Third and most importantly, youth and labor can vote against the regime with their bodies in the street, as they have repeatedly done. Moreover, it is not just high school and university students who protest on and around their campuses, or workers who demonstrate at their places of work. Professionals, whether lawyers, journalists, judges, doctors, or others, have also struck against hospitals and courts, barricaded their syndicate head-quarters, and even used them in attempts to provide safe havens from the regime for their members.

The "Midan al Tahrir Revolution" was the veritable apotheosis of protest uniting these constituencies, and so a signal lesson to the Sisi regime from which it has drawn the conclusion that the limited space granted them by Mubarak was excessive. It has emphasized the iron fist under the velvet glove in the bimodal strategy first devised by Nasser and subsequently utilized by all presidents toward these volatile constituencies. The prevailing general atmosphere of repression is particularly ominous for youths and labor, as it is intended to be. Lest they misread the regime's intent, it has supplemented the general crackdown with specific measures against student and youth organizations, unions, and even professional syndicates.

The very symbol and prime mover of the Midan al Tahrir uprising, the April 6 movement, was among the first to be targeted by Sisi, reflecting its particular threat as an organization seeking to unite students and workers. So named because in April 2008 it mobilized youths and especially university students in support of a strike in the industrial complex at al Mahalla al Kubra, in April 2014 it was declared an illegal organization and its leader, Ahmad Mahir, jailed. Tried in April 2016, he and four of his colleagues were given three-year sentences in addition to time already served in prison. The regime moved simultaneously against university student organizations, declaring on October 31, 2013 that police would be deployed on twenty-two campuses. A month later it abolished the requirement of a university president's consent or the Prosecutor General's authorization for police to be stationed on campus. It also replaced university security personnel with private security guards employed by Falcon Security, a firm founded by retired military officers some years previously and with close links to the Ministry of Defense. Thousands of protesting students were beaten and arrested. Similar tactics were employed against striking workers and even against the Journalists Syndicate, which was invaded on May 2, 2016 by security personnel to apprehend two journalists who were staging a sit-in protest against the inflammatory decision by Sisi to hand two Red Sea islands over to Saudi Arabia. When the head of the Syndicate, Yahia Qallash, protested against this unprecedented "invasion" of it by some fifty security personnel, who beat up the organization's own security guards and smashed furniture and equipment, he along with two other members of the board were sentenced to two years in jail in a trial that marked the first such event in the seventy-five-year history of the Syndicate. The Ministry of Interior denied using rough tactics and claimed implausibly that the journalists had turned themselves in, causing the international Committee to Protect Journalists to demand "an immediate investigation into this violent raid," the release of the two journalists, and that the regime "stop persecuting journalists for doing their jobs."[57]

The velvet glove, iron fist strategy originally conceived by Nasser to contain these three constituencies has under Sisi come to depend more upon the fist than even during the reign of its progenitor. Caught in a socio-fiscal trap, the regime lacks the wherewithal to provide velvet in the form of material rewards to youths, workers, and the state-employed professionals who constitute the largest single category of employees in most syndicates. It therefore now couples intimidation with increased efforts to prevent wildcat organization outside the framework of the state's approved bodies or the rise to power within them of dissidents. The protracted struggle to contain blue-collar labor since 2011 illustrates these dynamics.

In the wake of the coup-volution the minister of manpower, Ahmad al Burai, acceded to demands by workers to be permitted to form unions independent of the Nasserist-era Egyptian Trade Union Federation (ETUF), a hierarchical, corporatist body comprised of twenty-one national unions presiding in dictatorial fashion over their members. In this temporary climate of freedom the two most important arms of the labor movement, one based in traditional public sector enterprises such as spinning and weaving, the other and newer one in the civil service itself, managed to coalesce into the Egyptian Federation of Independent Trade Unions (EFITU). Although wary of it, the SCAF did not disband it out of the calculation that it would oppose the Brotherhood due to longstanding labor hostility toward that organization. And indeed, that turned out to be the case, with the EFITU supporting Sisi's 2013 coup. But once established in absolute power, the military had no further need of the EFITU, as indicated by its removal in March 2014 of minister of manpower Kamal Abu Aita, the former head of the Real Estate Tax Authority Union and a principal organizer of the EFITU. This signaled the intensification of the crackdown on labor unrest and the beginning of a protracted effort to subordinate the EFITU to the ETUF, or possibly to destroy the former altogether. In November 2014, the head of the General Union for Public Utilities Workers, which is within the ETUF, filed charges with the public prosecutor against EFITU affiliates in the public utilities sector. The charges were involvement in acts of sabotage and terrorism and posing a threat to national security. Since no specifics were ever adduced, presumably the case rested on the proposition that independent trade unionists must by definition be supporters or members of the Brotherhood, now officially a terrorist organization. The case was not pursued as the longstanding hostility between the Brotherhood and organized labor would have undercut the nebulous claims, but the EFITU was certainly put on notice of more trouble to come. On April 28, 2015, the Supreme Administrative Court outlawed the right to strike despite it being protected by the new constitution. Subsequent, now illegal strikes met ever increasing repression, such as that directed at the leaders of the Independent Trade Union for Public Transport Workers, an affiliate of the EFITU. When they announced a strike against the public transportation system in September 2016, security forces swooped on the union's headquarters, arresting its leader Tariq al Buhairy and six of his colleagues, the latter of whom were dispatched to the infamous Tora prison. The military sent fleets of vehicles to substitute for public buses halted by the strike, while a spokesperson for President Sisi labeled the event a "Brotherhood conspiracy," which stood in stark contrast to the SCAF's previous cultivation of transport workers, including inducements for them to strike when Mursi was president.[58] In the meantime, the ETUF, whose head had been restored to his usual position of minister of manpower, sent toughs to beat up EFITU members and lodged a case in the Supreme Constitutional Court against the EFITU, asking the court to declare it an illegal organization, forcing its members back into the ETUF. As the case was left pending in the typical sword of Damocles fashion much used by the regime, agents from the National Security Agency (formerly State Security Investigations) organized dismissals from their jobs of numerous EFITU activists.[59]

By comparison to the regime's heavy-handed treatment of organized blue-collar labor, which is the most threatening of the three constituencies because of its capacity to control public space and directly impact the economy, its treatment of youths, at the core of which are university students, and of professionals in syndicates, is relatively benign, at least in the context of unbridled, violent authoritarianism. Although youths can and do demonstrate, their primary threat to the regime, like that of syndicate professionals, is posed more by their minds than their bodies. Their views and actions can influence the broader public, as was the case in January–February 2011. They can serve as bases for recruitment into an alternative political elite, which was also illustrated in the lead up to and aftermath of the coup-volution. Finally, their treatment at the hands of the regime serves as a barometer of its broader acceptance and legitimacy—the greater the repression of students and professionals, the more the regime's lack of public acceptance and legitimacy is highlighted. Youths and professionals, in sum, have little hard power, unless they act in concert alongside organized labor, but considerable soft power. The regime's tactics to contain them are thus less directly physical, more manipulative, and aimed at their material well-being.

Just as the SCAF and then President Sisi harnessed the energy of workers, first as collaborators in their struggle against the Brotherhood, then to subordinate them to the regime instrument of the ETUF, so did they pursue much the same strategy toward students. The first step was to let them blow off the steam that had been generated by the coup-volution, while simultaneously reining in their street protests and general public presence. The SCAF gave them space on university campuses, but gradually restricted their activities elsewhere in urban areas, especially Cairo, with considerable force when necessary. Over time the struggle shifted to the campuses themselves and on them, to student unions, while in the broader public arena youths were harnessed to the purposes of the SCAF and then Sisi. Students who had been active in organizing during the coup-volution were drafted into the Tamarrud youth movement to serve as pawns in the struggle against the Brotherhood, from which many in turn were recruited by Military Intelligence to staff its newly created political party intended to soak up youthful activists and energies and occupy parliamentary seats.

Back on campuses the limited tolerance for independent organizational activity ended in the wake of the 2013 coup, just as it had for labor unions. Student unions have a venerable history in Egypt, having contributed significantly to the nationalist movement, then to mobilizing support for Nasser before becoming the vanguard of opposition to him, Sadat, and Mubarak, with Sisi clearly intent on trying to ensure that history not repeat itself yet again in his relations with them. In 2007 as part of his broader crackdown, Mubarak had decapitated the organized student movement, abolishing its elected national council to silence this student mouthpiece, leaving in place only single campus unions over which greater control was asserted, primarily through the recruitment of opportunists into leadership positions by agents of State Security Investigations. In 2013 the national Egyptian Student Union was reborn in response to intense demands from students over the previous two years. Elections to it were finally held in December 2015. In the interim the regime had sought to prepare the ground for the election of quislings by intimidating any and all perceived to be independent. In 2014 a law was decreed banning political organizations on campus, which had proliferated since 2011. Also in that year national student by-laws were amended to give university presidents the power to expel students without cause. Between 2013 and 2016, 3,000 students were arrested or incarcerated and twenty-one killed by security forces on campus. Presumably by the end of 2015 the National Security Agency assumed that it had softened up its student opponents sufficiently, so elections were allowed to proceed. But the students proved to be more obdurate than the NSA had calculated. In a high turnout they elected twelve prominent campaigners against the regime to the fourteen-member national executive, with the president from Cairo University, Abdullah Anwar, and vice-president from Tanta University, Amr al Hilw, both prominent voices for student independence, securing the top places. The minister of higher education responded by dissolving the board on a flimsy pretext and announcing that new elections would be held the following year. Then, in September 2016, the minister backtracked, declaring there would be no election for the national student union executive. Presumably a nose count by National Security agents had revealed that regime-backed slates would suffer another defeat. This interpretation was reinforced when in November 2016, a week before elections were scheduled to take place throughout the country for campus-based positions in the student organization, the minister cancelled them as well. The regime and university students thus appeared to be in a standoff, the former unable to impose its will on student organizations, the latter confined to campuses where they were unable to organize nationally.

The message of student and broader youth discontent, however, did apparently reach Sisi himself, possibly because by late 2016 his popularity was sliding downhill in inverse correlation to rising prices and unemployment rates, the latter of which in particular most directly impact youths, of whom by the end of 2016 about two in five were unemployed. So the president responded by declaring 2016 the Year of Youth and holding on October 25–7 a National Youth Conference at a Sharm al Shaikh luxury resort to which hundreds of student "leaders" were invited and in which he personally, along with the prime minister, promised to address grievances. At the closing ceremony Sisi declared that "this conference demonstrates that we are seeking dialogue rather than trying to monopolize power," a pledge that rang hollow in light of the cancellation of student union elections a week or so later.[60] One journalist objected to Sisi's reference to youths "as his sons and daughters," saying that they should be addressed as citizens with rights and duties.[61] But conferees were allowed to sound off a bit, criticizing the restrictive 2013 protest law and the incarceration of youths, including children under twelve, without trial. Shortly after the conference ended, eighty-two youths were pardoned by Sisi, albeit ones whose sentences had almost been served and who in any case were held on minor charges. With timing probably not coincidental, on December 3 the Supreme Constitutional Court struck down Article 10 of the 2013 protest law which had given the minister of interior the right to unilaterally cancel protests. The rest of the law was upheld. What the conference did undoubtedly produce was a storm of criticism on social media, with one wag commenting that "if Sisi had held the National Youth Conference in prison, there would have been a larger attendance than at Sharm al Shaikh."[62]

The cat-and-mouse game between students and the regime is paralleled by that played out with professional syndicates, which like student unions have a venerable, if less illustrious history of mobilizing members against first the monarchy, then successive republican governments. Nasser's repertoire of responses to contain syndicate activism included an effort to water down professional solidarity by forcing syndicates to include civil servants working in related areas, at one stroke vastly increasing their memberships but rendering them unwieldy and much more vulnerable to governmental intervention. Several of the larger syndicates, such as that of the agricultural engineers, underwent expansions of up to 500 percent between 1963 and the late 1970s. Sadat lifted several restrictions on syndicates, intended in part to facilitate their penetration by Brotherhood supporters who he was cultivating in his political struggle against leftists. The Brotherhood was happy to oblige. By the end of the first decade of Mubarak's rule it had come to dominate the boards of several of the most prestigious syndicates. Its proportion of elected seats on the board of the doctors' syndicate, for example, rose from one quarter when Mubarak became president to a majority a decade later. Out of its general strategy of cohabitation rather than confrontation with the regime, the Brotherhood did not seek to completely overwhelm this or other syndicates, as reflected by it desisting from offering candidates for the post of *naqib*, or chairman of the syndicate board.

Shortly after the Brotherhood won control of the lawyers' syndicate in 1993, however, Mubarak's patience snapped. He had passed in parliament the notorious Law 100, labeled in good Orwellian style, "Guaranteeing Democracy in Professional Syndicates." It stipulated that elections to syndicate boards would require half of the total membership to vote in the first round and, failing that, 30 percent in a second round for the outcome to be official. Otherwise, the syndicate would be "sequestered," meaning the government would itself appoint the syndicate's director. One by one all the leading syndicates lost their independence in this fashion, thereby alienating their professional members and contributing to their willingness to join demonstrators in Midan al Tahrir in 2011. One of the first decisions by the Supreme Constitutional Court in the wake of the coup-volution was to declare Law 100 of 1993 unconstitutional, thereby restoring syndicate independence.

It was destined not to last long. In the wake of the 2013 coup the new regime moved with alacrity to purge the syndicates of Brothers and to again subordinate them to government control. By the end of 2014 two of the largest ones, the teachers' and pharmacists' syndicates, had been placed again under sequestration by court order, their elected board members being replaced by government appointees. An independent council member of the pharmacists' syndicate likened sequestration to "collective punishment" against members and a "blatant violation of Article 77 of the Egyptian Constitution."[63] The language of that article is indeed quite unequivocal, stating that the "law shall regulate the establishment and administration of professional syndicates on a democratic basis" and "guarantee their independence." In its second paragraph it states that sequestration "may not be imposed nor may administrative bodies intervene in the affairs of such syndicates." The veterinarians' syndicate narrowly avoided a similar court order. Its head called on the government to issue the legislation necessary to implement Article 77, which it so far has ignored.

The treatment of the doctors' syndicate suggests that it is less the presence of Brothers than independence that is the regime's primary concern. In the initial election after the coup-volution the Brotherhood won the majority of seats on the board. In the second election, held in December 2013, the Brotherhood did not field candidates so the primary contest was between government-endorsed candidates and those supported by Doctors Without Rights, an activist group formed in 2011 focused on improving conditions for doctors and health care in general and a die-hard opponent of the Brotherhood. The latter candidates won 90 percent of the seats, thereby converting the syndicate into an effective voice for its members and for health-care reform. This began a guerilla war between it and the government that has seen many skirmishes of which the most notorious was in early 2016 when the syndicate held an extraordinary general assembly in protest against police beatings of doctors in the emergency room of a Cairo hospital. The cause of the aggression was that the doctors had refused to sign false reports to the effect that the police had suffered serious injuries at the hands of protestors. This much-publicized action, combined with campaigns against shockingly poor management of hospitals including lax hygiene, illustrated in graphic detail on social media, caused the government to indict Dr. Mona Mina, the leader of Doctors Without Rights and deputy head of the syndicate, the first ever woman in that role. The charges filed against her by the minister of health and the president of Cairo University were "disturbing security and social order, spreading panic among citizens, and defaming the state." She was released on bail in early December 2016, pending trial.[64] Thus far the regime has yet to devise an effective strategy to counter the broad public appeal of these doctor activists who have cleverly combined campaigns for improved health care with those for improving the status of doctors, which the public knows to be extremely poor regarding wages and conditions. Presumably the regime will just keep tightening the screws lest the example of the doctors' syndicate gives rise to emulators among the other professions.

Conclusion

Egypt's political and civil society superstructure is fragile and based on weak foundations. Its own deficiencies include its internal divisions, most vital of which is that between Islamists and their opponents, and its tendency to replicate hierarchical organizational models found in the government, in official Islam and the Christian churches, and in society more generally. Just as the government is stove-piped, so is political and civil society. But the government is more than partly to blame for these deficiencies. Vigorous gatekeeping of the limited access order by the state superstructure underpinned by the deep state ensures the weakness of any and all autonomous organizations. The channels of upward political and economic mobility, to say nothing of communications relevant to public policy making and implementation, are purposely blocked. The state wants to choose who it will admit and who it will listen to, rather than to be forced to give way to choices made by others. This pattern was established shortly after the 1952 coup and has persisted until today, but it is obviously increasingly difficult to sustain. Not only is the socio-fiscal trap undermining the resource base necessary to sustain the exclusionist model of government, but the sheer numbers of citizens, their deprivations, and their proliferating formal and informal organizations render the task of subordinating them ever more difficult. Overflow into the streets in 2011 and since, to say nothing of the insurgency in the Sinai and intensifying violence throughout the country, are clear manifestations of the blockage of channels into the limited access order, rising demands for entry, and the cracking of the once relatively coherent political community.

Thus far the regime's response has been to double down on the existing bet of containing political and civil society rather than offering to trade it access into the closed system in return for contributions in the form of ideas, activities, and resources. Among the consequences of trying to shore up the decaying limited access order is the failure of public brainpower to develop and be drawn upon in the making and implementation of public policy. Policy making in the Sisi regime is more isolated from political and civil society than in any of its predecessors in Republican Egypt, a failing which is reflected by the poor quality of policies and their erratic, frequently contradictory character. With the limited public brainpower inherited from preceding regimes having been lobotomized and the state's own institutional capacities having been further undermined by the military brushing them aside, the prospects of meeting the ever increasing economic, infra-structural, environmental, and foreign policy challenges are ever poorer. It is to those indicators of the state's performance that we shall now turn.

5 Reaping What is Sown _____

Whether in a communist, socialist, or capitalist system, the state operates as the brain, signaling if not directly controlling the direction it wants the economy to take, the ways and means by which human and physical resources are to be developed and deployed, and how the country is to relate to its neighbors and the world beyond. A state elite preoccupied with preserving and asserting its power against potential challengers that might arise from within or beyond the state is necessarily less intelligent in performing these functions than one freed from such worries. The deep state in Republican Egypt has been dedicated to preserving control of the limited access order it created, subordinating the remainder of the state, as well as political and civil society, to that end. As a result, the three branches of government could not develop infrastructural power with which better to perform their duties, relying instead on less efficient despotic power to crudely force compliance by citizens. Political and civil society, shackled by intrusive manipulation and outright repression, could not serve as arenas within which public brainpower could be developed and drawn upon by the state better to discharge its functions. State and citizens alike are caught in an ever-narrowing socio-fiscal trap in which there are insufficient resources to both sustain the political status quo and lay the foundations for future growth, which would in turn make possible an escape from the trap through the formation of a new, political support coalition.

The result has been a fierce but brittle state presiding over an increasingly divided nation beset with virtually life-threatening crises. The state's response since the 2013 coup has been to intensify repression and to distract its disillusioned citizens with pie in the sky promises of good things to come, so long as they are patient and docile. That a once proud, leading nation state in the developing world has been reduced to this parlous condition reflects accumulated failures. The state is reaping what it has sown with regard to the economy, human and physical resource development, and managing foreign affairs. State guidance of the economy has been inadequate in numerous respects, the most fundamental of which is that it has not conveyed to the nation either the direction in which the economy should grow, or the means by which that is to be achieved. The state has mouthed slogans about the economy, but not organized it according to a coherent model.

In Search of a Development Model

Egypt has been impacted by three economic "revolutions," or development models intended to facilitate rapid economic growth, that have swept across the MENA and much of the globe over the past two centuries. Under Muhammad Ali and then the British, Egypt was a progenitor of the nineteenth-century precursor to the "green" revolution in which agricultural growth was driven by intensified irrigation, improved cropping, and cultivars. That was followed by the onset of the "grey" revolution, or industrialization, which commenced under the monarchy but reached its apogee under Nasser. His rush to industrialize came at the expense of agriculture, from which a surplus was extracted to finance ill thought-out industrial projects, largely divorced from the once-vibrant agricultural sector and the green semi-revolution it had witnessed. A renewed effort to industrialize was stimulated by the "brown," or hydrocarbon revolution that began as a result of dramatic price rises in the wake of the October 1973 war. Under Sadat a half-hearted effort was made to capitalize on

Egypt's oil export earnings and those from the Gulf countries by again investing in manufacturing industry, this time with the private sector playing the lead role. It soon became evident, however, that large-scale private capital, able to capitalize on entry into the limited access order, sought virtually guaranteed returns in sectors other than comparatively risky manufacturing. This aborted effort to restart the country's industrialization drive was followed under Mubarak by significant upgrading of the country's energy-intensive processing industries, such as steel, fertilizer, and cement, all of which benefitted from the rapid expansion of natural gas production from 2002. But this brown revolution literally ran out of gas around the time of the coup-volution, as production of it tailed off. Before that, however, the oil and gas boom in Egypt and the MENA more generally had undermined industrialization by infecting it with Dutch Disease, undermining the cost competitiveness of all tradeable goods and services other than those directly connected to hydrocarbons. As Egypt lurched from one hoped-for engine of development to another, rather than seeking to integrate and build upon its comparative advantages in agriculture, manpower, and hydrocarbon endowment, the comparative performance of its economy deteriorated.

This outcome was not preordained. A reinforcing mix of green, grey, and brown was possible, the first two forming the classic agricultural-led model of development which much of Asia has followed. Egypt was in the vanguard of the nineteenth-century precursor green revolution and its associated infrastructure was the envy of the colonial world. Agriculture provided much of the capital for industrialization under the monarchy and then Nasser. In 1960, Egypt was as industrialized as Korea. Capital generated by the subsequent brown revolution could have energized the flagging industrial sector, especially if financial measures had been taken to inoculate the economy against the Dutch Disease. Expanding Arab demand could have stimulated the supply of larger quantities of Egyptian agricultural and industrial goods. Alas, instead of these three economic revolutions reinforcing one another within an integrated model of development, they worked at cross purposes, slowing rather than expediting growth. The primary cause of this failure was inappropriate government policies.

Republican governments all neglected the once dynamic agricultural sector so it did not partake in the 1960s green revolution that swept through South Asia and elsewhere. The decline of Egypt's once famous long staple cotton, referred to as the country's "white gold," is emblematic of the broader failure to both develop agriculture and to link it more effectively to industrialization. Due to chronic governmental mismanagement of cropping policies that discouraged farmers from growing cotton, by 2016 its harvest was the lowest since the days of Muhammad Ali when its cultivation commenced in earnest. This decline represents a huge foregone opportunity. Textiles and garments labeled as made of Egyptian cotton command a premium price worldwide, even though most of them are not made in Egypt nor even of Egyptian cotton.[1]

James Mayfield focuses on these shortcomings in comparing economic development in Egypt to that in South Korea and other Asian Tigers. Key to the latter's dynamic growth, in his view, was agriculture, which in turn depended upon land reforms, commodity prices that benefitted small farmers, and strengthened systems of local government, "including a willingness to allow local organizations, associations, cooperatives and other forms of grass roots participation."[2] These measures resulted in rapidly expanding rural incomes, creating new markets for demand-driven development of industry. Backward and forward linkages from small-holding agriculture nurtured economically and politically by government thus served as a motor force of growth in East Asia and, in Mayfield's view, should have done the same in Egypt. Two Egyptian economists, Hanaa Kheir-El-Din and Heba El-Laithy, reinforce and expand the argument, noting that "results from China, India and other Asian countries showed that agricultural growth is more important than manufacturing growth for poverty reduction."[3]

Why then did the Egyptian government not replicate established, successful models of agricultural-led growth, thereby reinforcing linkages with industry and reducing rural poverty? In assessing the failure of major efforts by the US government to help Egypt transform its agricultural sector for more than two decades from the late 1970s, Yahya Sadowski highlights the nexus of crony capitalists and public officials. Businessmen and bureaucrats colluded to subvert market-friendly reforms and preserve the rents derived from the state's domination of agricultural production.[4] But there was the additional problem of the inappropriate model of food self-sufficiency, as opposed to food security, driving government policy. The United States Agency for International Development (USAID) and other multilateral and bilateral donors have since the late 1970s sought to convince Egyptian governments that their goal for agriculture should be to dedicate more of the cropped area to horticulture, producing high-value crops for export to Europe, the Gulf, and beyond on land watered through micro-irrigation.[5] Egyptian decision makers, preoccupied with security concerns, remained unconvinced. Food security in their view required not strawberries and peaches for export, but basic foodstuffs for local consumption. So while neighboring Israel was shifting land out of field-crop production, such as wheat and barley, and into horticultural crops for export to Europe, Egyptian policy encouraged expanding acreage for food staples, especially wheat and rice. This goal was implied in Article 29 of the 2014 constitution, which states that "the state shall commit to providing the requirements for agricultural and livestock production, along with purchasing basic agricultural crops at suitable prices that provide a profit margin to farmers." In the face of an intensifying foreign currency crisis in 2016–17, the government announced it was increasing the acreage allocated to wheat from 3.4 to 3.5 million *feddans* (or from about 3.6 to 3.7 million acres), an area constituting approximately half the country's cropped land.[6] Key elements in the deep state helped propagate the view that American-Israeli efforts to revitalize Egyptian agriculture were really a plot, intended to undermine Egyptian food independence and security. The chief proponent of the "horticultural revolution," minister of agriculture Yusuf Wali, was vilified as an Israeli accomplice, if not agent.[7] Since Nasser, most of the political elite and, indeed, the population, has been entranced by the lure of food self-sufficiency, viewed as an indicator of governmental competence. President Mursi, for example, trumpeted the country's large wheat crop in April 2013.

Egyptian agriculture, like industry, suffers from misguided policies inimical to export growth which have no hope of achieving self-sufficiency. Inappropriate cropping patterns, which ignore the opportunity costs of using scarce land and water to grow grains, have undermined prospects for even a very pale green agricultural revolution. As one leading analyst of Egyptian agriculture notes, "self-sufficiency for most crops is only about 50 per cent of consumption."[8] The proximate cause of the failure to embrace reform is that lingering state controls are deemed necessary by the deep state to ensure rural political quiescence, while also providing rents to politicians, bureaucrats, and cronies. Included in the collateral damage of this state control is the "voice" of the agricultural sector, which like that for other sectors, including industry, has been stifled. Had those directly involved been encouraged to express their views, public brainpower would have generated a wider range of policy alternatives and better assessment of them.

But voice has been denied, so brainpower did not develop. Nasser's agrarian reforms politically decapitated large landowners. No rural lobby subsequently emerged to replace them.[9] Leonard Binder contended in his *Moment of Enthusiasm* that the country's rural middle class was remarkably politically resilient, holding on to substantial perches in local and national government during the Nasser and Sadat eras.[10] But this observation begs the question of whether the persistence of rural elites is evidence of the abiding political power of rural economic interests, or results from a regime strategy of co-optation that incorporated traditional elites into the centrally organized and focused national power structure. Unfortunately, there is no evidence of a rural lobby, so the co-optation explanation is much more plausible. Such evidence might include a prominent role for parliament's agriculture committee, for example, or the presence of high-profile landowners in the political elite, or even well publicized and hotly contested debates in the media about agricultural policy. In fact, there is little if any voice of this kind. Agriculture has had only marginal importance in the platforms of Egyptian political parties, whether governmental or opposition, since the Nasser era. In sum, rural Egypt lost its voice then and has never regained it. The steady decline in government spending on agriculture reflects the lack of articulation of interests by stakeholders in agriculture. Between 1980 and 1992 gross investment in agriculture fell by 31 percent. Between 2000 and 2007 annual public spending per capita on agriculture fell 6.1 percent, whereas in sub-Saharan Africa it rose during that same period by 6.6 percent and in the MENA by 1.1 percent.[11] Other sectors in Egypt were not as developed as agriculture so had less voice to lose.

Egypt's failure to renew its green revolution since the mid-twentieth century is both a reflection and cause of the wider failure to develop the economy. Globalization provided opportunities that the government failed to seize, preoccupied as it is with control rather than development. While that control seems to have been effective politically, as the relative quiescence of the countryside attests, it has come at a huge cost not just to agriculture and the countryside, but to the economy more generally. The multiple, inter- and intra-sectoral linkages required for development have never been built because the regime fears them, preferring to stove-pipe the economy just as it has the state superstructure. An agricultural-led model of development was dismissed in favor of a self-standing industrial one, which had little chance of success, largely disconnected as it was from agriculture and having few comparative advantages. The captains of what industry did exist were largely driven into exile, replaced typically by ill-prepared military officers. The grey revolution thus aborted, giving way to hopes for a brown or hydrocarbon one, which is itself now foundering as hydrocarbon supply is slowing relative to the size of the economy and population, while oil and gas prices have dramatically declined since June 2014, thereby undermining Egypt's comparative advantage in energy-intensive processing industries.

This economic history of sequential development models poorly thought out and inadequately applied was not a pre-ordained trajectory. Industrialization could have been based more directly on agriculture, as in East Asia, and in turn driven greater demand for its outputs, stimulating growth and rural incomes. Capital provided by oil and gas could similarly have been invested in a green/grey fusion, producing in turn more broadly based and sustainable growth. The agricultural, industrial, and hydrocarbon revolutions have been sequential and non-reinforcing, maybe even competitive, the result primarily of a government turning a deaf ear to its citizens and preoccupied with control rather than development.

Rent-Seeking in Lieu of Development

Unable to formulate a development model that would have successfully integrated and built upon the country's human and physical capacities, and tempted more by plunder than by the arduous and politically risky task of implementing a true development model, the deep state substituted rent-seeking for attempts at fixed capital accumulation. It plucked low-hanging economic fruit it could reach internally while organizing its external relations around the principle of rent-seeking from foreign patrons. That formula has not changed, although the relative abundance and type of the economic fruit plucked has.

The first crop to be plundered by the new republican regime was that of the accumulated capital of the royal family, followed by that of the various members of the bourgeoisie identified in Chapter 1. The nationalization of the Suez Canal Company in 1956 then provided a steady source of foreign currency, interrupted only by war and its aftermath in 1956 and again in 1967. Oil production commenced in Egypt even before World War I, and gas shortly before World War II, but they did not become major exports until the Sadat era when prices rose dramatically and Egypt regained fields in the Sinai and the Gulf of Suez lost to Israel in the 1967 war. The two other major sources of foreign currency earnings upon which Republican Egypt has come to depend also expanded rapidly under Sadat. Remittances exploded as Egyptians, who Nasser had discouraged from travelling, were encouraged by the new

Sadat government to take advantage of employment opportunities in the Gulf, Libya, and elsewhere, and to remit their earnings back to Egypt. Finally, the tourism industry, which was negligible under Nasser, was also cultivated by Sadat, becoming one of the world's largest and fastest growing.

Depending on these sources for foreign currency earnings, rather than upon exports of a wider range of goods and services, was parlous for several reasons. First, while relatively successful under Sadat and even for some part of the Mubarak era, this dependence obscured the need for broader, sustainable development. Second, it did not take account of the growing need due to a rapidly expanding population outpacing even rising earnings from these sources. Third, as mainly exogenous sources of income, they were all subject to conditions over which Egypt had little if any control. They were heavily dependent upon world hydrocarbon markets as well as the general well-being of the MENA region. These three deficiencies in Republican Egypt's rent-seeking strategy of development all became painfully manifest in the wake of the coup-volution. They have continued to intensify as the lethal cocktail of domestic instability, economic mismanagement, regional turmoil, and low prices for oil and gas has undermined foreign currency earnings from all the traditional sources.

In 2012 Egypt became a net importer of natural gas, despite possessing the third largest reserves in Africa, behind Algeria and Nigeria. A decade previously it had become a net importer of oil and oil products, its peak production of some 900,000 barrels per day having been reached in 1996, from which it has steadily declined. Egypt went from being the world's eighth largest exporter of LNG in 2009 to its eighth largest importer in 2016. This sudden and dramatic switch was due to mismanagement of both supply and demand. Egypt has never adequately developed its national domestic production capacities, the state-owned Egyptian General Petroleum Company, which serves as a holding company for most of the hydrocarbon sector, being one of if not the weakest national oil companies in the world given the country's level of reserves and long history of exploitation of them. Almost entirely dependent upon foreign companies to discover, develop, and export oil and gas, Egypt reneged on its contractual arrangements with virtually all those companies in the wake of the coup-volution. Owed in total almost $7 billion for gas fed into the national grid at low prices, and deprived of their share of production for export, the leading companies, including British Gas, BP, and ENI, ceased much of their maintenance activity and in at least one case commenced legal proceedings against the Egyptian government.[12] The consequence for gas production was that from 2012 it commenced a decline, paradoxically amidst reports of substantial discoveries of new fields. Egypt was sued by Israel for breach of contract for not supplying gas through the pipeline that links the two countries. In the face of declining supplies, demand reduction achieved by partially lifting subsidies for industrial and domestic consumers of gas was insufficient. Egypt was consequently forced to draw upon its scarce foreign currency reserves to import gas and even coal to fire its electrical generators.

Despite significant new discoveries of gas, especially in the offshore Zohr field, given the growing demand it appears unlikely Egypt will ever again be a net exporter. The country's energy-intensive processing industries, which had been able to purchase gas at less than $2 per million BTUs when the market price in Asia was as much as nine times that, were by 2016 paying some $5 per million BTUs, not much less than the global market price. The gas-fired boom from which Mubarak's cronies had reaped millions after 2002 has come to a sudden, dramatic end and is unlikely ever to be repeated. During that brief era gas and oil exports at one stage accounted for more than half the country's export earnings, suggesting the magnitude of the challenge of finding substitutes for those lost revenues.

Earnings from Suez Canal tolls are unlikely to pick up much if any of that slack because they depend heavily upon oil and gas tanker traffic as well as global trade, the latter of which is now growing at less than 2 percent annually, significantly below the rate of global economic growth, suggesting that globalization is slowing to a virtual halt. Suppressed tanker traffic also results from redirection of oil and gas exports away from Europe and North America to Asia, a trend that will continue to grow. Increased competition from the recently expanded Panama Canal is yet another cause of stagnant receipts from Suez Canal traffic. All these factors were known or predictable when in the wake of the 2013 coup the new military government decided to spend $8 billion digging a parallel channel to the Canal. It raised the funds by offering Egyptians a premium interest return on Canal certificates, which they purchased by transferring savings out of bank accounts and other government paper, thereby increasing the already severe budgetary pressure of debt service obligations. Faced with criticism of this decision, President Sisi's colleague, Admiral Mamish, head of the Suez Canal Authority, announced that by 2023 revenues would exceed $13 billion annually. This is extremely unlikely. The Central Bank announced in September 2016 that Suez Canal traffic had decreased by 4.5 percent in the fiscal year ending in June, with revenues falling from $5.4 billion in 2014–15 to $5.1 billion. The government had previously sought to disguise this downturn by not releasing the revenue figure in dollars.[13] Worse news was to come at the very end of 2016, when it was revealed that revenues had dropped to an almost two-year low.[14] Longer-term trends are equally ominous. According to the Suez Canal Authority, the maximum number of vessels to transit the Canal was attained in 2008, when it was 21,415. Since then annual vessel traffic has bounced along at around 17,000. Tolls also reached their peak in constant dollars in 2008 at $5.38 billion, since which time they have averaged $5.1–5.2 billion in current, so rather less in constant dollars. The steady decline of Suez Canal revenues as a percentage of GDP which commenced in 2008 will continue into the foreseeable future, unless GDP growth goes into reverse.

Remittances are subject to downward pressures similar to those pressing on Suez Canal revenues. Both are dependent on the Gulf Cooperation Council (GCC) states in general and, in the case of remittances, Saudi Arabia in particular, which with 1–1.5 million Egyptian expatriates accounts for just less than one half of Egypt's total remittances, the other large share coming from the US. Remittances from both sources are in decline, the latter because Egyptians who settle in the

US tend to do so permanently, gradually severing connections to Egypt. Remittances from Saudi Arabia are subject to bilateral relations between the two countries, the state of the global oil market, and the declared Saudi policy to nationalize as much of the labor force as possible. These three drivers are all depressing remittances to Egypt at present and into the indefinite future. Egypt is not alone among labor-exporting countries in facing a downturn in remittances, which to developing countries globally in 2015 amounted to $431 billion, the rate of growth from 2014 being the slowest since 2008. In its annual report on remittances, the World Bank singled out Egypt along with India as being the two countries which saw remittances contract the most in 2015, in which year Egypt's total remittances were the world's seventh largest, accounting for 6.8 percent of the country's GDP.[15] Average remittances per capita peaked in 2008 at $105, sliding to less than $60 by 2016. First-quarter remittances in 2016 were 15 percent less than the corresponding quarter in 2015. For some two decades remittances have amounted to more than five times Foreign Direct Investment (FDI) inflows and public foreign assistance, so they are of vital importance to the country's overall economy and its foreign reserves. As is the case with oil and gas and the Suez Canal, future revenue prospects are not bright. An authoritative forecast is that they will remain flat in current dollar terms until 2020, suggesting a small annual decrease in constant dollars.[16]

By the time of the coup-volution tourism had come to account for about 12 percent of GDP, with a slightly higher contribution to the share of employment resulting from the 3 million jobs generated by the industry, which rendered Egypt's labor market the 13th in the world most dependent upon tourism.[17] It has never recovered from those or subsequent dramatic events and broader turmoil in the region. Visitors fell by two thirds in 2013 from the preceding year, reaching the lowest number in a decade. The comparative magnitude of the impact is suggested by the fact that on a ranking of 184 countries according to economic dependence on tourism, it had fallen to 35th by 2014, while its ranking on prospects for tourism growth in 2014 was 174th.[18] That forecast was accurate and, indeed, the rate of decline subsequently steadily accelerated. In the first three quarters of the 2015–16 fiscal year, tourism revenues in comparison to the same period in 2014–15 fell by 40.5 percent, while the number of tourist nights decreased from 73.4 to 45.1 million. In the first quarter of 2016 tourism revenues were 62.2 percent less than in the same period in the previous year. Even more ominous was that "tourism payments," meaning travel by Egyptians outside their own country, increased in that period to $1.2 billion from $854 million in the first quarter of 2015, as compared to incoming tourist revenues of $550 million, sending the "tourist balance" into sharply negative figures for the first time in modern Egyptian history.[19]

As in the case of remittances, tourism revenues are unlikely to return to previous levels in the foreseeable future. Tourism depends heavily on security and the broader political environment, a fact of which jihadis intent on destabilizing the government are well aware. Attacks on tourists in Luxor and the Sinai in 2015, combined with the beheading of a kidnapped Croatian employee of a French energy company that year, followed by the downing in October 2015 of a Russian Metrojet airliner over the Sinai and then in March 2016 of an Egypt Air flight over the eastern Mediterranean, presumably due to terrorism, reflect this intent. On Christmas Eve 2016, the US State Department issued a renewed warning for Americans considering travelling to Egypt, noting that "terrorist attacks can occur anywhere in the country."[20] In January 2017, Israel warned its citizens of an impending attack in the Sinai and advised them to leave immediately.[21] Egypt's decline on the Global Peace Index in 2014 was the second largest among all countries ranked. By 2016 it had fallen to 142nd place out of the 163 countries ranked.[22] Even if the security and political environments in Egypt were somehow to improve, growing instability in the region, including in neighboring Libya, would still deter tourists. The Global Peace Index for 2016 identified the Middle East and North Africa as the world's least peaceful region. Egyptian and western educational, cultural, and other institutions based in Cairo or elsewhere in the country, including for example the American University in Cairo, have suffered sharp drops in foreign enrolments, with students, archeologists, and others establishing new institutional relationships in other countries, such as Morocco, considered a safer Arab location.

Stagnating remittances coupled with tourism's underperformance had by 2016 dramatically reduced the hitherto vital contribution of services and invisibles to the balance of payments. In the final decade of the Mubarak era annual tourism receipts alone averaged some $10 billion, typically offsetting the annual trade deficit in goods. Inadequate reserves of foreign exchange resulting from the decline of remittances and tourism, the latter which by 2016 was generating only some $2 billion annually, has in turn impacted on other productive sectors, most notably that of manufacturing, which depends heavily on importation of capital goods and raw materials, one of the reasons this sector has declined at a steadily growing pace since 2011. By 2016 the virtual collapse of non-oil merchandise exports, due in large measure to the inability of manufacturers and processers to import necessary inputs, caused the government to impose stiff tariffs on hundreds of imported goods, thereby signaling a retreat into economic isolationism, a stance which is impossible to sustain given the country's dependence on food imports.

Geo-strategic rents, like those from hydrocarbons, the Suez Canal, remittances, and tourism are in decline, with scant prospects for significant improvement. At the broadest level, geo-strategic rents are those provided through bilateral and multilateral public foreign assistance, of which Egypt has for decades been one of the world's most favored recipients. But the pie is steadily shrinking relatively, so Egypt's slice is as well. In 1990 the total overseas development assistance (ODA) provided to the developing world was $53 billion, whereas remittances totaled $29 billion and FDI $19 billion. By 2014 ODA had more than doubled, to $135 billion. But remittances in that period had increased by some fifteen times to $431 billion and FDI by more than thirty times to $662 billion.[23] Egypt's single largest source of ODA since 1990 has been the US, annual ODA from which other than military assistance has steadily declined from more than $1 billion to some $150 million by 2016. There is next to no chance that either global or US ODA provided to Egypt will increase relative to population growth or even in current dollar terms.

As that type of geo-strategic rent has gradually shrunk in proportion to Egypt's GDP and population, the country has turned increasingly to GCC states, especially since the coup-volution. Although there are no precise figures on the total transfers from 2011 to 2016, they are estimated at around $40 billion. Even more than is the case with ODA, however, subventions from the Arab Gulf countries have declined. Indeed, after Saudi Arabia, Kuwait, and the Emirates provided the military government with as much as $30 billion in the wake of the 2013 coup, subventions from Saudi Arabia have come to an almost complete halt, while those provided by the other two GCC states probably totaled less than $1 billion in 2016. The causes of this precipitate decline are the financial crisis in those GCC countries resulting from the downturn since 2014 in oil prices, and the souring of relations between Egypt and Saudi Arabia in particular and, to a lesser extent, Kuwait and the UAE. While those relations could improve, subventions of the magnitude transferred between 2011 and 2014 are virtually impossible to imagine occurring again. Sisi's effort to substitute for those lost geo-strategic rents by seeking replacements from Russia, Iran, and China have thus far produced little other than promises and some long-term contracts for the supply of goods ranging from nuclear reactors to consumer durables, but those contracts call for payments by Egypt, sometimes in local currency, and will, therefore, only be implemented if it finds the wherewithal. World Bank and IMF loans extended in 2016 for some $13 billion are on concessional terms, but they do bear interest and must be repaid.

Rent-seeking, as an alternative to articulating and implementing a coherent development strategy that integrates various sectors and draws upon the country's comparative advantages, thus has bleak prospects. Indeed, the grim future has already arrived. In the second half of 2016 Egypt confronted both fiscal and balance of payments crises, the consequences of which could be described as "20/20." Having to float the Egyptian pound as a condition for obtaining the IMF loan, the government could only sit by helplessly as the pound immediately sank from 8 to 20 to the dollar. Inflation, which had risen from about 9 percent at the time of the coup-volution to 13 percent at the time of the devaluation, immediately shot up to 20 percent. By the end of 2016 Egypt was in danger of succumbing to runaway inflation coupled with a collapsing currency.[24] Its foreign currency reserves, bolstered by the IMF loan, were still less than sufficient for three months' imports, well below the recommended minimum and causing the government to slap increased tariffs on 364 imported commodities, ranging from chewing gum to tennis shoes to electrical appliances, in order to save precious funds to pay for food and other necessities.[25] But there were insufficient funds even to cover such basic goods as medicines for chronic diseases, to say nothing of inputs into industrial production. Over 40 percent of the country's imports are of semi-finished and intermediate goods, suggesting the profound dependence of the industrial sector on its external ties. Imports and exports began to spiral down together in unison, with the latter at $18 billion amounting to less than one third of the former's $56 billion in 2016, raising the question of where Egypt would find the foreign currency required to sustain its population, of which by this time some 30 percent were living in dire poverty. The answer was through more foreign borrowing, the door to which was opened by the IMF loan of late 2016. In January 2017 Egypt floated a dollar-denominated Eurobond issue of $4 billion, but it had to pay dearly for those dollars. The interest rate on the ten-year bonds was 7.5 percent, while that on the thirty-year bonds was a staggering 8.5 percent, rates typically associated with struggling sub-Saharan African countries and equal to that paid by the EU laggard Greece. With its foreign debt now approaching $70 billion, servicing requirements were coming to constitute a huge drain on its foreign currency earnings. Already in 2012 Egypt had scored lower on *The Economist*'s "Wiggle Room Index," which measures the scope to ease fiscal and monetary policies, than any other country. By 2016 it would have dropped off the chart had *The Economist* repeated the exercise.

The government's response to the crisis was to charge the military with yet more economic tasks, such as importing cattle, providing baby milk powder to mothers who could prove they were incapable of breast feeding, establishing pharmaceutical and cement companies, engaging in fish farming, distributing a million food hampers in Sinai and Upper Egypt, and undertaking more construction projects, including that of the $45 billion new capital in the desert between Cairo and the Gulf of Suez. Despite the manifest increase in the military's economic role, and presumably as a result of public criticism of it, Sisi declared in October 2016 that the military's share of GDP was stagnant at only 1.5 percent, a figure impossible to challenge because no public information is available on the size of the military economy.[26] He did not mention that in 2015 Egypt imported $5.3 billion of arms, ranking it first among developing countries, or that it committed to $12 billion in arms transfer agreements, making it the world's second signer of such agreements, immediately after Qatar.[27] In January 2017, as the military was expanding its economic activities, Sisi explained that it was "using its own budget without burdening the state's general budget...in efforts to preserve the national pride and dignity...of the Egyptian people." He added that "the army has built-up its economic capabilities over many years; for the last three-and-a-half-years, the armed forces haven't used any money from the general budget to buy its weaponry."[28]

What was made clear by these scattered efforts was that neither the government nor the military upon which it rests were capable of addressing the fundamental causes of the economic crisis, or maybe even of recognizing it, as suggested by the profligate arms purchases. In addition to woeful transient management of the macro economy, those causes are the accumulated consequences of the socio-fiscal trap, which have made it impossible to invest adequately in human resources and physical infrastructure.

Human Resources Imperiled

Egypt is facing a population boom it can ill afford. The government announced in November 2016 that there were 100 million Egyptians, of whom 92 million reside in Egypt. Egypt is the fifteenth most populous country in the world and its share of the global population has risen from 0.86 percent in 1955 to 1.26 percent in 2016. In 2017 Cairo became the world's fastest growing city, projected to add half a million residents in that year.[29] The population growth rate of 2.4 percent per annum is "five times that of developed countries and double the average for developing countries."[30] The UN projects this rate to slow, but still predicts that by 2050 the population will exceed 150 million and by the end of the century over 200 million. By 2040 Egypt will be more populous than either Russia or Japan.[31] Although the birthrate declined during the first decade of the Mubarak era, it began to grow again after that as a result of female members of the "youth bulge" reaching child-bearing age, coupled with an unexpected increase in fertility rates driven by increasing poverty and decreasing female participation in the labor force.[32] In 2013, almost 50 percent more babies were born than a decade previously. Ragui Assaad and Caroline Crafft observe that the "echo" effect of the youth bulge, whereby the leading edge of that bulge come of age to be parents, is beginning to be felt. The cohort of 0–9-year-olds is much larger than that of 10–19 years. In 2008 2.1 million children were born, whereas 2.6 million were born in 2012. The increase in births between 2010 and 2012 was "the largest two-year increase since records began.[33] A source of further concern is that a primary cause of the rebound in the fertility rate is declining employment of females of child-bearing age. In 1998, 22 percent of female high-school graduates were employed, whereas in 2012 only 17 percent were. The comparative percentages for female university graduates were 56 percent dropping to 41 percent in 2012. Further deterioration of female employment will presumably drive up the fertility rate yet more, exacerbating the already daunting challenge of job creation which requires at least 800,000 new positions annually just to maintain existing employment rates. The rate of economic growth required to produce this number of jobs, in excess of 8 percent, was only almost achieved during one year of the Mubarak era. The IMF and World Bank do not forecast a growth rate for Egypt in excess of 5 percent per annum in the decade to come.

Egypt is neither educating nor employing its youths adequately. On the United Nations Development Program's overall Human Development Index, Egypt scores twenty places below its ranking on GDP per capita, while on the narrower Education Index it is thirty-five places below the level it should achieve according to its GDP per capita.[34] Only about two thirds of adult Egyptians are literate, a ratio somewhat below that for the Arab world as a whole (71 percent), but far behind that of Turkey at 89 percent or Thailand at 94 percent.[35] More than two in five of Egyptian women are illiterate.[36] The educational system emphasizes quantity over quality and largely fails to address the needs of the poor. Combined gross enrollment in education of those in the relevant age cohorts is 76 per cent, which exceeds the Arab country average of 66 per cent and even that of Turkey, which is 71 per cent.[37] Yet the quality of that education, as indicated not only by comparatively high illiteracy rates, but by international test results, is relatively low. Egyptian pupils' performance on the Trends in International Mathematics and Science Study (TIMSS) tests administered in 2003 were well below international averages in mathematics and science and fell yet further when retested four years later.[38] In analyzing the results the World Bank noted the comparatively high proportion of Egyptian students who failed to reach the low benchmark of 400—40 per cent, compared to 32 and 23 per cent for Lebanese and Iranian students, respectively.[39] The Bank's explanation of Egypt's lopsided result is that the two lowest income quintiles perform extremely poorly, the gap between rich and poor students being greater in Egypt than any other MENA country.[40]

While inequality is one explanation of educational underperformance, inadequate government expenditure is another. Relative to GDP per capita, Egyptian teachers are the lowest paid in the MENA region, their average salary being only one and half times per capita GDP.[41] As comparatively low as Egypt's spending on education is, it is money not well invested. Male high-school graduates earn only 6 per cent more over their lifetimes than those who had no schooling whatsoever. Returns to educational expenditure in Egypt are lower than in all regional comparators, including Morocco and Tunisia.[42]

The 8 per cent return achieved in 2000 compared poorly to more than double that rate achieved by Argentina, Chile, and Uruguay.[43] One careful study of the impact of public expenditures in Egypt concluded that "as a whole [education spending] has a negative effect on growth."[44] The World Economic Forum ranked Egypt's higher education 126th out of 134 countries and 128th on the degree to which it satisfied the needs of the country's labor market.[45] Ten per cent of graduates from tertiary educational institutions are in science and engineering, about half the average share in the MENA as a whole. In Turkey and China the comparative percentages are 24 and 30, respectively.[46]

Given that the overall recruitment pool from which the labor force is drawn is comparatively poor as well as poorly and even mis-educated, it is not surprising that the labor force is relatively non-competitive. The overall labor force participation rate of 49 per cent compares to Bangladesh's 71 per cent and Thailand's 72 per cent.[47] Female labor force participation at 24 per cent is half the total of males and females combined. In Bangladesh and Thailand the female rates are 57 and 64 per cent, respectively.[48] Egypt ranks 108th on the "Third Billion Index" of 128 countries on the economic empowerment of women.[49] Booz and Company estimates that Egypt's GDP by 2020 would grow by an additional one third if the female matched the male employment rate. This is the highest potential increase in the countries studied, outpacing even India's projected gain, despite the fact that India ranks lower on the female empowerment index.[50] The Egyptian labor force is widely perceived as being poorly trained, a standard lament of potential investors.

But it is not just inadequate education and training coupled with underinvestment that pose problems for job creation. Key features of the limited access order also present obstacles. One is that cronyism in the form of politically connected firms deters employment growth in the sectors into which those firms expand, as was reported in a 2015 World Bank study of the impacts of cronyism on the economy.[51] Another, related problem is that "there is little mobility between labor market segments," as the rigid, limited access order stove-pipes the

entire political economy, largely as a result of heavy dependence on public employment.[52] These constraints have some
rather bizarre consequences, including shortages of labor in
some important segments of the economy. In health care, for
example, there is a superabundance of doctors, but such a
shortage of nurses that thousands of non-Egyptians have to
be hired to fill vacancies. Lack of foreign exchange has slowed
this hiring, resulting in Egypt having 14.8 nurses for every
10,000 inhabitants, about half the global benchmark figure
for developing countries of 28.6 nurses.[53]

Not surprisingly, unemployment is a chronic problem that
has been further aggravated by the coup-volution, rising from
less than 10 per cent to 15 per cent in official figures, which
understate the magnitude of the problem because the definition of employment used is a minimum of one hour of
work per week to qualify as employed. *The Economist* claims
that the unemployment rate for youths in 2016 was at least
40 percent and that for university graduates 34 percent.[54]
The International Labor Organization reported in 2014 that
91.1 percent of employed youths aged between fifteen and
twenty-nine worked in the informal sector, meaning without
contracts, health insurance, or pensions.[55] The Global Youth
Development Index of the British Commonwealth, which
measures "multi-dimensional progress on youth development
in 183 countries," ranked Egypt 138th out of 183 countries in 2016, a decline of fifty-two places from 2013. On
the "employment and opportunity" indicator, Egypt ranked
174th.[56]

Associated with rising unemployment is growing poverty.
In 2000 the overall poverty rate was 16.7 percent.[57] By 2017,
28 percent of Egyptians were officially living below the poverty
line of an income less than $2 per day, but unofficially in the
wake of the November 2016 devaluation, probably as much
as 40 percent.[58] In Upper Egypt poverty grew from 43.7 per
cent in 2009 to some 55 percent in 2016. Increasingly the
impacts of poverty are being reflected in the physical well-
being of Egyptians. Malnutrition is becoming common, with
Egypt, according to UNICEF, among the twenty countries in
the world with the highest incidence of chronic malnutrition.

About one in every three children under five is stunted, their growth impeded by inadequate diet. Half of children under five are suffering from anemia resulting from iron deficiencies.[59] Egyptians suffer from the world's highest rate of hepatitis C, partly the result of a national campaign under Nasser, then Sadat, from the 1950s till the mid-1980s, which relied on intravenous tartar emetic to treat bilharzia. Re-use of needles spread the virus.[60]

As a result of these parlous conditions Egyptians, especially youths, are increasingly desperate. In September 2016, campus protests included groups of graduates burning their PhD and MA diplomas in protest at the lack of suitable jobs.[61] Those further down the social ladder take more drastic measures. Egypt has become a major supplier for organ transplants as impoverished citizens sell them. In 2010 it was named as one of the top five countries for illegal organ trade by the World Health Organization, which said that poor Egyptians sold kidneys and other organs to "buy food or pay off debts." An organ-trafficking ring of doctors, nurses, and professors was rounded up by the authorities in 2016 and proclaimed by the government to be the world's largest, operating out of a range of public and private health centers and hospitals as well as the faculties of medicine at Cairo and Ain Shams Universities.[62] By 2017 the price of a black-market kidney in Egypt had reached $100,000.[63] Egypt ranks second among African countries for the number of drug trials conducted by pharmaceutical companies, as citizens submit themselves to trials for payment and to receive treatments they otherwise could not afford.[64] As the economic crisis intensified in 2016–17, consumption of donkey and even cat meat intensified, with the police intermittently seizing tons of such meat unfit for human consumption.[65] A survey conducted by the government's Central Agency for Mobilization and Statistics in 2016 found that only 15 percent of citizens report they have a decent living with access to education and nutrition, whereas 85 percent state that they and their families lack such access to the degree that it affects their physical and mental health.[66] The World Economic Forum's Inclusive Development Index for 2017 placed Egypt 73rd out of 79 developing countries, noting that "the country struggles with many aspects of inclusive growth."[67]

It is unsurprising that Egyptians are unhappy and alienated. The Arab Barometer survey conducted in 2013 revealed that only 6 percent of respondents thought the current economic situation in Egypt was "good", 6 percent that the state was doing a good job in creating employment opportunities, and 15 percent reporting health services as good but over 80 percent as bad or very bad. That these negative assessments are coupled with political alienation is suggested by the findings that only 2.9 percent of respondents were members of a political party, 2.6 percent a member of a charitable organization, and 2.6 percent a member of a professional association or trade union. Their evaluations of the country's institutions revealed that only 7 percent thought parliament was "good," and 11 percent that the cabinet was "good."[68] Presumably declining support for the military caused the government to prevent a question about it being asked in the most recent "wave" of the Barometer, that of 2015.

Faced with these dire circumstances, an increasing number of Egyptians are voting with their feet. A growing percentage of Mediterranean boat people and the human traffickers transporting them are Egyptian nationals, as reflected by the country being placed in July 2015 on the US State Department's "Watch List" for Global Trafficking in Persons.[69] Government data, which no doubt understates the numbers, provided the figure of 90,000 youths departing Egypt illegally in 2015, as compared to 15,000 in 2009; 3,720 such illegal youth migrants hoping to reach Europe were apprehended in a three-month period ending in June 2016.[70] In late 2016 the minister of immigration and Egyptian expatriate affairs announced that Egypt "ranks first in illegal immigration rates worldwide."[71] Egypt was among the twenty countries worldwide with the highest number of people living abroad in 2015, in part, *The Economist* notes, "because of a surging volume of refugees."[72]

Egypt's limited access order, in sum, has little room for its citizens, especially young ones. Indeed, it has not bothered to properly educate and train them, nor to ensure even their basic nutrition. As a consequence, the labor force is steadily losing its competitiveness to other middle and lower middle income countries, including neighboring ones such as Morocco and Tunisia. The attractiveness of cheap, unskilled labor to investors is in decline as labor-saving technologies render it ever more redundant. So Egyptians are rushing to the exits in ever greater numbers. An increasing proportion of them are doing so as illegal migrants, thus facing uncertain futures in an increasingly hostile Europe. They have limited prospects for sending back remittances as previous generations of Egyptian migrants to the Gulf, Libya, and the US have done. The regime's policies signal that it does not want its own people, but no other country does either.

Physical and Environmental Decay

Just as Egypt has not invested adequately in its people, so has it neglected its physical infrastructure and environment, the key elements of which are water, land, air, housing, and transportation and communication networks. Gross fixed capital formation is the best measure of a country's commitment to its physical infrastructure and environment as it includes spending on land improvements; plant, machinery, and equipment purchases; the construction of roads, railways, private residential dwellings, and hospitals, schools, commercial and industrial buildings. Comparative rates of gross fixed capital formation reflect both its steady decline in Egypt and its low level by regional and other standards. For the period 1987 to 1991 as a percentage of GDP it was 28.3, whereas for the period 1997–2001 it sagged to 19.3 percent. By comparison, lower middle income country averages from 1987 to 1991 were 26.4 percent, roughly the same as Egypt's, but they then accelerated in the 1997–2001 period to 28.1 percent, almost 10 per cent of GDP more than Egypt's. By 2014 Egypt was investing just 13.2 percent of its GDP in gross fixed capital. The world average in that year was 23 percent. Egypt's rate of gross fixed capital formation as a share of GDP has since 2000 been below that of all Arab countries other than Yemen.[73] But even this exceedingly low rate is unlikely to be sustained

in light of the country's economic crisis. The currency devaluation coupled with accelerating inflation at the end of 2016
is predicted to drive debt servicing up from 29 percent to 37
percent of the 2016–17 budget, which, combined with the
costs of subsidies and the public service wage bill, will devour
at least 90 percent of the entire budget, possibly even more
as the cost of energy subsidies was rising along with global
oil prices.[74]

The pressure on Egypt's physical infrastructure and environment is comparatively great because of its population
density. About 95 percent of the population live along the
banks of the Nile, in the Nile Delta, and adjacent to the Suez
Canal. These regions are among the world's most densely
populated, containing an average of 1,540 persons per square
kilometer. This makes the core of Egypt the eighth most densely
inhabited "country" in the world, but the seven preceding
ones are city states such as Singapore, Macao, Gibraltar, or
the Holy See. The Netherlands, which is the most densely
settled European country, has just under 500 people per square
kilometer, or about one third the density of Egypt's core regions.
Israel, generally thought of as having relatively little land for
its people, has 372 persons per square kilometer. The challenges of managing so many people in such a confined area
while sustaining the quality of the land, water, and air essential
to their lives are beyond the government's abilities. In Cairo
alone the failure to protect public land is bemoaned by the
city's governor as resulting in 17,000 separate pieces of land
comprising 3.6 million square meters having been encroached
upon.[75]

Egypt's infrastructure, including power generation, sewer
and water treatment, railways and roads, and so on, have
steadily deteriorated since the Sadat era, lacking adequate
investment from both foreign assistance and indigenous funding
sources.[76] Electricity outages had become commonplace
throughout the country by 2014. Poor maintenance of rural
and urban water delivery systems resulted in the drying up
of potable and irrigation water to literally millions of rural
and urban dwellers. Accompanying and in many cases caused
by the deterioration of the physical infrastructure were growing

environmental problems, including poor air and water quality, resulting in turn in increased incidence of health problems such as bronchial and intestinal diseases. Particulate-matter concentration in the air in Egypt's cities with populations above 100,000, for example, is only worse in some six other countries, a result primarily of congested roads and inadequate alternative modes of transport.[77] Road transport has become exceedingly dangerous. The World Health Organization places Egypt in the top ten countries for the number of fatal road accidents, which it attributes primarily to the poor conditions of roads. Other sources report it is the world's second most dangerous country in which to drive, with more than 25,000 road deaths annually.[78] The World Economic Forum ranks Egypt 135th out of 141 countries in terms of travel safety.[79] Maritime safety is little if any better, largely because of deficient investment in search-and-rescue capacities, the shortcomings of which were revealed in grisly fashion in September 2016, when a boat carrying 600 illegal migrants floundered just off the coast of al Rashid, within cell-phone reach of Alexandria. Despite frantic calls there was no response for hours, during which time at least a third of the passengers drowned.[80] As with transportation infrastructure, that for communications is substandard. Agreement on terms for the purchase of licenses to operate the 4G network of high-speed telecommunications and data transfer was delayed for several years as state-owned Telecom Egypt vied with the military and three private companies over terms and conditions. 4G systems were introduced in Japan in 2004, in the US in 2010, and in the GCC states in 2011. Egypt will not have that technology before mid-2017 at the earliest.

Important as transport and communications infrastructures are, they are not as central to the concerns of citizens as their personal housing. The state's response to steadily rising housing demand reflects its reliance on despotic as opposed to infrastructural power. Unable to calibrate a housing policy that would expand supply on the basis of reasonable burden and benefit sharing between stakeholders, under Nasser it decreed a draconian rent-control policy that discouraged new housing construction. That policy, with modification, remains in place.

Its consequences have been deterioration of existing housing stock, combined with the private sector focusing on new construction for wealthier Egyptians, leaving the middle and lower ends of the housing market to the state. Nasser's reaction was to build public housing of the type common in Europe and North America at the time, concentrating the poor in substandard high rises in undesirable areas with predictable negative consequences. Since then the state has addressed the housing shortage in two other ways. Under Sadat it commenced building "new cities" in remote locations, typically on the fringe of the Delta or Nile Valley. President Sisi has reinvigorated this approach, placing the military in charge of such constructions, which again are meeting with only tepid approval from prospective inhabitants. The problem has been that these austere, poorly situated cities are unpopular with potential residents because they are far from places of work and lack the urban infrastructure upon which many depend for their livelihoods, such as informal markets and meeting places.

The second, rather more successful approach was essentially to do nothing other than turn a blind eye to encroachments on land not owned by those building or living upon it. This is the so-called "informal" housing sector, known as *ashwa'iyyat*. Such housing has mushroomed throughout Egypt since the Sadat era and has come to account for as much as 70 percent of the housing in Cairo, occupying more than 40 percent of its built-up area in some 100 settlements. Similar if somewhat lower proportions obtain elsewhere. The land illegally built upon is typically owned by some government instrumentality, by the military, or by private owners, especially of land zoned as only for agricultural purposes, the owners taking side payments for permitting transgressions. Lacking legal status, these informal settlements cannot easily obtain public services, such as water, sewerage, electricity, garbage collection, schools, etc. Most, however, do have police stations, reflecting the government's preoccupation with security and its disinterest in other services. Typically, the buildings are several stories high, noncompliant with building codes, lacking elevators, and crammed together, admitting neither light nor air into apartments and being inaccessible by automobile. During the Mubarak era, they became hotbeds of Islamist organization precisely because they were not easily penetrated by security forces and housed vast numbers of poor citizens attracted to radical Islamism. Police in informal housing areas are notoriously corrupt, sometimes running shakedown rackets and pushing drugs. The chaos associated with the coup-volution and its consequences opened the door to intensification of construction of *ashwa'iyyat* and further elevated the importance of housing as a public policy issue, not the least reason being that these informal settlements continued to pose security threats. One consequence was that *ashwa'iyyat* made it into the 2014 constitution in the form of Article 78, which requires the government to take steps to improve them as follows: "The State shall devise a comprehensive national plan to address the problem of unplanned informal settlements, which includes re-planning, provision of infrastructure and utilities and improvement of the quality of life and public health." In June 2014, in one of his initial acts as president, Sisi created the Ministry of Urban Renewal and Informal Settlements, charging it with the responsibility to implement this constitutional article. Like his predecessors, however, Sisi lacked ongoing commitment to tackle this issue. The thrust of his government's policy, as was that of Sadat's and Mubarak's, has been to build yet more "new communities," this time with the military as the prime contractor. In the meantime, Egypt's poor and members of the aspiring middle class look after their housing needs as best they can, surviving with minimal public services and lacking the title deed that would enable them to capitalize their housing asset.

Preservation and appropriate utilization of land and water resources is inherently difficult in such a densely populated area that depends almost entirely on one freshwater source, the damming of which has raised the water table from Aswan to the Mediterranean, thereby imperiling many agricultural crops and exacerbating the problems of water delivery and wastewater removal and treatment. Some of these problems would have been at least partially resolved and water conservation maximized had micro-irrigation supplanted open drains as the principal means of delivering water to crops, but since the state was reliant on despotic rather than infrastructural power it was unable to engineer that shift. Irrigation and drainage canals do double or even triple duty as refuse dumps, open sewers, and providers of "potable" water to rural residents. Virtually all of rural Egypt lacks adequate wastewater treatment facilities, a deficiency that accounts in part for the country's world-leading rates of hepatitis and gastro-intestinal diseases. Soils have been contaminated not just by waterborne bacteria, but also by overuse of herbicides and pesticides, a problem exacerbated by the re-use of drainage water for irrigation. One consequence of the degradation of water and soil resources has been contamination of crops, a problem left unaddressed for crops intended for domestic consumption, but which has increasingly disrupted Egypt's agricultural exports. Recipient countries, whether in Europe, North America, or the Gulf, have rejected a growing range of agricultural commodities on phytosanitary grounds. Russia, for example, the second largest market after Saudi Arabia for Egyptian fruit and vegetables, rejected shipments of oranges, tomatoes, and potatoes in the fall of 2016 on the grounds of bacterial contamination. At about that time the US placed at least a temporary ban on the importation of strawberries from Egypt in the wake of the Food and Drug Administration's finding that more than 100 Americans contracted hepatitis A from eating them. The EU has over the years rejected shipments of various horticultural products ranging from onions to green beans. Egypt's salt-water resources of the Mediterranean and Gulfs of Suez and Aqaba are at risk from sewerage runoff and damage to coral reefs by pollution and uncontrolled touristic exploitation. Much of the country's built cultural heritage, from Aswan to Alexandria, is threatened by the high water table and encroachment from the Mediterranean. Dewatering projects conducted with the support of the United States Agency for International Development have done more to save Pharaonic, Islamic, and Christian built cultural heritage than any actions by the Egyptian government, despite the fact that admissions to those sites has over the years provided it with substantial revenues.

Egypt's remarkable inheritance, including one of the world's greatest rivers, the most fertile soils, an extraordinary cultural heritage, magnificent beaches, and what until the late 1960s was relatively pristine air, with the scent of jasmine even detectable in downtown Cairo, is under profound threat. These resources underpin the basic health and well-being of residents and in some cases, once destroyed, can never be replaced. The government has taken few meaningful steps to protect this patrimony despite the immediately perceptible costs of not doing so, such as those resulting from rejection of exports. It has neither the will nor the capacity to act. It is concerned overwhelmingly with controlling citizens, not improving their lives.

Foreign Policy Adrift

A discussion of foreign policy is included in this chapter primarily because it has been a key aspect of the rent-seeking upon which successive republican regimes have based their economic strategy, and secondarily because Egypt's rulers have relied upon their foreign patrons to reinforce their personal power. Such stubborn persistence in the face of changing regional and global realities has been due in part to the relative success enjoyed by Nasser and Sadat in obtaining geostrategic rents during the Cold War, first from the Americans, then the Soviets, then, after 1973, the Americans again, this time with more backing from Europe. The last hurrah of this strategy came in 1990–1, when Mubarak sent troops to Kuwait to participate in the US-led Desert Storm operation to throw Iraqi troops back across the border. He garnered about $25 billion in debt forgiveness for what was symbolic rather than real military participation. This dramatic event was virtually coterminous with the end of the Cold War, which undermined one pillar upon which geo-strategic rent-seeking had rested.

The second, more important pillar for success of the strategy was Egypt's relative power, primarily hard but also soft. When Egypt could threaten neighboring states with substantial, even overwhelming military power, and could mobilize Arabs wherever they were in its support, it could either be opposed or supported, but both East and West had to deal with it. Generally, it was easier to pay than to fight, so with the exceptions of 1956, 1967, and 1973, that was the normal modus operandi in relations with Cairo. Egypt became one of the world's largest recipients of public foreign assistance and, since 1980, the world's second largest beneficiary of military assistance, the first being Israel. But the relative value of that assistance has declined in tandem with Egypt's shrinking power, both hard and soft. Preoccupied with its own welfare, the military has lost the will and capacity to fight substantial opponents and is even increasingly wary of quite weak ones, lest the Argentinian or Greek scenarios of military adventurism gone bad undermine the regime's popularity. Soft power has similarly abated as the Arab center of gravity has shifted in general to the Gulf and state-based nationalisms have grown in virtually every Arab state at the expense of Arab nationalism. Egypt no longer has much to offer potential patrons, so they are offering less to it. US aid has declined steeply in proportional terms and even in nominal ones, whereas the key GCC countries, originally willing to bankroll Sisi as a useful counterweight to the Muslim Brotherhood, have all but stopped doing so. In their view, Sisi's regime was providing too little in return for their investment, and in any case could do little to threaten them.

This leaves Egypt having to depend for continued rents on being seen as either too big to fail by its traditional supporters, key of which are the US, Europe, and the GCC states, or being viewed by the opponents of those supporters, including Russia and China, as a new entry point into the region, or as a counterweight, in the case of Iran, to its own regional antagonists. Neither option is likely to produce geo-strategic rents in the magnitude of the glory days of the Cold War, nor even of the very recent past when Gulf shaikhs supported the Egyptian military to crush the Brothers.

The too-big-to-fail scenario is based on relatively small sticks and carrots. The major stick is undocumented immigration. Egypt can flood southern Europe with boat people, a potential threat which has been a driving force in Italian policy toward it since at least the 1990s. As if to remind European decision makers of the threat, and in response to US criticism of the country's increasing role in human trafficking, the government passed an anti-trafficking law in 2016 while also reporting more cases of interdiction of human smuggling even as the numbers of those transiting from Egypt continued to increase.[81] Just as the legislation was being enacted, the Egyptian Foreign Ministry responded to the Italian government's suspension of delivery of F16 spare parts in retaliation for non-cooperation in investigating the murder of Giulio Regeni, by stating that the Italian government's choice "would affect bilateral, regional and international cooperation between the countries, particularly concerning immigration across the Mediterranean Sea."[82] The implied threat was painfully obvious. The far bigger threat is simply that Egypt collapses, becoming a failed state like Libya, but with a population almost twenty times larger. In this scenario, the eastern Mediterranean would swarm with boat people as at least some regions in the Nile Valley and Delta became terrorist havens within easy striking distance of Israel and Europe.[83]

As for carrots, the key one is cooperation in "counterterrorism," whether in Egypt itself or more widely in the region, most notably in Libya and Gaza. As regards the latter, Sisi has built upon cooperation with Israeli security authorities to contain Hamas so that his relation with Israel has become his country's most vital regional tie, in large measure because of support extended to Egypt by the pro-Israeli lobby in the US. The strength of the relationship was demonstrated in December 2016, when Egypt, holding the chair of the UN Security Council, sought unsuccessfully to postpone a vote condemning Israeli settlements on the West Bank as illegal. In the event, New Zealand led a group of four countries overturning Egypt's decision and the vote was held, with the US abstaining, hence allowing the resolution to pass, 14–0. That Egypt had become more supportive of Israel than even New Zealand was cause for outrage throughout the Arab world. This episode illustrates the limits of a rent-seeking foreign policy in today's complex, conflict-ridden MENA, as the payoffs from serving the interests of external parties are relatively small and typically come at the cost of losing payments from other, competing parties. Similarly, while external actors are willing to pay off Egypt to deter yet more undocumented immigration and out of the hope of averting the country's collapse, such payments are not of the magnitude of Cold War geo-strategic rents and are insufficient to tackle the fundamental development deficiencies just discussed.

As for potential support from challengers to western hegemony in the eastern Mediterranean and North Africa, led by Russia and China and including Iran, Sisi has been in pursuit of it, but with mixed results. One problem is that gains from these sources are offset by losses from traditional backers, including both the GCC and western states. In the case of the former, the potential gains from Iran are miniscule in comparison to forgone rents from just Saudi Arabia. Another problem is that these "meddlers" do not perceive fundamental geo-strategic interests being served by improved relations with Egypt. Rather, they perceive some marginal gains at the expense of the US and Europe and a card to play in, say, dealings over Eastern Europe. Egypt is a second-order priority for both Russia and China and their financial support for it will necessarily be limited. Finally, Russia and Iran clearly lack the resources to supplant the magnitude of support that Egypt previously received from the West and until recently from GCC states. While China has the resources, nowhere else has it invested heavily in geo-strategic rents, as opposed to entering into commercial relations from which it also obtains benefits, and it is unlikely to make an exception in Egypt's case, as its withdrawal in February 2017 from the project to construct a new capital suggests.

Egypt's foreign policy under Sisi, in sum, is similar to that of his predecessors in that it is based primarily on the pursuit of geo-strategic rents. But the growing magnitude of Egypt's needs, combined with the changed regional and global environments, render this strategy redundant. Sisi is presumably aware of the inevitable diminished returns from his rent-seeking strategy, but continues to pursue it through a diversification of supporters because their support is a useful counterbalance to the US and Europe. The US in particular is distrusted by Sisi because it jettisoned Mubarak so unceremoniously and, in his view, supported the Brotherhood. He fears that the US, backed by Europe, could exert pressure on him as a result of human rights and other abuses, including the failure to deliver on promises of democratization, possibly even seeking to replace him. This is almost reason enough to cultivate Moscow, Beijing, and Tehran, whatever the consequences for rent-seeking. Tweaking the nose of Americans and Gulf Arabs is also popular precisely because of their unpopularity among Egyptians. The regime's foreign policy, in short, is intended to maximize rents while preserving the regime. Neither is a suitable or appropriate objective. The rents are increasingly marginal, while the primary threats to the regime are overwhelmingly domestic, beyond the capacity of any external actor to substantively influence or counter. Posturing against Washington or Riyadh can provide only very short-term benefits.

The ill-founded foreign policy also bears significant opportunity costs, chief of which is alienation of traditional governmental and public sources of support. The US, for example, "re-directed" over $100 million of foreign assistance committed to Egypt away from it in 2016, on the grounds that agreement was not reached on its utilization, suggesting that tension in the relationship would cause Washington to ignore Egypt's financial plight, possibly even to use it to pressure the government. Loss of support from the GCC amounts annually to billions of dollars. Increasing tension between their governments and that of Egypt are an additional reason why high-spending Gulf Arabs have drastically reduced their touristic presence there. Lack of suitable attention to normal bilateral consular relations is reflected in Egypt's dropping from 88th to 162nd place out of 199 countries between 2016 and 2017 on Passportindex's measure of visa-free travel for a country's citizens.[84] The regime's foreign policy, in sum, is not emerging from a national consensus on how Egypt should relate to the world, nor is it focused on serving the needs of its citizens. Egypt's cozying up to Israel and Iran is highly unpopular, as are various other aspects of its policies. Sisi's foreign policy reflects short-sighted opportunism propelled more by his regime's needs than the country's. Still based on foundations that crumbled years ago, Egypt's foreign policy does not assist it in addressing pressing domestic issues, rather it renders that task yet more difficult.

Conclusion

The limited access order established almost seventy years ago has steadily undermined the country's performance and well-being, bringing it to crisis point. Concerned primarily with preserving its power and rewards, the deep state and the regimes based on it opted for rent-seeking rather than a structural development of the economy based on a thoughtful consideration of alternative models. As rents have declined, so has the comparative and, in all too many cases, absolute quality of human and physical resources. Egypt has been steadily falling behind comparator countries across a wide range of development measures, while its environment is increasingly degraded. Its relations with the world reflect its declining capacities, as its chief card now is not to exert soft or hard power beyond its borders, but simply to threaten collapse, leaving a failed state and ungoverned spaces in its wake. Given the lessons of Afghanistan, Syria, Yemen, and Libya, to name some regional examples, it should be clear enough to the Egyptian regime that while the world will take some actions to try to save failing states, those actions will be limited and unlikely to be decisive.

The Rocky
Road Ahead

Egypt's squandered inheritance and present plight suggest that the primary challenge is no longer that of developing the nation, but of holding it together. The political community which underpins the state is dissolving while the state itself is ever more concerned with countering threats to it rather than acting as the "brain" to think out and direct a national development effort. But even were the regime to seriously attempt to reverse the country's accelerating economic downhill slide, it would be hard to do. Egypt has become a "late, late developer," when some seventy years ago it was poised to be a leader of Third World efforts to overtake the First.

During these three generations of lost time the world has moved on, rendering classic development models virtually obsolete. Global competition in agriculture, industry, services, information technology, and indeed all economic sectors, has intensified, with the successful relying ever more heavily on capital, technology, skilled labor, and effective management, what the economists call Total Factor Productivity, rather than simply increasing the quantity of factors of production. It is no longer possible to move up industrial production ladders, as much of Asia has done, by starting at the very bottom with labor-intensive, poorly capitalized, technologically deficient enterprises. The world is being economically partitioned, with Asia becoming the primary industrial workshop, especially for consumer durables, rendering successful industrialization efforts by other aspiring regions ever more unlikely. Moreover, the MENA, with its dependence on hydrocarbon exports, its ubiquitous Dutch Disease, its relatively poorly developed human resources, and its globally leading rates of instability and conflict, is possibly the least hospitable global region for late, late development efforts by countries with large populations and few indigenous resources. Egypt is highly unlikely to overcome these barriers to more rapid economic growth, so the pressure on its political community and state are bound to intensify as more of the population suffers from ever greater hardships.

The country's future thus turns on whether or not the pressures resulting from development failure can be managed sufficiently to prevent breakdown of the nation state. There appear to be two possible scenarios in which this could be accomplished. The first is that the country's remarkable endowments of state and nation, although much degraded, are sufficient to enable it to continue to limp along more or less as it is at present, aided by some good luck. President Sisi's dogged determination in this scenario begins to pay dividends. On the security front his forces gradually succeed in defeating the insurgency in the Sinai while stamping out acts of political violence elsewhere in the country. Greater confidence resulting from this success would enable him to reach a favorable accommodation with the Brotherhood and other Islamists, presumably weakened by that very success. Levels of external support for Egypt might also rise, both to help it meet the security challenge and then, once that was accomplished, to consolidate at home while assisting external benefactors in their counterterrorism efforts elsewhere, most notably Libya. Reconciliation with GCC states could be achieved and result in a resumption of subventions, albeit in lesser magnitude than in the 2012–15 period. President Trump might see a kindred spirit in President Sisi and throw considerably greater American weight behind him, maybe in turn causing the Russians and Chinese to follow suit in a renewed version of Cold War competition. Progress in resolving the Israeli–Palestinian conflict, possibly through the revival of the Arab and matching Israeli Peace Initiatives, which Egypt would ardently support, would entitle it to a claim on new public foreign assistance funds, to say nothing of it benefitting from intensified economic relations with Israel. Fearful of undocumented immigration from Egypt, the EU might also increase its levels of support.[1] New oil and gas discoveries could restore the country's status as a net exporter of fuels. Improved security in Egypt and neighboring states, combined with the attraction of low prices, could lure back an increasing number of tourists, while Suez Canal revenues could rise due to a resurgence of global trade. On the political front, grudging admiration for Sisi's accomplishments would solidify his position vis-à-vis the population as a whole and within the deep state. He would not only win re-election in 2018 for another four-year term, but would amend the constitution so he could be president for life.

Clearly it would be very unlikely for all of this good luck to bless Sisi and Egypt, but sufficient of it could enable them to persist as is into at least the immediate and medium-term futures. While a bit of a stretch of the imagination, this scenario is possible precisely because of Egypt's continuing relative strengths in a region beset with failing states and ungoverned spaces. In the land of the blind, the one-eyed man is king.

A second scenario involves political change engineered by and largely limited, at least at the outset, to the deep state. One version of this is the "Mubarak option," whereby the military decides that carrying the political baggage of an increasingly unpopular, discredited Sisi is dragging it down, so it replaces him with another officer, whether through an absolutely pre-emptive coup, or one in response to growing political troubles, including demonstrations. Following Sisi's removal his successor would undertake some liberalization measures akin to those launched by Sadat and Mubarak in the early days of their presidencies. Reconciliation would be sought with GCC states, possibly in the form of a new military alliance directed against Iran, an alliance that Trump's America might welcome and further support.

Another, less likely version, is that reformers from within the deep state dispatch Sisi as well as the high command beholden to him, reaching out to civilian elements, possibly including Islamists, in order to rebuild an at least semi-civilian political order, say more or less along the lines of Sadat's, but with some similarities to Tunisia's more democratic order. A "corrective revolution" of this sort would reduce the primacy of the security and armed forces, shifting power into the presidency, which would be more accessible to civilian political actors. This liberal version of Egypt's standard republican regime would be more attractive to the West, so presumably garner more support from it. Indeed, like present-day Tunisia, it could be trumpeted as a beacon of democracy in a region shrouded in political fog. Gatekeeping into the limited access order would be relaxed and the military economy partially civilianized. Were such reform initiatives to meet with political and economic success, they could gather momentum and begin to propel Egypt back up the slopes of authoritarian decay and material decline down which it has long been sliding. Europe in particular might be encouraged to engage more heavily with a reformed Egypt, investing in a variety of shared projects such as solar energy to be fed into grids on both sides of the Mediterranean, just-in-time manufacturing for fashion-conscious markets in trendy Europe, or intensification of horticulture for exports north into receptive winter markets.

These two versions of the scenario in which Sisi is replaced depend largely on political pressure mounting to the point that key actors in the deep state decide they have to take action, either stubbornly to preserve the status quo, or to reform it. Were either to occur, the flow-on effects, including at least some of the good luck associated with the first scenario, might be sufficient to sustain for some years the updated but still fundamentally authoritarian version of republican government from Nasser to Sisi; or in the case of more thoroughgoing reform, assist the semi-liberal government in consolidating itself while energizing the economy.

Finally, a breakdown scenario is regrettably also possible. It can be envisioned as taking any one of at least three forms. The first, but not most likely, is that the confrontation between Islamists and the government intensifies, essentially paralyzing the nation and ultimately fragmenting the deep state, some elements of which then join the Islamists. Ensuing developments come to resemble those in Libya, Yemen, or Syria, as the contending forces fragment, are joined by newly mobilized regional, tribal, and other elements, all of which square off against one another in Hobbesian fashion. But this version requires a stronger and more united Islamist opposition to the government than presently exists or is likely to emerge.

The second variation is a rerun of the "Tahrir Revolution," in which massive numbers of Egyptians pour into the streets in largely peaceful protests. This time around, however, the army and the people are not of one hand, with troops opening fire on demonstrators. Reactions then intensify on both sides, ultimately splitting the deep state's forces, some of which defect to increasingly well-armed, combative opposition forces. The situation spirals downhill in similar fashion to that just described, with power, as is typically the case in revolutions, shifting into the hands of the most radical elements. But this version of a largely middle-class uprising being transformed into a revolution or just system breakdown, requires that middle class to be willing again to enter the squares and the deep state to confront them and then to fragment. At present the middle class seems unlikely to find the energy to try the Midan al Tahrir option again, whereas the coherence of the deep state under pressure is unknown, although it is presumably much greater than in Libya, Yemen, or Syria.

Finally, there is the truly Hobbesian version of general system breakdown from the bottom. The accumulating hardships and misery of inhabitants of impoverished rural areas and urban slums, coupled with some mobilization by Islamists and clan and tribal leaders, causes them to become increasingly restive throughout the country, with security forces dashing from one locale to another to put them down with increasing force, in turn stimulating yet more uprisings. These amorphous, anomic outbreaks then merge into a more coherent, nation-wide challenge to the regime, which is unable to keep the lid on, in part because the Central Security Force, composed primarily of the very same poor, marginal elements contesting the regime, defects. And in this fashion Egypt, as above, comes to resemble other failed Arab states, with normal living no longer possible amid endemic violence and the collapse of services. That such miserable outcomes, even if unlikely, are imaginable, is testament to the current state of political and economic decay and the possibility it may intensify. It is thus an open question whether the country's much squandered inheritance of a relatively unified political community shaped and guided by a once more capable state will remain sufficient to weather approaching storms and hold the nation state together.

Notes

1 Eroding Historical Legacies

1 Nathan W. Toronto, "Egypt's 'Coup-Volution'," *Middle East Insight* (February 16, 2011).
2 For a concise, retrospective view of those bloody events, see Shahira Amin, "Three Years on, Wounds of Egypt's Deadly Sit-in Dispersals Linger," *Al Monitor* (August 21, 2016).
3 Ishac Diwan, "Understanding Revolution in the Middle East: The Central Role of the Middle Class," *Middle East Development Journal* 5:1 (March 27, 2013), http://belfercenter.hks.harvard.edu/files/Understanding%20Revolution.pdf.
4 Facundo Alvaredo and Thomas Piketty, "Measuring Top Incomes and Inequality in the Middle East: Data Limitations and Illustrations with the Case of Egypt," Working Paper 832, May 2014, Cairo, Economic Research Forum, http://erf.org.eg/wp-content/uploads/2014/07/832.pdf.
5 Roger Owen, *The Rise and Fall of Arab Presidents for Life*, Cambridge, MA: Harvard University Press, 2012.
6 Discrimination against Christians is reflected in legal restrictions on their building of churches. President Sisi promised to lift these legal restrictions and legislation to that effect was introduced in parliament in early 2016, but it has not been acted upon. The impact of this discrimination is reflected in the comparative numbers of churches and mosques, there being 2,869 of the former but 108,395 of the latter. Thus churches constitute some 2.5 percent of total places of worship, whereas their proportion of the population may be about three times greater. There is no

accepted official figure on the religious composition of the population. Its Christian component is estimated to be as low as 6 and as high as 15 percent. See "Under the Gun," *The Economist* (August 20, 2016), p. 42.

7 For a review of these dimensions and the research upon which they are based, see Robert Springborg, "The Precarious Economics of Arab Springs," *Survival* 53:6 (2011), pp. 85–104.

8 *Pocket World in Figures*, 2016 edition, London: The Economist, p. 23.

9 http://www.tradingeconomics.com/egypt/gdp-per-capita-ppp.

10 "World Bank: Egypt's Middle Class Shrank in the Lead-up to the Arab Spring," *Mada Masr* (May 22, 2016); Sherine Abdel-Razek, "Caught in the Middle," *Al Ahram Weekly* (December 22, 2016).

11 Study conducted by Omnia Helmy of the Egyptian Center for Economic Studies, cited in Nesma Nowar, 'Education Challenge', *Al Ahram Weekly*, 14–20 July 2011.

12 "World Bank: Egypt's Middle Class Shrank in the Lead-up to the Arab Spring."

13 "How to Improve, Through Skills Development and Job Creation, Access of Africa's Youth to the World of Work," *Egypt Country Report for the 2014 Ministerial Conference on Youth Employment*, Abidjan, Côte d'Ivoire (July 21–3, 2014), http://www.adeanet.org/min_conf_youth_skills_employment/sites/default/files/u24/Egypt%20Country%20Report_0.pdf.

14 Robert Springborg, "Effects of Patronage Systems and Clientelism on Citizenship in the Middle East," in Roel Meijer and Nils Butenschon (eds), *The Crisis of Citizenship in the Arab World*, Leiden: Brill (forthcoming 2017).

15 The survey was conducted by James B. Mayfield, who reports its findings in his *Field of Reeds: Social, Economic and Political Change in Rural Egypt*, Bloomington: AuthorHouse, 2012.

16 For a brief review of that evidence, see "Degrees of Democracy," *The Economist* (June 25, 2011), p. 88.

17 "Egypt's Illiteracy Rate Increases in 2013: CAPMAS Report," *Ahramonline* (September 7, 2014).

18 Sarah Elmeshad, "University Rankings: How Significant are They?," *Egypt Independent* (October 12, 2012); QS World University Rankings, 2015–16, http://www.topuniversities.com/university-rankings/world-university-rankings/2015#sorting=rank+region=6+country=21+faculty=+stars=false+search=.

19 "From Zero to Not much More," *The Economist* (June 4, 2016), p. 46.
20 http://siteresources.worldbank.org/INTMENA/Resources/EDU_02-Chap02-Education.pdf.
21 Cited in Clement Moore Henry and Robert Springborg, *Globalization and the Politics of Development in the Middle East*, Cambridge: Cambridge University Press, 2010, p. 188.
22 http://info.worldbank.org/governance/wgi/index.aspx#home.
23 For an assessment of the judiciary under the military, see David Risley, "Egypt's Judiciary: Obstructing or Assisting Reform?," Middle East Institute (January 13, 2016), http://www.mei.edu/content/at/egypt%E2%80%99s-judiciary-obstructing-or-assisting-reform.
24 The study is cited by Ahmid Hidji, "Sisi on Corruption in Local Governments: What Can I do About It?," *Al Monitor* (August 24, 2016).
25 On the increasing mobilization of Nubians and the bases for their claims, see "Egypt's Nubians: Let Them Go Home," *The Economist* (September 17, 2016).
26 Zeinab Abul-Magd, *Imagined Empires: A History of Revolt in Egypt*, Berkeley: University of California Press, 2013, pp. 3–4.
27 Charles Issawi, "The Japanese Model and the Middle East," in *The Middle East Economy: Decline and Recovery*, Princeton: Markus Wiener, 1995, pp. 165–84.

2 The Deep State Presides: Military, Presidency, and the Intelligence Services

1 For the history of the value of the pound, see "Timeline: The Egyptian Pound Over the Last Five Decades," *Egypt Independent* (November 4, 2016).
2 Douglass C. North, John Joseph Wallis, Steven B. Webb, and Barry R. Weingast, "Limited Access Orders: Rethinking the Problem of Development and Violence," Stanford University (January 25, 2011), https://web.stanford.edu/group/mcnollgast/cgi-bin/wordpress/wp-content/uploads/2013/10/Limited_Access_Orders_in_DW_-II_-2011.0125.submission-version.pdf.
3 Steffen Hertog, "Is There an Arab Variety of Capitalism?," Working Paper 1086, Cairo: Economic Research Forum, December 2016, p. 2.

4 Ishac Diwan, Philip Keefer and Marc Schiffbauer, "Pyramid Capitalism: Political Connections, Regulation, and Firm Productivity in Egypt," World Bank Group, Policy Research Working Paper 7354, July 2015, p. 9.
5 Neveen Wahish, "Egypt: The Importance of Connections," *Al Ahram Weekly* (January 26–February 1, 2017).
6 Ibid., p. 23.
7 Hazem Kandil, *The Power Triangle: Military, Security and Politics in Regime Change*, Oxford: Oxford University Press, 2016, p. 239.
8 Ibid., p. 247.
9 Waguih Ghali's fine novel, *Beer in the Snooker Club*, captures the sense of alienation felt by Copts from the new order. It was republished in London by Penguin, Vintage Editions, 2014.
10 Michael Mann, "The Autonomous Power of the State: Its Origins, Mechanisms and Results," *Archieves europeennes de sociologie* 25 (1984), pp. 185–213, https://www.sscnet.ucla.edu/soc/faculty/mann/Doc1.pdf.
11 Ibid., p. 113.
12 Ibid.
13 Ibid., p. 114.
14 "Reforming Taxation," *Al Ahram Weekly* (October 25, 2016).
15 http://taxfoundation.org/article/sources-government-revenue-across-oecd-2015.
16 "Reforming Taxation," *Al Ahram Weekly*.
17 "Reforming Taxation," *Al Ahram Weekly*.
18 Samer Soliman, *The Autumn of Dictatorship: Fiscal Crisis and Political Change in Egypt*, Stanford: Stanford University Press, 2011; Amr Adly, "Beyond Crony Capitalism: Failed Economic Transformations in North Africa," submitted for publication to *The Middle East Journal* (January 2017).
19 http://data.worldbank.org/indicator/GC.TAX.TOTL.GD.ZS; https://en.wikipedia.org/wiki/List_of_countries_by_tax_revenue_as_percentage_of_GDP.
20 Amr Adly, "Beyond Crony Capitalism," p. 10. See also https://knoema.com/atlas/Egypt/topics/Tourism/Capital-Investment/Capital-Investment-percent-share; *Survey of Social and Economic Developments in the ESCWA Region, 1999–2000, Part II*, Beirut: United Nations Commission for West Asia, 2001, p. 48; http://countrystudies.us/egypt/74.htm
21 Adly, "Beyond Crony Capitalism," pp. 8, 10.

22 Ibrahim Saif and Ahmed Ghoneim, "The Private Sector in Post-revolution Egypt," Carnegie Middle East Center, June 2013.
23 Adly, "Beyond Crony Capitalism," p. 11.
24 John Sfakianakis, "The Whales of the Nile: Networks, Business-men and Bureaucrats During the Era of Privatization in Egypt," in Steven Heydemann, *Networks of Privilege in the Middle East*, New York: Palgrave Macmillan, 2004, pp. 77–100.
25 Niveen Wahish, "The Importance of Connections," *Al Ahram Weekly* (January 26–February 1, 2017).
26 By 2017 GRU, or Russian Military Intelligence, was making a comeback at the expense of the FSB as Putin sought to balance off the two competing agencies. See Michael Weiss, "The GRU: Putin's No-Longer-So-Secret Weapon," *The Daily Beast* (December 31, 2016).
27 Anouar Abdel-Malek, *Egypt: Military Society. The Army Regime, the Left, and Social Change Under Nasser*, New York: Random House, 1968.
28 Kandil, *The Power Triangle*, pp. 285–8.
29 Philippe Droz-Vincent, "The Enduring Role of Egyptian Officers," unpublished ms (2017).
30 Active Military Manpower by Country, http://www.globalfirepower.com/active-military-manpower.asp.
31 Countries Ranked by Military Strength, http://www.globalfirepower.com/countries-listing.asp.
32 Ahmed Eleiba, "Looking South: The Expansion of Egypt's Naval Operations," *Ahramonline* (January 15, 2017).
33 The term "officer republic" is borrowed from Yezid Sayigh, "Above the State: The Officers' Republic in Egypt," *Carnegie Papers—Middle East*, Washington, DC: Carnegie Endowment for International Peace, 2012. On the role of officers in the state, see also Zeinab Abul-Magd, *Militarizing the Nation: Army, Business, and Revolution in Egypt, 1952–2015*, New York: Columbia University Press, 2016. For comparative information on the power of MENA militaries, see Elke Grawert and Zeinab Abul-Magd (eds), *Businessmen in Arms: How the Military and Other Armed Groups Profit in the MENA Region*, London: Rowan and Littlefield, 2016.
34 The term "Military Inc." is borrowed from Ayesha Siddiqa, *Military Inc.: Inside Pakistan's Military Economy*, London: Pluto, 2007. On the size and growth of Egypt's military economy in comparative perspective, see Grawert and Abul-Magd, *Businessmen in Arms*. See also Shana Marshall, "The Egyptian Armed

Forces and the Remaking of an Economic Empire," Washington, DC: Carnegie Middle East Center, April 2015; and Shana Marshall, "Egypt's Other Revolution: Modernizing the Military-Industrial Complex," *Jadaliyya* (February 10, 2012).

35 Egyptians consistently profess a higher level of trust in their military (over 80 percent) than any other Arabs, according to the Arab Democracy Barometer conducted by the Arab Reform Initiative, http://www.arabbarometer.org/content/online-data-analysis. For a review of the public opinion data on the military and on Sisi, see Robert Springborg, "President Sisi's Delegative Authoritarianism," Rome, Istituto Affari Internazionale, Working Paper 15 (July 26, 2015).

36 On the role of Military Intelligence in selecting candidates for the 2015 parliamentary elections, see Hossam Bahgat, "Anatomy of an Election: How Egypt's 2015 Parliament was Elected to Maintain Loyalty to the President," *Mada Masr* (March 14, 2016).

37 Florence Gaub, "Civil-Military Relations in the MENA: Between Fragility and Resilience," European Union Institute for Security Studies, *Chaillot Papers*, No. 139 (October 2016), p. 16.

38 Ibid.

39 For an assessment of the military's relations with global capital, see Shana Marshall and Joshua Stacher, "Egypt's Generals and Transnational Capital," *Middle East Report* 262 (Spring, 2012).

40 On the military's manipulation of school history curricula since 1952, see Sudarsan Raghavan, "In New Egyptian Textbooks: 'It's Like the Revolution Didn't Happen'," *Washington Post* (April 23, 2016).

41 Nevine El-Aref, "New Project to Showcase Egypt's Ancient Military History," *Ahramonline* (April 6, 2016).

42 "Shocking Historical Errors leave Egypt's Military Museum Curator Red-Faced," *The New Arab* (September 23, 2016).

43 Ibid.

44 Khalid Hassan, "How Far is Egypt Willing to Go to Have Strong Grip on Media?," *Al Monitor* (February 12, 2017).

45 For a discussion of the range, quality, and prices of military supplied goods and services, see Abul-Magd, *Militarizing the Nation*.

46 Sayed Elhadidi, "How Will Egypt Police its Police Force?," *Al Monitor* (May 11, 2016).

47 Kandil, *The Power Triangle*, p. 236.

48 David Kirkpatrick, "Recordings Suggest Emirates and Egyptian Military Pushed Ousting of Morsi," *New York Times* (March 1, 2015).

49 Robert Springborg, "Abd al Fattah al Sisi: New Face of the Old Guard," BBC World Service (March 26, 2014), http://www.bbc.com/news/world-middle-east-26188023. See also David Kirkpatrick, "Egypt's New Strongman: Sisi Knows Best," *New York Times* (May 24, 2014).

50 Hossam Bahgat, "A Coup Busted: The Secret Trial of 26 Officers for Plotting 'Regime Change' with the Brotherhood," *Mada Masr* (October 14, 2015).

51 Bahgat, "Anatomy of an Election."

52 "When Will Cairo Recognize its Responsibility for the Death of Italian Student," *al Quds al Arabi*, reported in *Mideast Wire* (April 8, 2016), https://mideastwire.com/page/articleFree.php?id=60223; "Italian Judicial Sources Refute Anonymous tip on Regeni's Death to La Repubblica," *Mada Masr* (April 6, 2016).

53 The Nation's Future Party more or less disintegrated as a result of infighting during its first year in parliament, with many of its members using the connections it had provided to move on to better things. Muhammad Badran himself resigned as leader in September 2016, saying he was taking up a scholarship at an unnamed American university. He had been absent from Egypt from January 2016. See "Mohamed Badran Resigns as President of Nation's Future Party," *Mada Masr* (September 27, 2016).

54 Sisi's reliance on Military Intelligence and the subordination to it of General Intelligence is reflected by the continual purging of generals from the latter, of which 113 have been removed in eight separate waves between July 2014 and February 2017. "Egypt's Sisi Threatens to Remove Dissidents Within State Institutions," *The New Arab* (February 10, 2017).

55 The Civil Service Reform Act, Law 18, decreed in 2015 before parliament convened, was the only decree of 342 laws issued in its absence which the parliament then rejected, presumably at least in part out of MP's fear of the political consequences of reducing salaries and limiting employment in the public service. That President Sisi fully endorsed the draft legislation is suggestive of his contempt for the civilian administration, his need to reduce its cost, and his willingness to bear the political costs of cracking down on it. For a discussion of its content and proposed revisions to it following its rejection, see Doaa Abdel-Moneim,

"Losing Hard-Earned Gains?," *Al Ahram Weekly* 1291 (April 14, 2016).

56 In 2015 the World Economic Forum ranked Egypt's educational system 139th out of the 140 countries assessed. Klaus Schwaub, *The Global Competitiveness Report, 2015–16*, Geneva: World Economic Forum, 2015, http://www3.weforum .org/docs/gcr/2015–2016/Global_Competitiveness_Report _2015–2016.pdf.

57 Israeli–Egyptian cooperation has grown under Sisi to include virtually all areas of mutual concern, including intelligence sharing. "Israel Reports Unprecedented Intelligence Cooperation with Egypt," *Middle East Online* (April 20, 2016), cited in *Marsad Egypt* (April 21, 2016) http://www.marsad.eg/en/2016/04/20/israel-reports-unprecedented-intelligence-cooperation-egypt.

58 Kirkpatrick, "Recordings Suggest Emirates and Egyptian Military Pushed Ousting of Morsi."

59 Hazem Kandil, *Soldiers, Spies, and Statesmen: Egypt's Road to Revolt*, London: Verso, 2012, p. 40.

60 For an overall review of human rights and their violation in 2015, see *Egypt: Country Reports on Human Rights Practices for 2015*, Washington, DC: US State Department, Bureau of Democracy, Human Rights and Labor, April 2016. For "disappearances" in 2016 see "Giulio Regeni: The Face of Egypt's Dark Disappearances," *The New Arab* (April 5, 2016). See also Viviana Mazza, "Egypt: Enforced Disappearances under Sisi Explained: Giulio and the Others," *Corriere della Sera* (April 4, 2016); and "Egypt: Children Reported Tortured, 'Disappeared,'" Human Rights Watch (April 21, 2016), https://www.hrw.org/news/2016/04/21/egypt-children-reported-tortured-disappeared?mc_cid=10401a78d1&mc_eid=aff1f61ec0.

61 Kandil, *The Power Triangle*, p. 267.

62 Nadeen Shaker, "College Students in Egypt Keep Getting Arrested, Disappeared and Killed," *Vice News* (June 12, 2015).

63 Egypt's ranking on the Press Freedom Index fell from 127th in the world at the end of the Mubarak era to 159th under Sisi in 2016. In April of that year at least twenty journalists were under detention "for trumped up charges," making the country "one of the world's biggest prisons for media personnel." "Egypt Falls Again in Press Freedom Index, Now Ranked 159th," Reporters Without Borders (April 20, 2016), https://rsf.org/en/news/egypt-falls-again-world-press-freedom-index-now-ranked-159th?mc_cid=e1709a9dcd&mc_eid=aff1f61ec0. Egypt fell several places

from 2014–15 to 2015–16 on Freedom House's Press Freedom Index, with that organization noting that only China detained more journalists during the year. "Egypt: Freedom of the Press, 2016," Freedom House, April 2016, https://freedomhouse.org/report/freedom-press/2016/egypt?mc_cid=57e1b9c79f&mc_eid=aff1f61ec0

64 Jannis Grimm, "Repressing Egypt's Civil Society," *SWP Comment*, Berlin: German Institute for International and Security Studies, August, 2015; and Todd Ruffner, "Under Threat: Egypt's Systematic Campaign against NGOs," Washington, DC: Project on Middle East Democracy, March 2015.

65 Kandil, *Soldiers, Spies and Statesmen*, p. 22, citing Niccolo Machiavelli, *The Prince*, Indianapolis: Hackett Publishing, 1995, p. 20.

66 Kirkpatrick, "Egypt's New Strongman, Sisi Knows Best."

67 Ibid.

68 Ibid.

69 Karl Vick, "Egypt's al-Sisi: The Field Marshal Who Could be Pharaoh," *Time* (January 27, 2014).

70 Alex Wright, "Sisi Declares Himself God-Send," *The New Arab* (June 8, 2015).

71 "Cry me a River: Sisi Tears up During Speech," *The New Arab* (December 27, 2016).

72 Kandil, *Soldiers, Spies, and Statesmen*, pp. 24–5.

73 On Sisi's religiosity, see Robert Springborg "The Man on Horseback," *Foreign Policy* (July 2, 2013), and "General al Sisi's Islamist Agenda for Egypt," *Foreign Affairs* (July 28, 2013).

74 A December 2014 poll conducted by the Egyptian Center for Public Opinion Research (Baseera) revealed an overall approval rating of 86 percent, with 79 percent of respondents reporting they would vote for him in a presidential election. The overall approval rating was down slightly from the same organization's poll results in the previous month, although the fall in "highly approve" responses was from 66 percent to 58 percent and yet more substantial among youths, where it fell from 57 percent to 49 percent. In the November poll 82 percent of Egyptians reported they would vote for Sisi. "Sisi's Approval Rating Shows Signs of Slipping, Suggests Poll," *Mada Masr* (December 15, 2014). Sisi's approval rating bounced back up by May 2015, when the same organization's polling found it at an all-time high of 89 percent, with 72 percent of those over 50 highly approving of his performance, compared to 55 percent of those under

30. Emir Nader, "President al Sisi's Rates at all-time High Despite Worsening Security," *Daily News Egypt* (May 9, 2015). Data on polls conducted by Baseera are reported on the organization's website, www.baseera.com.eg. For a report on the October 2016 Baseera poll results, see Hend el Behary, "Sisi's Satisfaction Rating Among Egyptians Falls to 68 Percent: Baseera Poll," *Egypt Independent* (October 23, 2016).

75 See Mona El-Nahhas, "Resurrecting a Ruling Party?," *Al Ahram Weekly* (October 25, 2016).

76 The rankings are included in *The Economist*'s annual publication, *The World*. For the most complete discussion of the indices, see Laza Kekic, "The Economist Intelligence Unit's Index of Democracy," *The World in 2007*, http://www.economist.com/media/pdf/DEMOCRACY_INDEX_2007_v3.pdf.

77 Democracy Index, Economist Intelligence Unit, 2014, http://www.sudestada.com.uy/Content/Articles/421a313a-d58f-462e-9b24-2504a37f6b56/Democracy-index-2014.pdf.

78 Guillermo A. O'Donell, "Delegative Democracy," *Journal of Democracy* 5:1 (January, 1994), pp. 55–69.

79 Ibid., p. 61.

80 Ibid., p. 62.

81 Ibid., p. 60.

82 Ibid.

83 Tom Rollins, "Egypt's Poor Expect Sisi to Deliver on Campaign Promises," *Al Monitor* (January 27, 2014).

84 Stephen Kalin, "Sisi's Economic Vision for Egypt: Back to the Future," *Reuters* (May 22, 2014)

85 Ibid.

86 "Egypt's Largest Church and Mosque to be Built at New Capital: Sisi," *Ahramonline* (January 6, 2017).

87 O'Donell, "Delegative Democracy," p. 61.

88 Ibid., p. 60.

89 Ibid., p. 67.

90 Ibid.

3 Under the Thumb: Bureaucrats, Judges, and Parliamentarians

1 Sarah Smierciak, *Assembling Egypt's Business-State Relations: Cosmopolitan Capital and International Networks of Exclusion, 2003–2011*, PhD thesis submitted to Oxford University, January 2017.

2 Nathan Brown, "Egypt's Wide State Reassembles Itself," Carnegie Endowment for International Peace (July 17, 2013), http://carnegieendowment.org/2013/07/17/egypt-s-wide-state-reassembles-itself/gfvk.

3 Ahmed Aleem, "Egypt Swears in New Cabinet Members After Tough Search," *Al Monitor* (February 16, 2017).

4 Emir Nader, "Off the Books: Egypt's Hidden $9.4 Billion," *Daily News Egypt* (June 24, 2015).

5 Hazem Beblawi, *Arba Shuhur fi Qafas Al Hukuma* (Four Months in the Government's Cage), Cairo: Shrouk Publishing House, 2012.

6 Nathan Brown, "Egypt Has Replaced a Single Dictator With a Slew of Dictatorial Institutions," Carnegie Endowment for International Peace (January 26, 2014), http://carnegieendowment.org/2014/01/26/egypt-has-replaced-single-dictator-with-slew-of-dictatorial-institutions-pub-54322.

7 Robert Bianchi, *Unruly Corporatism: Associational Life in Twentieth Century Egypt*, Oxford: Oxford University Press, 1989.

8 Brynjar Lia, *The Society of Muslim Brothers in Egypt: The Rise of an Islamic Movement, 1928–1942*, London: Ithaca Press, 1999.

9 Mona El-Ghobashy, "Dissidence and Deference Among Egyptian Judges," *Middle East Research and Information Project* 279 (Summer 2016), http://www.merip.org/mer/mer279/dissidence-deference-among-egyptian-judges?ip_login_no_cache=905ed a51dfb54f07f1ef9a08f1292966; "Judicial Diversity Statistics 2015," Judicial Office Statistics Bulletin, https://www.judiciary.gov.uk/wp-content/uploads/2015/07/judicial_diversity_statistics_20151.pdf.

10 See http://www.doingbusiness.org/rankings.

11 See http://worldjusticeproject.org/rule-law-around-world.

12 Tamir Moustafa argues that the oversupply of lawyers has rendered litigation very inexpensive, thus stimulating frivolous lawsuits of all kinds. Tamir Moustafa, "The Islamist Trend in Egyptian Law," *Politics and Religion* 3 (2010), pp. 610–30.

13 "National Salvation Front and Tamarod Call on Army to Intervene," *Daily News Egypt* (July 3, 2013).

14 Nasser had created a "constitutional court" in 1969 staffed by judges on two-year appointments and intended not to reinforce constitutionalism but to undermine it. Its purpose was to prevent other courts from applying judicial review, a practice referred to as "abstention control" in which they had increasingly engaged. It took until 1979 for enabling legislation to be passed and judges to be appointed to Sadat's SCC.

15 El-Ghobashy, "Dissidence and Deference Among Egyptian Judges."
16 Ibid.
17 Sahar Aziz, "The Expanding Jurisdiction of Egypt's Military Courts," *Sada*, Carnegie Endowment for International Peace (October 12, 2016), http://carnegieendowment.org/sada/index.cfm?fa=64840.
18 Rana Allam, "Egypt: What is Done in the Name of Stability," *LobeLog Foreign Policy* (October 28, 2016), https://lobelog.com/egypt-what-is-done-in-the-name-of-stability.
19 Sahar Aziz, "Egypt's Judiciary, Coopted," *Sada*, Carnegie Endowment for International Peace (August 20, 2014), http://carnegieendowment.org/sada/?fa=56426, p. 2.
20 Ibid.
21 Nathalie Bernard-Maugiron, *Judges and Political Reform in Egypt*, Oxford: Oxford University Press, 2009. Republished by Cairo Scholarship Online, January 2012, http://cairo.universitypressscholarship.com/view/10.5743/cairo/9789774162015.001.0001/upso-9789774162015-chapter-4.
22 Aziz, "Egypt's Judiciary, Coopted."
23 For details of how such cooperation worked under Sadat and Mubarak, see Tamir Moustafa, *The Struggle for Constitutional Power: Law, Politics, and Economic Development in Egypt*, Cambridge: Cambridge University Press, 2007.
24 Brown, "Egypt's Wide State Reassembles Itself."
25 Nathan Brown, "Egypt's Constitutional Cul-De-Sac," Carnegie Endowment for International Peace (March 31, 2014), http://carnegieendowment.org/2014/03/31/egypt-s-constitutional-cul-de-sac-pub-55310.
26 Ibid.
27 "Egypt: Hundreds Disappeared and Tortured Amid Wave of Brutal Repression," Amnesty International (July 13, 2016), https://www.amnesty.org/en/latest/news/2016/07/egypt-hundreds-disappeared-and-tortured-amid-wave-of-brutal-repression.
28 Allam, "Egypt: What is Done in the Name of Stability."
29 Aziz, "The Expanding Jurisdiction of Egypt's Military Courts."
30 Ibid.
31 Aziz, "Egypt's Judiciary, Coopted."
32 "State Council Senior Employee Was Killed in Custody," *Egypt Independent* (January 4, 2017).
33 "Egypt's SJC Warns Judges of Publishing News Related to Judiciary Affairs on Social Media," *Ahramonline* (January 9, 2017).

34 Philippe C. Schmitter and Terry Lynn Karl, "What Democracy Is...And Is Not," *Journal of Democracy* (summer 1991), pp. 3–16 (p. 9), http://www.ned.org/docs/Philippe-C-Schmitter-and-Terry-Lynn-Karl-What-Democracy-is-and-Is-Not.pdf.

35 Since the Nasser era the lower house had been named the *Maglis al Shaab*, meaning the House of the People, a leftist/populist reference. That "Deputies" were substituted for "People" may be reflective of the broader shift to the right of Sisi's regime and its desire to embed it in Egyptian history prior to the Republic.

36 Scott Williamson and Nathan J. Brown, "Egypt's New Law for Parliamentary Elections Sets up a Weak Legislature," Atlantic Council (June 24, 2014), http://www.atlanticcouncil.org/blogs/menasource/egypt-s-new-law-for-parliamentary-elections-sets-up-a-weak-legislature.

37 Ibid.

38 See the report by the Tahrir Institute for Middle East Policy at: http://timep.org/pem/elections-summary.

39 See https://www.humanrights.gov/dyn/2015/12/egyptian-parliamentary-elections.

40 The nominal upgrading in the 2014 constitution of the powers of the cabinet at the expense of those of the president also have little if any actual impact. According to Ziad Bahaa-Eldin, "In reality executive power rests with the presidency and the government is not an active partner in defining state policy. Its role is limited to practical implementation...the Cabinet's circumscribed role and powers denies it the ability to think in the long term, coordinate effectively among ministries and state agencies, and respond swiftly to developing events and crises." "Egypt: Do we really need a Cabinet Shuffle?," *Ahramonline* (January 12, 2017). The cabinet did not consider the 2016 IMF loan approved by the president in November until January 2017. "Egypt's Cabinet Approves IMF Loan Agreement," *Ahramonline* (January 11, 2017).

41 Williamson and Brown, "Egypt's New Law for Parliamentary Elections Sets up a Weak Legislature."

42 See open budget index at http://www.internationalbudget.org/opening-budgets/open-budget-initiative/open-budget-survey.

43 Gamal Essam El-Din, "MP Sadat to be Investigated for 'Leaking Draft NGO Law to Foreign Embassies'," *Ahramonline* (November 13, 2016).

44 Ibid.

45 Gamal Essam El-Din, "Conflict of Loyalty?," *Al Ahram Weekly* (October 25, 2016).
46 George Mikhail, "Why a Cop Controls Human Rights in Egypt's Parliament," *Al Monitor* (November 9, 2016).
47 "Egypt Parliament Speaker Warns MPs Not to Criticize Monetary Policy," http://english.alarabiya.net/en/News/middle -east/2016/05/23/Egypt-parliament-speaker-warns-MPs-not-to-criticise-monetary-policy.html.
48 Ahmed Hidji, "Just How Independent is Egypt's Parliament?," *Al Monitor* (May 9, 2016).
49 "Parliamentary Speaker Warns MPs to Stay Mum on Monetary Policies," *Mada Masr* (May 23, 2016).
50 Ibid.
51 "Egypt Parliament Divided: Representatives' Budget or Not?," *Egypt Independent* (February 4, 2017).
52 Mohamed Hamama, "Has Parliament been Sidelined in Egypt's Loan Approval Process?," *Mada Masr* (November 14, 2016).
53 Gamal Essam El-Din, "Leftist MP to be Investigated," *Al Ahram Weekly* (November 10–16, 2016).
54 See http://worldjusticeproject.org/rule-law-around-world.
55 Ahmed Aboulenein, "Challenging Government, Egypt's Parliament Approves 'Repressive' NGO Bill," *Reuters* (November 15, 2016).
56 Rana Mamdouh, "What has Happened to the NGO Law?," *Mada Masr* (January 8, 2017).
57 Ayah Aman, "Why Was Pro-Government TV Host Taken Off Air?," *Al Monitor* (January 23, 2017); "Tarek Nour's le Marche Rescheduled for April, Newspaper," *Egyptian Independent* (February 19, 2017).

4 Political and Civil Society: Little Room to Breathe

1 Indra Overland, "Civil Society, Public Debate and Resource Management," in Indra Overland (ed.), *Public Brainpower: Civil Society and Natural Resource Management*, London: Palgrave Macmillan, 2017.
2 The former head of Egypt's General Authority for Investments, Ziad Bahaa-Eldin, lamenting the lack of input into critical economic decision making that he considered responsible for the deepening economic crisis in early 2017, wrote that, "It isn't every day the General Federation of the Chambers of Commerce

together with the biggest Investors' Association in Egypt—
representing most of the Egyptian private sector—publish an
appeal to the president complaining about the policies adopted
by the government and the central bank, as they did last week.
The call for help is illustrative both of economic mismanagement
and the lack of mechanisms and channels to resolve differences
and manage competing interests in society." "Before the Economy
Sinks," *Ahramonline* (January 4, 2017).

3 See http://www.prosperity.com.
4 Michael Lipka, "Muslims and Islam: Key Findings in the U.S.
and Around the World" (December 27, 2015), http://www.
pewresearch.org/fact-tank/2016/07/22/muslims-and-islam-key-
findings-in-the-u-s-and-around-the-world.
5 See http://www.pewforum.org/2013/04/30/the-worlds-muslims-
religion-politics-society-beliefs-about-sharia.
6 Ibid.
7 Gamal Soltan et al., "The Arab Barometer Project," Cairo: al
Ahram Center for Political and Strategic Studies, June 2011, pp.
13–14, accessed through http://www.arabbarometer.org/content/
arab-barometer-ii-egypt.
8 Cornelius Hulsman, "Discrepancies Between Coptic Statistics in the Egyptian Census and Estimates Provided by the
Coptic Orthodox Church," Cairo: MIDEO, June 2012, http://
www.arabwestreport.info/sites/default/files/pdfs/AWRpapers/
paper52.pdf.
9 Mai Shams El-Din, "Copts Debate Abolishing Marriage Prepa
ration Sessions in Churches," *Mada Masr* (November 10, 2016).
10 Georges Fahmi, "A New Law in Old Bottles," *Diwan*, Carnegie
Middle East Center (September 16, 2016), http://carnegie-mec.org/
diwan/64602.
11 Mona Eltahawy, "Egypt's Cruelty to Christians," *New York
Times* (December 22, 2016).
12 Philippe Droz-Vincent, "The Enduring Role of Egyptian Officers,"
unpublished ms, 2017.
13 "Naguib Sawiris 7th Richest Billionaire in Africa, Second in
Egypt," *Egypt Independent* (January 13, 2017).
14 George Mikhail, "Leader of Egypt's Winning Party Outlines
What's Next," *Al Monitor* (December 3, 2015).
15 Asmaa Naguib, "The Elephant in the Room (Part I): The State
and Sectarian Violence," *Mada Masr* (September 26, 2016).
16 Demonstrations against the government by young Copts in front
of Cairo's Coptic Cathedral, in the wake of the December 11,

2016 bombing of a church in the cathedral complex that claimed twenty-six lives, focused on the state's laxity in protecting Christians. Ahmed Hidji, "Is Egypt's Sisi Losing Coptic Support?," *Al Monitor* (December 26, 2016).

17 Ahmed Morsy and Nathan Brown, "Egypt's al-Azhar Steps Forward," Carnegie Endowment for International Peace (November 7, 2013), http://carnegieendowment.org/2013/11/07/egypt-s-al-azhar-steps-forward-pub-53536.

18 H.A. Hellyer and Nathan Brown, "Leading from Everywhere: The History of Centralized Islamic Religious Authority," Carnegie Endowment for International Peace (June 15, 2015), http://carnegieendowment.org/2015/06/15/leading-from-everywhere-history-of-centralized-islamic-religious-authority-pub-60413.

19 "Rift Escalates, Becomes Public between Sisi, Al Azhar," *Egypt Independent* (January 26, 2017).

20 Morsy and Brown, "Egypt's al-Azhar Steps Forward."

21 This figure is given by the Central Agency for Public Mobilization and Statistics, according to Steven T. Brooke, "Mr. Morsi's Machine: Islamic Infrastructure and Electoral Mobilization in Egypt's 2012 Presidential Election," paper delivered to the annual conference of the Middle East Studies Association, Boston, MA, September 19, 2016.

22 "Egypt Cracks down on Quran Schools," *Gulf News* (November 16, 2016).

23 Brynjar Lia, *The Society of the Muslim Brothers in Egypt: The Rise of an Islamic Mass Movement, 1928–1942*, London: Ithaca Press, 1999.

24 Hazem Kandil, *Inside the Brotherhood*, Cambridge: Polity Press, 2014, p. 1

25 Hazem Kandil, *The Power Triangle: Military, Security and Politics in Regime Change*, Oxford: Oxford University Press, 2016, p. 17.

26 Stéphane Lacroix, "Egypt's Pragmatic Salafis: The Politics of Hizb al-Nour," Carnegie Endowment for International Peace (November 1, 2016), http://carnegieendowment.org/2016/11/01/egypt-s-pragmatic-salafis-politics-of-hizb-al-nour-pub-64902.

27 Ibid., p. 4.

28 "Egypt Police Arrest Suspects Allegedly Behind Murder of Top Prosecutor," *Ahramonline* (November 4, 2016).

29 Ibid.

30 Scott Stewart, "Tracking the Hasam Movement, Egypt's Ambitious New Militant Group," *Stratfor Report* (October 6, 2016).

31 "Security Forces in Hunt for Terrorists in Assiut Mountains," *Egypt Independent* (January 29, 2017).

32 *Egypt Security Watch, Quarterly Report*, The Tahrir Institute for Middle East Policy, Washington, DC, September 2016, https:// timep.org/commentary/quarterly-report-2016-q2.

33 Ibid., p. 18.

34 "Army Has Killed 500 Militants in North Sinai Operations," *Ahramonline* (February 10, 2017).

35 "Egypt's Counterterrorism Efforts Taking Toll on Resources: Sisi," *Ahramonline* (January 10, 2017).

36 "MPs Criticize Interior Ministry Over Reported False Info," *Egypt Independent* (January 16, 2017).

37 Steven A. Cook, "Egypt's Nightmare: Sisi's Dangerous War on Terror," *Foreign Affairs* (November/December, 2016).

38 "Security Forces in Hunt for Terrorists in Assiut Mountains," *Egypt Independent* (January 29, 2017).

39 Cook, "Egypt's Nightmare."

40 Ibid.

41 "ElBaradei: 'Government Threatened to Destroy Me Over Rabaa Opposition,'" *The New Arab* (November 15, 2016).

42 "Who Murdered Giulio Regeni?," *Guardian* (October 4, 2016).

43 Khaled Mansour, "The Stasi, Freud and Egypt's Predicament (Part I)," *Mada Masr* (October 21, 2016).

44 "Journalists Sentenced to Prison Over Offending Interior Ministry," *Egypt Independent* (November 16, 2016).

45 "Bank Account of Egyptian Torture Victim Centre Suspended," *The New Arab* (November 11, 2016).

46 "HRW Criticizes Placement of Over 1,500 People in Egypt on Terror List," *Egypt Independent* (January 25, 2017).

47 "Infinite Eyes in the Network: Government Escalates Attack on Secure Communication," *Mada Masr* (January 25, 2017).

48 See http://pomed.org/civil-society/ngos/egypt-under-president-sisi-worse-than-under-mubarak-or-morsi.

49 Ahmed Morsy, "Poison in the Honey," *Al Ahram Weekly* (December 1, 2016).

50 World Justice Project, http://worldjusticeproject.org/rule-law-around-world.

51 Ziad Bahaa-Eldin, "Can the Revision of the Protest Law Open a Fresh Page?," *Ahramonline* (November 3, 2016).

52 Amr Hamzawy, "Egypt's Parliament Opens the Door for More Repression," Carnegie Endowment for International Peace (September 22, 2016), http://carnegieendowment.org/2016/09/22/egypt-s-parliament-opens-door-for-more-repression-pub-64666.

53 Diaa Hadid and Nour Youssef, "Egyptian Police Officer Gets Life Term for Killing in Dispute Over Tea," *New York Times* (November 16, 2016).
54 Ibid.
55 Amr Mostafa, "Egypt Seeks to Crack Down on Killings by Police," *Al Monitor* (October 9, 2016).
56 Atef Said, "Egypt's Long Labor History," *Solidarity* (September–October 2009)
57 "Egypt Police Raid Journalists' Syndicate, Arrest Two Journalists," Committee to Protect Journalists (May 2, 2016), https://cpj.org/2016/05/egypt-police-raid-journalists-syndicate-arrest-two.php.
58 Haitham Gabr, "Public Transport Workers: Dissidents Across Different Regimes," *Mada Masr* (November 18, 2016).
59 Ibid.
60 Gamal Essam El-Din, "Towards a Politics of Consensus," *Al Ahram Weekly* (November 3, 2016).
61 James M. Dorsey, "Under Pressure, Egyptian President Promises Change," *The World Post* (October 30, 2016), http://www.huffingtonpost.com/james-dorsey/under-pressure-egyptian-p_b_12709666.html.
62 Ibid.
63 Jano Charbel, "Out of the Syndicates," *Mada Masr* (December 11, 2014).
64 El-Sayed Gamal El-Din, "Deputy Head of Doctors Union Mona Mina Released on Bail After Questioning," *Ahramonline* (December 3, 2016).

5 Reaping What is Sown

1 The Egyptian Cotton Association estimates that 90 percent of global textiles labeled as containing Egyptian cotton do not in fact do so. Arwa Gaballa and Eric Knecht, "Crackdown on Fake Cotton Helps Revive Egyptian Crop," *Business Report* (February 13, 2017).
2 James B. Mayfield, *Field of Reeds: Social, Economic, and Political Change in Rural Egypt: In Search of Civil Society and Good Governance*, Bloomington, IN: Author House, 2012, p. 289.
3 Hanaa Kheir-El-Din and Heba El-Laithy, "Agricultural Productivity Growth, Employment and Poverty in Egypt," Working Paper 129, Cairo: Economic Research Forum, February 2008, p. 3.

4 Yahya M. Sadowski, *Political Vegetables? Businessman and Bureaucrat in the Development of Egyptian Agriculture*, Washington, DC: The Brookings Institution, 1991.
5 The scores of studies and reports produced by USAID/Cairo during this period can be found online at the Agency's Development Experience Clearinghouse, https://dec.usaid.gov/dec/(F(5jvMjqkbC8sj1Zzn5zyej9C_K2L5gsdnBJLOS5r2Ay7p_ADwR6hTD4aaHZeP5-si3FVirW6EJrHFIg1SE1sOsHusTz-5tAUIeKsYfW7t3Q81))/home/Default.aspx.
6 "Egypt's Wheat Reserves Enough to Last for Five Months: Supply Minister," *Ahramonline* (January 3, 2017).
7 Sadowski, *Political Vegetables?*, pp. 149–90.
8 Ray Bush, "Food Security in Egypt," in Zahra Babar and Suzi Mirgani (eds), *Food Security in the Middle East*, London: Hurst and Company, 2014, p. 92.
9 Bent Hansen, *Egypt and Turkey: The Political Economy of Poverty, Equity, and Growth*, Oxford: Oxford University Press, 1991, see esp. pp. 532–6; and Roger Owen, "Large Landowners, Agricultural Progress and the State in Egypt, 1800–1970," in Alan Richards (ed.), *Food States and Peasants*, Boulder: Westview Press, 1986.
10 Leonard Binder, *In a Moment of Enthusiasm: Political Power and the Second Stratum in Egypt*, Chicago: University of Chicago Press, 1978.
11 Bush, "Food Security in Egypt," p. 99.
12 By 2017 arrears to international energy companies had been reduced to $3.5 billion, which the minister of petroleum pledged in January to continue to pay off in monthly installments, noting however that the foreign currency shortage would make "the drawing down of those debts more difficult." "Egypt Committed to Repaying $3.5 bln to Foreign Firms Says Minister," *Al Arabiya Net* (January 24, 2017).
13 "Egypt Suez Canal Revenue Drops to 3.108 bln EGP in Feb," *Reuters* (March 22, 2016).
14 "Egypt Reports 21 Month Low in Suez Canal Revenues in November," *Ahramonline* (December 22, 2016).
15 "Remittances to Developing Countries Edge up Slightly in 2015," World Bank, press release (April 13, 2016), http://www.worldbank.org/en/news/press-release/2016/04/13/remittances-to-developing-countries-edge-up-slightly-in-2015; *Migration and Remittances Fact Book, 2016, Third Edition*, Washington, DC: World Bank, 2016, http://siteresources.worldbank.org/INTPROSPECTS/

Resources/334934–1199807908806/4549025–1450455807487/
Factbookpart1.pdf

16 See http://www.tradingeconomics.com/egypt/remittances/forecast.
17 *Travel and Tourism: Economic Impact 2014, Egypt*, World
    Tourism and Travel Council, 2014, http://sp.wttc.org/-/media/
    files/reports/economic-impact-research/country-reports-2014/
    egypt2014.pdf.
18 Ibid.
19 "Balance of Payments Performance During July/March 2015/2016,"
    Central Bank of Egypt, press release, available via https://ace-
    notebook.com/press-release-central-bank-of-egypt-free-related-
    pdf.html.
20 "US Urges Citizens to Consider Risks of Travel to Egypt," *Aswat
    Masriya* (December 24, 2016).
21 "Israel Advises its Nationals in Sinai to Leave, Citing Attack
    Risk," *Egypt Independent* (January 25, 2017).
22 See http://economicsandpeace.org/wp-content/uploads/2016/06/
    GPI-2016-Report_2.pdf.
23 *Migration and Remittances Fact Book, 2016, Third Edition*,
    Washington, DC: World Bank, 2016, http://siteresources.
    worldbank.org/INTPROSPECTS/Resources/334934–
    1199807908806/4549025–1450455807487/Factbookpart1.pdf.
24 By the end of 2016 core inflation was running at 26 percent and
    the most vital retail inflation index, that for food, at over 28
    percent. "Egypt's Cost of Living Soars as Currency Dives," *Aswat
    Masriya* (January 10, 2017).
25 "Tariffs for 364 Commodities to Increase," *Egypt Independent*
    (December 2, 2016).
26 Mohamed Hamama, "Sisi Says Military Economy is 1.5% of
    Egypt's GDP, But How Accurate is This?," *Mada Masr* (Novem-
    ber 2, 2016). That criticism of the growth of the military's role
    in the economy continued to mount was suggested by Sisi's state-
    ment a few weeks later in which he dismissed rumors that its
    share was 20–50 percent, saying this time it was only 2 percent.
    He made the statement while opening a production line at the
    military-owned Nasr Company for Chemicals, which operates
    twenty-five factories. "Egypt's Sisi Dismisses Claim That Army's
    Economy Stands at 20–50% of GDP," *Ahramonline* (December
    24, 2016). According to Transparency International, "Egypt's
    entire defence budget (estimated to be around $4.4 billion) is
    classified as a state secret and no details on defence spending
    are available." Transparency International Defence and Security,

Global Defence Anti-Corruption Index, Egypt, http://government.defenceindex.org/countries/egypt-arab-rep.

27 Thom Shanker, "U.S. Sold $40 Billion of Weapons in 2015, Topping Global Market," *New York Times* (December 27, 2016); "US Report: Egypt Topped Developing Countries in Arms Imports in 2015," *Mada Masr* (December 27, 2016).

28 "Egypt Govt Will Build 'Parallel Commodity Market' to Combat Price Hikes: Sisi," *Ahramonline* (January 16, 2017).

29 "Cairo is Fastest Growing City Worldwide in Terms of Population in 2017: Report," *Egyptian Independent* (February 27, 2017).

30 "Number of Egyptians Worldwide to Reach 100 Million on Thursday," *Ahramonline* (November 23, 2016).

31 Paul Rivlin, "Egypt's Economy: The Agony Continues," *Middle East Economy* (July 31, 2016), http://dayan.org/content/egypts-economy-agony-continues.

32 Caroline Krafft and Ragui Assaad, "Beware of the Echo: The Impending Return of Demographic Pressures in Egypt," *Policy Perspective* 12, Cairo: Economic Research Forum, May 2014.

33 Paul Rivlin, "Sisi as Sisyphus: Egypt's Economic Emergency," *Middle East Economy* (June 19, 2014), p. 4, http://dayan.org/content/iqtisadi-sisi-sisyphus-egypts-economic-emergency.

34 Clement M. Henry and Robert Springborg, *Globalization and the Politics of Development in the Middle East*, Cambridge: Cambridge University Press, 2010, p. 27.

35 Ibid.

36 Farzaneh Roudi-Fahimi and Valentine M. Moghadam, "Empowering Women, Developing Society: Female Education in the Middle East and North Africa," Population Reference Bureau, November 2013, http://www.prb.org/pdf/EmpoweringWomeninMENA.pdf.

37 Knoema Education Statistics, September 2016, https://knoema.com/WBEDS2016Apr/education-statistics-world-bank-september-2016?country=1002400-middle-east-north-africa.

38 World Bank, Human Development Department Middle East and North Africa Region, *Arab Republic of Egypt. Improving Quality, Equality, and Efficiency in the Education Sector: Fostering a Competent Generation of Youth* (June 29, 2007), p. 9, http://documents.worldbank.org/curated/en/796151468021861883/pdf/428630ESW0P08910gray0cover01PUBLIC1.pdf; National Center for Educational Statistics, "Trends in International Mathematics and Science Study 2007," http://nces.ed.gov/timss/table07_3.asp.

39 World Bank, *Arab Republic of Egypt. Improving Quality, Equality, and Efficiency in the Education Sector*, p. 11.
40 Ibid., p. 1.
41 Ibid., p. 29.
42 Ibid., p. 26.
43 Yasmine Fahim and Noha Sami, "Adequacy, Efficiency and Equity of Higher Education Financing: The Case of Egypt," *Prospects* 41 (2011), p. 52.
44 Clemens Breisinger et al., "Beyond the Arab Awakening: Policies and Investments for Poverty Reduction and Food Security," Food Policy Report, International Food Policy Research Institute, February 2012, p. 27.
45 Cited in Fahim and Sami, "Adequacy, Efficiency and Equity of Higher Education Financing," p. 58.
46 Marcus Noland and Howard Pack, *The Arab Economies in a Changing World*, Washington, DC: The Peterson Institute, 2011, p. 36.
47 See http://data.worldbank.org/indicator/SL.TLF.CACT.ZS/countries.
48 See http://data.worldbank.org/indicator/SL.TLF.CACT.FE.ZS/ countries.
49 "Economic Contribution of Women," *The Economist* (October 20, 2012), p. 85.
50 Ibid.
51 Ishac Diwan, Philip Keefer, and Marc Schiffbauer, "Pyramid Capitalism: Political Connections, Regulation, and Firm Productivity in Egypt," World Bank Group, Macroeconomics and Fiscal Management Global Practice Group, July 2015, p. 27.
52 Steffen Hertog, "Is There an Arab Variety of Capitalism?," Working Paper 1068, Cairo: Economic Research Forum, December 2016, p. 14.
53 David Wood, "Why are Private Egyptian Hospitals Recruiting Nursing Staff from Overseas?," *Mada Masr* (September 27, 2016).
54 "Egypt's Economy: State of Denial," *The Economist* (August 6, 2016), p. 35. "Look Forward in Anger," *The Economist* (August 6, 2016), pp. 16–18.
55 Cited in Amr Adly, "Egypt's Oil Dependency and Political Discontent," The Carnegie Endowment (August 2, 2016), http://carnegie-mec.org/2016/08/02/egypt-s-oil-dependency-and-political-discontent-pub-64224.
56 "Egypt Retreats 52 Spots in Global Youth Development Index," *Aswat Masriya* (October 26, 2016).

57 "Government Report: The Poor Represent a Quarter of Egypt's Population," *Egypt Independent* (October 16, 2012); and Sherine Abdel-Rezek, "Living in Poverty," *Al Ahram Weekly* (February 9–15, 2011).

58 Sherine Abdel-Razek, "Caught in the Middle," *Al Ahram Weekly* (December 22, 2016).

59 See http://data.unicef.org/topic/nutrition/malnutrition.

60 I am indebted to Dr. Soha Bayoumi of the Department of the History of Science at Harvard University for this information.

61 Nader Habibi and Fatma El-Hamidi, "Why Are Egyptian Youth Burning their University Diplomas? The Overeducation Crisis in Egypt," Crown Center for Middle East Studies, Brandeis University, September 2016, http://www.brandeis.edu/crown/publications/meb/meb102.html.

62 "Egyptian Authorities have Arrested Doctors, Nurses and Professors Suspected of Being Involved in an International Organ Trafficking Ring," BBC News (December 6, 2016), http://www.bbc.com/news/world-middle-east-38224836; Mohamed Abdel-Baky, "Organ Trafficking Bust," *Al Ahram Weekly* (December 8, 2016).

63 "Saudi Brothers Held in Egypt Over Illegal Donor Trade," *The New Arab* (January 16, 2017).

64 "Pharma Companies Targeting Poor Egyptians for Drug Trials: NGO," *Egypt Independent* (October 21, 2016).

65 Robert Cusack, "What's the Beef?: Another Poison Donkey Meat Discovery in Egypt," *The New Arab* (January 6, 2017).

66 Mohamed Abul Ghar, "Egypt's Only Way Out," *Ahramonline* (November 20, 2016).

67 The World Economic Forum, *The Inclusive Growth and Development Report 2017*, http://www3.weforum.org/docs/WEF_Forum_IncGrwth_2017.pdf.

68 See http://www.arabbarometer.org/content/arab-barometer-iii-0.

69 "Egypt Downgraded to 'Watch List' in Fighting Human Trafficking: U.S. Report," *Cairo Post* (July 28, 2015).

70 Mira Tzoreff, "From Great Expectations to Bitter Disappointment: Egypt's Youth, After Three Years of al-Sisi's Presidency," *Tel Aviv Notes* 10:16 (September 26, 2016).

71 "Egypt Ranks First in Illegal Migration Worldwide: Minister," *Egypt Independent* (November 25, 2016).

72 "Look Forward in Anger," *The Economist* (August 6, 2016), pp. 16–18.

73 See https://knoema.com/med_ec3/gross-capital-formation?tsId=1000110.

74 Niveen Wahish, "Fallout on the Budget," *Al Ahram Weekly* (November 10, 2016).
75 "Cairo Sees Encroachments on 3.6 mln Square Metres of Land: Governor," *Ahramonline* (December 30, 2016).
76 As a consequence Egypt has been facing increasingly frequent power and water shortages of ever greater duration. See for example, Sherine Abdel-Razek, "Power Deficits to Continue," *Al Ahram Weekly* (August 16–22, 2012); Reem Leila, "Power to the People?," *Al Ahram Weekly* (July 25–30, 2012); and "Market Thirsty for Bottled Water," *Al Ahram Weekly* (August 9–15, 2012).
77 World Bank, World Development Indicators, http://data.worldbank.org/products/wdi.
78 "Egypt in Top 10 for Road Traffic Deaths, Officials Still Seeking Solutions," *Egypt Independent* (October 7, 2016).
79 Kamal Tabikha, "Egypt Ranked 6th Most Dangerous Travel Destination in WEF Report," *Egypt Independent* (October 14, 2016).
80 "Report from Rashid: Where Was the State When Hundreds Drowned?," *Mada Masr* (October 13, 2016).
81 Sofian Philip Naceur and Tom Rollins, "Europe's Migration Trade with Egypt," *Mada Masr* (February 1, 2017).
82 "Egypt to 'Review' Joint Immigration Measures Following Italy's Decision to Cut Military Supplies," *Mada Masr* (July 7, 2016).
83 The Hungarian Minister of Defense on a visit to Cairo in February 2017 speculated that "instability in the North African country would trigger the departure of about ten million migrants to Europe." "Egypt, Hungary Defense Ministers Discuss Military Cooperation, Migrant Crisis," *Ahramonline* (February 22, 2017).
84 "World's Most Powerful Passports Revealed, Egypt's Ranking Declines," *Egypt Independent* (January 23, 2017).

6 The Rocky Road Ahead

1 For an analysis of how the EU is already linking "development" funding to migration control, see Sofian Philip Naceur and Tom Rollins, "Europe's Migration Trade With Egypt," *Mada Masr* (February 1, 2017).

Index

World Justice Project
    2016 Rule of Law Index 88,
        114–15, 145–6

Yazal, Samih Saif al 59–60
Year of Youth 155
Yemen 6, 15, 19, 26, 57, 119,
    184, 195, 200
Young Egypt 84

youth
    demonstrations/protests 148,
        149, 150
    migrants 183
    population bulge 178
    unemployment 6, 155, 181
    see also education

Zind, Ahmad al 92